Managing Hedge Fund Managers

Quantitative and Qualitative Performance Measures

EDWARD J. STAVETSKI

John Wiley & Sons, Inc.

I want to thank my wonderful wife, Hilary, and my children, Laura and Alec, who give me strength every day. They continue my parents' efforts to make me a better human being, husband, and father, and I am very grateful for them.

Contents

Preface   xi

   Highlights of the Book   xii

Acknowledgments   xiii

INTRODUCTION
**The Art and Science of Hedge Fund Investing—Are You
Precisely Wrong or Approximately Correct?**   1

   The Explosion of Hedge Funds   1
   What Are Hedge Funds?   5
   Finding a Comfort Zone   7
   A Look beneath the (Book) Covers   8
   As You Begin   9
   Madoff   10

CHAPTER 1
Asset Allocation and Fiduciary Duty   11

   Determinants of Portfolio Performance   12
   Why Alternate Investments?   13
   A Closer Look at Hedge Fund Structures   16
   The Rise of Socially Responsible Investing   20
   Fiduciary Responsibility   20
   Where Do I Start?   24

CHAPTER 2
Large versus Small Funds   27

   Research Confirms Small Fund Advantage   29
   Performance of New Small Funds   34
   Attrition Rates   36
   Drivers of Outperformance   37
   Invested Interests   37

Aligned Interests   38
Point of Diminishing Returns   39
Master of Trend Line Analysis   40

CHAPTER 3
The Search for an Honest Man   **41**

Prime Brokers   43
Conferences and Industry Events   45
Industry Publications   46
Incubators and Platforms   47
Industry Web Sites and Databases   48
Building Your Own Database   53
Unconventional Sources   53
Six Steps to Kevin Bacon   54
Sizing up the Flock   56
What's in the DDQ?   57
Summary   60

CHAPTER 4
Performance Analysis   **61**

The First Step: Understand What Is Being Measured   63
Two Sides to Hedge Fund Performance: Long and Short   65
Performance Standards   66
Check the Entry   67
Finding a Benchmark   68
Peer Analysis   71
Confusion from the Best and the Brightest?   73
A Practitioner's View   74
Examine the Bad   77
Examine the Good   78
Expect the Improbable   79
I Surrender   79

CHAPTER 5
Risk in Hedge Funds   **81**

Major Risk Categories   84
Liquidity Risk   85
High Watermark Risk   87
Concentration Risk   89

Operational Risk   89
Liquidity Mismatch Risk   90
Transparency Risk   90
Risk Process   91
Leverage Risk   91
Short Selling Risk   92
Reputation Risk   93
Submerged Risk   94
Counterparty Risk   94
Market Risk   94
Credit Risk   95
Model Risk   96
Complexity Risk   98
Key Person Risk   99
Sensitivity to Assumptions Risk   99
NAV Instability Risk   99
Derivatives Risk   100
Summary   101

CHAPTER 6
You Only Find Out Who Is Swimming Naked When the Tide Goes Out   103

Filling Out the DDQ   103
Form ADV Part II   109
Fund Brochures and Documents   110
Planning the On-Site Visit   111
Summary   112

CHAPTER 7
Let the Games Begin   115

The Process   115
Examining the Organization   119
Preparing for the On-Site Visit   120
Preparing the Final Evaluation   126
In Conclusion   137

CHAPTER 8
Getting Ready Is the Secret of Success   139

Top-Down Strategy Analysis   140
Bottom-Up Manager Analysis   141

Test or Model the Portfolio 142
Portfolio Optimization 147
Summary 153

CHAPTER 9
Navigating Buyers' Remorse **155**

Long Term Capital Management: Poor Diversification
and High Leverage Are a Dangerous Combination 156
Bayou Group, LLC: Due Diligence Is a Must 158
Wood River Capital Management: A Lack of
Experience and Auditing 160
MotherRock: The Liquidity Squeeze in a Small Market
Will End Badly When Volatility Increases 162
Amaranth: Liquidity and Concentrated Portfolios Can
Drag a Fund Down as the Trend of Any Trade
Eventually Reverses 165
Recent Events: Ospraie Fund 168
Your Final Exam 169
Applying Your Education 170
The Importance of Second Acts 171

CHAPTER 10
Monitoring Your Flock **173**

Everyone's Favorite Metric: Performance 174
Portfolio Exposures 175
Performance Trends 179
Peer Group Analysis 181
Strategy Reviews 182
Fund Size and Performance Impact 183
Management and Personnel Reviews 185
Third-Party Vendors 186
Regulatory and Legal Risk 188
Business Continuity Risk 188
A Final Word on Monitoring 189

APPENDIX A
Sample Investment Policy Statement **191**

I. Statement of Investment Objectives 191
II. Asset Allocation and Rebalancing 192
III. Guidelines for the Selection of Fixed-Income
Securities 195

IV. Guidelines for Selection of Equity Investments 196
V. Standards of Performance 196
VI. Selection of Managers 199
VII. Responsibilities of Managers 200

APPENDIX B
Sample ADV Part II with ADV Schedule F 203

APPENDIX C
Hedge Fund Manager Due Diligence Questionnaire 219
I. Background 219
II. Investment Process, Strategy, and Philosophy 221
III. Business Plans 221
IV. Manager Selection and Research 222
V. Manager Monitoring and Risk Management 222
VI. Performance and Fees 222
VII. Compliance and Client Reporting 223
VIII. Personnel 223
IX. Operations and Administration 223
X. Taxes 224
XI. Performance (See Appendix 6) 224
Attachments 226

APPENDIX D
U.S. Equity Long/Short Managers 229
A. Organization 229
B. Investment Professionals (Product Specific) 230
C. Investment Philosophy and Process 231
D. Trading Process and Systems 232
E. Performance 233
F. Composite/Product Information 244
References 248

Bibliography 249

Index 253

Preface

To many investors, the hedge fund world is shrouded in secrecy and compounded by complicated structures and investment vehicles. Even some investment professionals view hedge funds as Satan here on earth. The horror stories of investors losing millions of dollars while greedy hedge fund managers collect rock star salaries make for great headlines and raw meat for governments and regulators, but do little to advance the education of the investing public.

Understanding and investing in hedge funds can be a daunting task. Not everyone will have the resources or opportunities presented to them that a Harvard or Yale endowment fund has. This does not mean that if you are a qualified investor, in the legal sense, you should avoid the hedge fund space or, even more importantly, blindly invest in a fund on the basis of a tip you received at a cocktail party. The main goal of this book is to remove some of the shroud of secrecy in the hedge fund world and provide practical tools for investing in this space. Whether you consider hedge funds an asset class or just an investment vehicle, you need to understand some of the technical aspects of structure, the comparative performance statistics, and the continual vigilance needed to successfully navigate this investment field.

In this book, the process of investing in a hedge fund proceeds from the guidelines of an Investment Policy Statement, through investing in a chosen fund, and then to the follow-up monitoring that is needed. We will break down each step of the due diligence process and focus on critical tasks, reviews, and questions. Knowledge of some financial calculations is imperative, but equally important is being able to realize that sometimes the numbers don't add up, or notice something inconsistent in the responses and answers you get from a fund. Time and time again the book stesses that numbers and calculations do not provide answers but only questions. Investing in hedge funds is as much art as science; faith versus reason. Some of the smartest, well connected funds have gone down in flames. As an old mentor once told me, sometimes I would rather be lucky than smart. And I believe the harder you work the luckier you become.

HIGHLIGHTS OF THE BOOK

Following is a brief overview of the contents of this book:

- A comprehensive Investment Policy Statement including hedge funds (Chapter 1).
- The virtues of emerging managers versus well established ones and the risks involved in choosing either type (Chapter 2).
- Casting a wide berth to search for a new manager (Chapter 3).
- How to decipher the mind-numbing statistics that rise up around hedge fund investing (Chapter 4).
- The various concepts of risk and the real exposure you face as an investor (Chapter 5).
- Performance is important but is the hedge fund a real business? (Chapter 6).
- Researching qualitative factors that impact a hedge fund (Chapter 7).
- Portfolio construction goes beyond high performance numbers (Chapter 8).
- A review of highly detectable factors that imploded several funds (Chapter 9).
- The work is never done; the ongoing monitor is very important since real money is now at stake (Chapter 10).

I hope that the knowledge you acquire in this book will be useful in helping you to become a successful hedge fund investor. New information and methods to understand hedge funds are being discovered every day. There is no one formula or specific way to analyze every fund. But you must understand the process and be comfortable with your decision and your investment.

Acknowledgments

I would like to thank Vitaliy Katsenelson for his enthusiasm and persistence in encouraging me to take on this project. I owe a special thanks to the editors at John Wiley & Sons who provided advice, guidance, and assistance throughout this process.

Moreover, I want to voice my appreciation to the people who gave generously of their time and knowledge during my inquisitive years before I began writing this book. A mix of practitioners, including Ted Aronson of AJO Partners and Sam Kirschner of Mayer & Hoffman Capital Advisers, helped shape the practical aspects of this book, along with academics Dr. Andrew Lo and Dr. David Hsieh, who provided outstanding insights and research to complement the others. I also want to thank some old colleagues, Brain Kraus, PJ Grzywacz, and Andrew Elkin, who always made due diligence interesting.

Finally, I want to thank my family and friends, whose continued support I greatly appreciate.

The Art and Science of Hedge Fund Investing—Are You Precisely Wrong or Approximately Correct?

Hedge funds have been around for more than 50 years, but their impact in the investment world has increased since the 1990s. Alfred Winslow Jones, trained as a sociologist and known professionally as a journalist, established a partnership in New York in 1949 that has become known as the first hedge fund. Jones wanted to protect his investments from market risk, and by shorting stocks he calculated he could sufficiently defend his portfolio against declining markets. Feeling confident that his strategy would be successful, Jones borrowed capital (leverage) to increase his long and short positions. So successful was this strategy that Jones saw his funds appreciate 670 percent between 1955 and 1965.

The interest in hedge funds remained relatively flat until the 1990s, when hedge fund managers Julian Robertson, Michael Steinhardt, and George Soros hit the news with the force of rock stars. In 1990, there were about 100 hedge funds with approximately $38.9 billion in assets under management. By 1995, there was about $185.7 billion invested in only about 170 funds. In 2005 the amount of assets under management rose to over $1.1 trillion invested in approximately 8,500 funds; however, 196 hedge funds controlled approximately $730 billion of the total.

THE EXPLOSION OF HEDGE FUNDS

There are currently over 15,400 single strategy hedge funds and over 6,100 funds of funds (FOFs), depending on the day and source you use. There are approximately 800 to 1000 new hedge funds every year. Of the single strategy hedge funds, 36 percent are U.S. domiciled and 64 percent are domiciled offshore. Among FOFs, approximately 18 percent were domiciled onshore while 82 percent were offshore. Assets Under Management (AUM) at the end of 2006 (the most recent year for which data is available) rose to over $1.4 trillion. Prior to the bear market debacle in 2008, the hedge fund industry was expected to maintain its torrid growth. It now appears that growth will be halted as hedge funds continue to suffer from the credit squeeze. Hedge funds are imploding and gates are going up in an attempt to bring orderly redemptions to the process. It is now estimated that 20 to 30 percent of the hedge funds in existence may close over the next few quarters.

The recent activity in the hedge fund world should serve as a huge wake-up call to investors. It is not just the small out-of-the-garage type of funds that are closing. Many of the large, well-established funds have closed their doors. It is too early to do a final analysis of this downfall. The credit crisis has cut hedge funds in several ways. First, they have been subject to a swift downdraft in security prices. While many folks believe that hedge funds actually hedge the portfolio, they have been surprised at how poorly hedged many have been. Second, the credit squeeze has created a liquidity squeeze on several fronts for hedge funds. Many large funds leverage trades in order to produce any alpha. Leverage, once again, has proven to be a source of alpha in up markets and poison in down markets. As investors begin to panic, redemption notices have poured in and funds have been forced to put up gates, as due to market conditions they cannot sell portions of the portfolio without substantial damage to the NAV. This is also creating a problem with high watermarks. Steep declines in NAV will eliminate any performance bonuses managers hope to get. Keeping investment talent without the high bonus payment will cause a run on talent.

Several funds are attempting to do right by investors. They have temporarily halted redemptions and have asked for new lock-ups in order to provide orderly liquidation. In exchange for these new lock-ups, they are waiving or reducing management fees and/or performance fees until investors are righted.

The lessons to investors will be many. Safety by investing in large funds proved to be nonexistent. Investors need to pay particular attention to the short side of a manager's book or how well the manager hedges the portfolio. Finally, character as much as pedigree is determining how managers are treating investors in this troubled time. And possibly the ultimate lessons are that excesses do eventually get worked out of the system and risk is always a major factor in the investment world.

This meteoric growth has also affected the type of funds that are now available to investors. In 1990, approximately 71 percent of the assets were invested in global macro strategies; relative value arbitrage funds ranked next in AUM with about 10 percent. Equity long/short and equity market neutral funds combined accounted for only 7 percent of the invested assets in 1990. By the end of 2005, global macro was about 11 percent of invested funds while equity long/short funds accounted for 30 percent of the assets invested.

To further illuminate how fast the hedge fund industry has grown in recent years, 22 percent of the funds have been in existence for less than 2 years and approximately 62 percent have been in existence for less than 5 years (HFR Industry reports 2007). The explosion in assets shifting to hedge funds and the growth in the number of funds, however, do not mean the monies are being equally distributed across all funds. Less than 15 percent of the funds have more than $500 million in AUM. In fact, over 60 percent have less than $100 million in AUM (according to PerTrac Financial Solutions). There are risks, albeit quite different risks, for investors at either end of the AUM spectrum.

This growth spurt is reminiscent of the prolific growth of mutual funds in the 1980s. Investors have been jumping into the fray with a similar reckless abandon. The buzzword is performance, real or imagined. The investor's ability to make an educated decision about a hedge fund is fully jaded by the most recent performance dot and cocktail party chatter. In recent years, many have been forced to learn painful lessons that performance can be fleeting glory. For example, top performing funds like MotherRock and Amaranth saw a huge influx of dollars to their funds based on strong short-term performance. In what seemed like an instant, more than a billion dollars in assets evaporated as oil went from around $40 per barrel to nearly $100.

Or, take the case of Eric Mindich and Eaton Park. In 1994, at the age of 27, Mindich became the youngest partner ever in the history of Goldman Sachs. In 2000 he became co-chief operating officer of the equities division, and in 2002 he became co-head of the equities division. In 2003, Mindich joined the Executive Office and became chair of the Firmwide Strategy Committee. In November 2004, he launched Eton Park, a global multi-disciplinary hedge fund. The fund essentially began and stopped taking assets in its opening week with commitments of $3.5 billion. The terms were a 2 percent management fee and 20 percent take of profits. The fund had a two-year lock-up, after which investors could redeem one-third of their assets over the next three years. The fund would allocate a portion of the assets to private equity and the majority of them to multi-strategy investments (CV arbitrage, capital structure, credit arbitrage, and long/short equity). There is no question that Mr. Mindich had what the hedge fund world calls pedigree. According to the cocktail chatter, this was a "must-have" investment. Some astute observers were rankled about the rather severe lock-up period, and some wondered aloud how folks could invest money with a manager who had, by some accounts, worked in an administrative capacity and not in an investment one for about four years. Time will be the true judge as to who did the best due diligence on this fund. After a slow start, Eaton Park had a strong year in 2007. The long-term outcome is yet to be written.

It is no secret that the hedge fund industry has received a great deal of headline attention over the past few years. Enormous paydays for hedge fund managers coupled with, in some instances, mediocre performance have led to the typical cries for regulatory or Congressional intervention. The lack of regulation and transparency of the investments have led to much speculation about the operations, functions, and use of hedge funds. The outcry began after the tech bubble burst, when markets crashed and asset flow to hedge funds soared. The tabloid headlines in the popular press led the SEC to call for the registration of all hedge fund managers in its October 1, 2003, report. There were almost daily articles in the major national newspapers, the *New York Times* and the *Washington Post* among others, criticizing hedge funds for the crash, lack of regulation, and what was perceived as excess salaries. In fact, many likened hedge funds to a fee scheme rather than an investment option.

In an effort to protect investors from themselves, Congress sprang into action by holding post-mortem hearings, followed by the SEC requirement that hedge funds had to be registered by February 1, 2006. Phillip Goldstein of Bullfrog Investors took up the cause of the hedge funds and sued the SEC. He won his case, and the SEC has since thought better of its course of action. Subsequent to that victory, Mr. Goldstein took up another hedge fund cause that addresses transparency: He is seeking an exemption from having to file 13fs. A 13f requires an investment manager to list all equity holdings when that manager's discretionary assets under management exceed $100 million. A victory here would add some additional wrinkles to due diligence, since the holdings transparency will be reduced. Whether Mr. Goldstein will win is unknown at this point. He is arguing that there is no legitimate government interest and his intellectual property rights are being violated.

The current cause célèbre seems to be hedge fund compensation. The same cast of characters from the press are leading the shrill chorus. Is the compensation too high? Yes! Again, we are seeing efforts to protect investors from themselves. The key point is that no one forces anyone to invest in a hedge fund. As part of their due diligence, investors need to check out the fees. Compensation is a side issue in the fee discussion. Investors need to be aware of exactly what they are paying for in the fund. The task is not always an easy one. Fee structures are not always straightforward and can include a variety of expenses that are readily discernable. The key point: If you are not comfortable with the fees, don't invest.

The background noise continues, however, and even the regulators and legislators are aware that they must not kill the golden goose. Carefully selected hedge funds have provided higher risk-adjusted returns to pension

funds and endowments. Higher returns have allowed pension plans of corporations, states, and municipalities to return to a status of near full funding.
This rise has allowed politicians to ignore issues facing an aging population
and their retirement benefits, which in turn may be especially pertinent to
states and municipalities confronted with underfunded pensions and raising
taxes by punitive amounts in order to meet mandatory benefits.

WHAT ARE HEDGE FUNDS?

Quite simply, a hedge fund is a business structure, typically a limited partnership or private pool. It may be organized in any number of legal jurisdictions and, through what is known as a master feeder structure, could be
organized simultaneously in several jurisdictions. The strategies and investments employed are wide ranging. Most funds fall into broad based strategic
categories and then can be further classified into smaller subcategories by
style, geography, industry, or sector. It is usually helpful to divide the hedge
fund universe into the following eight broad strategies:

1. Arbitrage
2. Event-driven
3. Fixed Income
4. Long-Short
5. Macro
6. Multi-strategy (or fund of funds)
7. Sector
8. Trading

In order to gain a better understanding of some strategies the following
definitions will be helpful.*

> **Arbitrage** strategies seek to capitalize on price inefficiencies between
> securities and markets on a nondirectional basis. Leverage is fre-
> quently used. Arbitrage (or arb, as is the common Street name)
> strategies include capital arbitrage, closed end fund arbitrage,
> convertible arbitrage, credit arbitrage, and statistical arbitrage.

---

*None of the firms or hedge funds mentioned in the definitions is issuing an invitation
or an offer to purchase an interest in any of the listed funds. Such an offer can only
be extended after an investor has received a confidential offering memorandum
concerning the fund. All investors must be qualified purchasers as defined in the
securities laws.

Wolverine is an example of a fund that uses different arbitrage strategies.

Event-Driven strategies seek to capture gains from price movements that are the result of an anticipated or announced corporate event. These strategies include merger arb, corporate restructurings, and activist strategies. Contrarian Capital is a hedge fund that uses event-driven strategies in its portfolio.

Fixed Income strategies focus on the inefficiencies in fixed income securities from temporary dislocations between related types of bonds or other instruments related to troubled companies or debt issuers in some crisis. Duration Capital and Lancelot are hedge funds that implement fixed income strategies in different ways.

Long-Short strategies focus on the simultaneous investment stance of being long and short, typically in equity assets or derivative financial instruments. The portfolio may be net long, net short, or neutral. Braeside Capital and Oak Street Capital are two hedge funds that implement equity long/short portfolios.

Macro strategies may be long or short in a multitude of financial instruments globally including equities, bonds, currencies, or commodities. These funds tend to be highly leveraged and rely on rapid trading execution. Quantum and Highbridge are two large and infamous hedge funds that play the global macro hedge fund game.

Multi-Strategies funds employ multi-fund or multi-manager strategies that provide lower volatility though broad-based diversification. This strategy may also be organized as a fund of funds. These funds will allocate across multiple styles, strategies, and trading strategies. Halcyon, 1794 Commodore, and Guidant Capital are examples of a single hedge fund and fund of funds that utilize a multi-strategy approach.

Sector strategies will focus on investment activities not closely aligned to a market or investment technique, such as emerging market debt or emerging market equity that focuses on analysis of nondeveloped countries, capital flows, and economic development. Sector funds may also be employed to establish long or short positions in specific sectors such as health care/biotechnology, energy, or electronics. Sail Pacific Explorer, CCI Healthcare, and NS Utility fund are examples of different types of sector specific funds.

Trading strategies are dynamic trading programs that are characterized by high trading volume and high volatility. The instruments used may be currencies, managed futures, or options. John W. Henry and Renaissance Asset Management are two well known hedge funds that implement diverse trading strategies.

These brief descriptions will serve as a guide to the due diligence discussion. There are many variations of the theme; however, most hedge fund strategies can easily be placed in one of the above categories. The operations of any given fund may use one or several different methods to implement their strategy with little to no leverage or a lot of leverage. Each manager tries to implement the strategy in such a way that it provides an edge, or an ability to provide alpha.

FINDING A COMFORT ZONE

The understanding of what is the strategy employed is only the first step. Investors also need to be comfortable with the type of underlying instruments the fund may invest in. A general rule of thumb, used by many seasoned investment professionals, is if you don't understand the strategy or instrument, run, don't walk to the nearest exit. Performance, leverage, and fees are essential to understanding the underlying business sense of a hedge fund. The level of detail an investor receives from the fund with regard to fund performance, fees, and operations gives the investor confidence that the general partners share some of his interest in the success of the fund, as well as taking prudent actions to limit excessive risk on investors' capital. An investor needs to fully examine how performance and fees are reported in order to evaluate whether or not he will earn sufficient return on capital, the sources of those returns, and whether he is ultimately getting what he paid for.

A deeper understanding of a hedge fund is not limited to its investment program. The majority of hedge fund failures have been caused by operational inadequacies. Examinations of past failures by EdHec shows that 50 percent of the failures were due to operational issues and 38 percent were due to investment issues. Additionally, some strategies are more prone to failure than others. More than with other investment vehicles, hedge fund analysis requires a quantitative and a qualitative review. Rigorous analysis can lead to uncovering shortfalls in the business or the investment process. Sometimes a simple telephone call to the named auditor or reviewing third-party vendors for an affiliation to the fund can save investors pain. This first-hand lesson was learned by investors in Bayou and Wood River, whose stories we will discuss in Chapter 10.

Despite all the academic work that is being done, analysis of hedge funds is as much an art as a science. Many of the mathematical measures that work nicely with traditional long-only investment vehicles are not effective in providing significant insights into hedge funds. As newer, statistically significant methods are being developed, reliance on qualitative measures has increased in importance. It is instructive to note that, when examining hedge funds, quantitative analysis provides questions, not necessarily answers. Numbers viewed in isolation do not provide adequate information. For example, a manager reports a return in a high yield fund of 18 percent. Did he do well? Maybe. How did the high yield index perform? What level of leverage did he or she take? Did the fund successfully make money throughout the year? Did it make money in the long book *and* the short book? What was the gross and net exposure throughout the year? How does that return look in view of the prior year's performance? All of the numbers need to be examined in context of the overall objectives and operations of the fund. This will be further discussed in Chapter 7.

A LOOK BENEATH THE (BOOK) COVERS

One of the most effective ways to analyze these shadowy beasts known as hedge funds is to divide the analysis between art and science. The science deals with the litany of Greeks (alpha, beta, and so on) that are the result of some mathematical measurement of financial activity. Quantitative number crunching is the hallmark of most due diligence processes. The qualitative view deals in the literary aspect of the fund and its terms: SEC registration, broker/dealer affiliation, pricing policies, and third-party vendors only begin the list.

Whether you use a routine screening process or are a one-off buyer, the first cut is undoubtedly alpha or Sharpe Ratio, standard deviation, and may be drawdown (a losing period in the investment record). This is typically followed by a perusal of marketing material and maybe a call to the fund itself. Taking the guided tour of a hedge fund is not a sound way to invest your dollars. The important issue that needs to be remembered is that, regardless of whether you are an institutional investor or a recreational user of hedge funds, the process by which you compare and evaluate the funds should be in-depth and consistent each and every time.

In the chapters that follow, I offer some other measures for analyzing hedge funds. The Sharpe Ratio is widely used as a measure of risk-adjusted performance. Unfortunately, the mathematical precision of this measure is better suited for investment vehicles with normally distributed returns, or traditional long-only funds. The use of standard deviation as a measure of risk will also be discussed. Standard deviation in essence gives equal weight to upside and downside risk. Investors do not. I, like others much smarter than I, have difficulty grasping a concept as upside risk. I tend to believe that an investor would take all of the upside risk he could carry. Additionally, the measure adds little value to the asymmetric returns of hedge funds. Later we will take a closer look at downside deviation and downside capture.

In the global markets, investors are beginning to see some weakness, and those using concepts of normal distribution curves and randomness of returns will see their portfolios become quite vulnerable. The statistical 100-year events are now happening at a pace of every three to four years. The use of well structured hedge funds will allow investors to garner higher risk-adjusted returns and ride through what is beginning to be an interesting period in the financial markets. By their very nature, picking appropriate hedge funds is more complex than picking long-only funds, and the analysis is deeper and more complex.

Analyzing past performance is the science part of the process. Investors should be cautioned, however, that past performance is indicative of nothing. It does provide insight and a bit of direction on how a hedge fund manager may have allocated his or her capital under different conditions; however, it will tell you little if anything about the future. More importantly, investors need to pay particular attention to operational and business due diligence. The majority of funds that default or close do so because of operational issues. Uncovering these defects requires more leg work and understanding of the business itself. This is the art part of the equation.

In the upcoming chapters, the discussion will flow from the Investment Policy Statement (IPS), where investor guidelines and expectations are set, to the quantitative measures, qualitative rankings, and monitoring your managers. I have found over the years that quantitative numbers have generally raised more questions than they have answered. In the quantitative section, there will be some discussion on whether investors should focus on what appears to be high risk emerging funds, or gravitate to the perceived safer, more established larger funds. Regardless of the precision of the mathematics, investors will learn more about the fund itself from a close-up look at the people in the fund and how they manage the business. This matrix of art and science opens a picture into the soul of a hedge fund operation. It is imperative that investors use a consistent roadmap to due diligence and do not get consumed with an arrogance that will surely lead to missing an opportunity, or worse, to a downfall. The hedge fund business is full of intelligent people. You do not need to be the sharpest knife in the drawer, just the most diligent.

AS YOU BEGIN

The process of beginning a hedge fund search must start with an investor's Investment Policy Statement, or IPS. The comfort offered by past returns should be only of passing interest. How the funds are currently investing, operating, and dealing with the markets and investors should be of paramount concern to you. The past is not always prelude to the future, and with a certain stick-to-itiveness and unconventional views, you can help improve your portfolio returns and avoid some common landmines that often plague hedge fund investors.

MADOFF

I would like to add one final note. Subsequent to this book being written, the investment world has been shaken once again with the discovery of the largest Ponzi scheme in history allegedly perpetrated by Bernard Madoff, the former chairman of NASDAQ. What is most surprising is that many sophisticated investors and hedge funds were taken in by Mr. Madoff. The truly unfortunate part of this tragedy is that many folks are financially ruined as a result of this scheme.

As future hedge fund investors, it will be invaluable to follow the Madoff scandal. Many of the red flags of problem investments were waving long before the end arrived. Investors violated tenets of diversification by placing all or substantially all of their assets with the fund. Conflicts of interest arose from trading and brokerage, audited statements provided by a storefront entity, manual confirms from a makeshift back-office, and returns that defied reason, probability, and belief. Add this to an unbelievable stealth atmosphere of the fund and bells should have been ringing even for the tone deaf.

As with all examples, the purpose is to learn and not make light of the tragic losses people have suffered. It is important as you read the following chapters that a healthy skepticism along with hard work may keep you out of a similar situation.

CHAPTER 1

Asset Allocation and Fiduciary Duty

Investment Policy Statement: The Roadmap

Diversification is for those investors who don't know what they are doing.

—Warren Buffett

The Wizard of Omaha takes the approach that a savvy investor should concentrate his money in only his best ideas, but this is a difficult approach for mere mortals. Instead, it is much more advisable to develop a long-term plan that encompasses the investor's goals and expectations and tells how best to achieve these goals. The basic building block for any investment portfolio should be the Investment Policy Statement (IPS). Whether you are a small individual investor, a foundation or endowment, or a multi-billion dollar global pension fund, the initial step before investing the first dollar should be the written guidelines of an IPS. The IPS is now part of accepted best practices.

The Investment Policy Statement serves as a roadmap for investors, consultants, and fund managers. There are four basic purposes of an IPS regardless of the size of the investor's portfolio.

1. Identify the objectives that the investor expects from these funds. Time horizons, liquidity, and risk/return expectations will be quite important as to which investments will be most suitable. The required rate of return should drive much of the design process.

11

2. Define the asset allocation policy. Asset allocation may arguably be the most important part of the IPS.
3. Create guidelines for selecting investment options.
4. Establishes guidelines to monitor the portfolio.

The IPS outlines the how and why of investing in alternative investments. It will provide a detailed explanation of the returns expected, the risk level, and the type of fund the investor is willing to assume. Appendix A contains a sample IPS.

DETERMINANTS OF PORTFOLIO PERFORMANCE

The publishing of the Brinson, Hood, and Beebower research study (1986 and 1991) on the contributions of asset allocation over the long term to investment returns has increased focus on the need for diversification of investment portfolios. Once the time horizon, risk tolerance, and asset allocation policies have been established, the selection of managers becomes a critical part of the implementation of the asset allocation policy. Much of the benefit of a sound asset allocation plan may be undermined or negated by a manager selection process that is ineffective or inefficient. If the selection leads to poorly-performing managers, asset allocation will not save the investor. The Brinson et al. study and results were reprinted in the July-August 1995 *Financial Analysts Journal* during the roaring bull market of the 1990s, in which concerns for diversification were lost in the rising euphoria of the tech bubble.

As a brief review, the study compiled data from 91 pension plans that had complete quarterly data for a 10-year (40-quarter) period, beginning in 1974. The study measured actual and passive returns for the portfolios, which contained allocations to stocks/bonds/cash equivalents. The results showed the average plan lost 66 basis points per year in market timing, and another 36 basis points per year from security selection. Or more succinctly, the study concluded that asset allocation explained 93.6 percent of the variation in a portfolio's investment returns. Another interesting but little discussed result reflected the historical tendency of investors to move to the same policy mix.

Over the past 20 years, this study has been the focal point of many debates on the importance of asset allocation in portfolio management. Further analysis concluded that the actual result of the study was not total return, but volatility. The two are related but invoke an entirely different result that investors must remain aware of.

Of the basic four parts of the IPS (objectives, asset allocation policy, investment guidelines, monitoring) the first three have the largest impact on persons contemplating investments in hedge funds. Monitoring deals primarily with the aftermath of the decision process and communication procedures, including guidelines, benchmarking, and reporting results.

One essential thing to be considered in the asset allocation process is the investment impact of hedge funds on the overall portfolio construction. A portfolio that includes hedge funds can offer investors a better risk/return profile than one that relies solely on traditional asset classes.

WHY ALTERNATE INVESTMENTS?

The objectives determine the time horizon and time frame, while asset allocation determines permissibility of asset classes. Historically, the typical asset allocation generally begins with an allocation between the three large asset classes: cash, fixed income, and equities. Investors who face longer-tailed liabilities or intergenerational concerns such as pension funds, endowments, and ultra-high net worth (UHNW) also allocate to nontraditional or alternative investments such as real estate, private equity, and hedge funds. As David F. Swensen, chief investment officer at Yale University's endowment, outlines in his book *Pioneering Portfolio Management*, hedge funds serve certain investors well. Swensen has been highly successful in managing Yale's funds.

Pensions, endowments, foundations, and family offices (UHNW), through a different approach to traditional asset allocation, can be successful buyers of illiquidity. These funds, by being buyers of illiquid assets, gain several advantages in this investment approach, including increasing the return/risk ratio and non correlation of the assets, and targeting absolute returns instead of relative returns. This book does not intend to debate whether hedge funds are a separate asset class but addresses the uses and risks in hedge fund selection in a fully diversified portfolio.

From the standpoint of an Investment Policy Statement, hedge funds are usually classified under alternative investments in the asset allocation process, as private equity and other similarly structured investment vehicles would be. A further breakdown is the classification of absolute return and directional hedge funds. The arguments for and the distinctions between the two subcategories get blurry at times, since many folks believe that a hedge fund's goal is to provide absolute returns.

As stated in the Introduction, the typical structure for hedge funds is some form of limited partnership. Although there are institutions that require the use of Separate Account Management (SAM, discussed in Chapter 8), giving hedge funds more transparency provides investors with the ability to better monitor the risk profile of their entire portfolio. Also, the limited partnership structure may not be a practical option for some entities.

The hedge fund itself may be structured in any number of jurisdictions. It may also be effectively organized in several jurisdictions simultaneously by employing what is called a master feeder structure with a common investment portfolio. In addition to restrictions outlined by an IPS, there are legal and tax issues that may limit how and where an investor may allocate funds to a particular hedge fund. The practicalities of these structures are further discussed in Chapter 7, as well as investor issues in regard to tax status and fees associated with these vehicles.

Traditional asset allocation typically breaks out along the lines of range of percentages to equity, fixed income, and cash, with further breakdowns among domestic, international, and style types. As seen in Table 1.1, historically a typical allocation would be 50 to 60 percent equity, with a token allocation to alternative assets (hedge fund or private equity) and the balance to fixed income and cash—depending on liquidity needs and risk tolerance.

In the past few years pension and endowment funds have seen the effects of the tech bubble, which have led a large number of pension funds to be seriously underfunded. Historically low interest rates have compounded the need to find nontraditional investments with higher risk-adjusted returns. In Figure 1.1, for the period 1987 through 2006, annualized compounded returns and standard deviation are plotted for several of the major equity and bond indexes. Included in the chart is the same representation for a hedge fund index (Hennessee Hedge Fund Index). Leaving aside the issue of survivor bias that does impact hedge fund indexes, Figure 1.1 demonstrates the potential impact of including hedge funds in a portfolio. The hedge fund

TABLE 1.1 Typical Asset Allocation Profiles

	Typical	Family Office	Yale University
Domestic Equity	50%	15%	11%
Foreign Equity	10%	20%	14%
Fixed Income	32%	15%	4%
Hedge Funds	3%	25%	24%
Real Assets	—	10%	27%
Private Equity	—	10%	19%
Cash	5%	5%	2%
Yale University data as of June 30, 2007.			

Source: Wilmington Family Office, Chronicle of Higher Education.

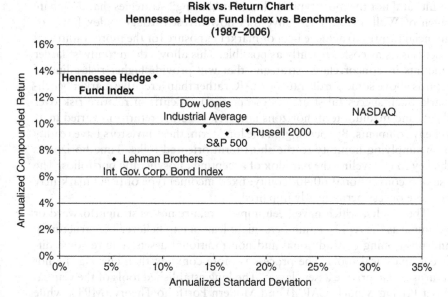

FIGURE 1.1   Risk/Return Comparison of Indexes
Source: Hennessee Group LLC.

index provided over 30 percent higher returns with, on average, half the
risk as measured by standard deviation. One can certainly argue from the
chart that the starting point of 1987 disadvantages traditional investments
(it does), but it also shows that investors can survive bad markets with the
downside protection hedge funds offer.

The endowment world is quite aware of this advantage and has taken a
more nontraditional approach over the past decade. Asset allocation to U.S.
equity and fixed income decreased and funds were shifted to non-traditional
hedge funds (real assets and private equity). The result was higher risk-
adjusted returns that had low correlations to the traditional equity and
fixed income allocations. More to the point, hedge funds are being used to
provide equity-like returns with bond-like volatility. As the success of these
strategies expanded, so did the popularity of hedge funds. See Table 1.1.

Pension and endowment funds, in an effort to close the funding gap,
and ultra-high net worth investors seeking to preserve capital, have quickly
warmed to the concept of adding hedge funds to their asset allocation
schemes. Pension funds, through Liability Driven Investing (LDI) and the
ultra-high net worth investors, are implementing a post-modern portfolio
theory of Minimum Acceptable Returns (MAR) that focuses on long term

results and not the more typical "liquidity chasing" strategies that dominate much of Wall Street. These investors now invest through index funds or financial futures to achieve beta or market exposure for the more traditional asset classes as cost-efficiently as possible. This allows them to invest larger amounts in noncorrelated strategies that will provide higher risk-adjusted returns above some hurdle rate or MAR, rather than a relative market benchmark. Such successful strategies escape the handcuffs of relative risk over short- and medium-term horizons and seek absolute returns in varied market environments. By focusing on the long term, these investors have readily been supplying liquidity to the short-term oriented folks. Time horizon is the key to unraveling the paradox of accepting idiosyncratic portfolios. The use of a conventional 60:40 (equity: fixed income) type of benchmark may be more or less permanently impaired.

The results, which have been impressive, are not as straightforward or as simple as the reported numbers might lead one to believe. The structuring and positioning of traditional and nontraditional assets require some different analytical tools. The process is more complex than chasing the hot returns of the private asset classes. The long established tools of the Capital Asset Pricing Model (CAPM) and Modern Portfolio Theory (MPT), while still the basic tenets of portfolio construction, do not lend themselves easily to analyzing hedge funds and constructing portfolios with hedge fund allocations.

A CLOSER LOOK AT HEDGE FUND STRUCTURES

Before we can begin to examine the operations and performance of the hedge fund, it's important to first understand the structural nature of a hedge fund. The hedge fund vehicle is typically a limited partnership between the management company serving as the General Partner, or GP, and investors, through an offering memorandum, and subscription documents become limited partners, or LPs, by allocating their dollars to the fund. The structures and documents are covered more fully in the chapter on due diligence (Chapter 7). The main consideration in the IPS is that the document make clear to interested parties the limits or objectives relating to approval of LP structures, leverage limits, allowable strategies, SEC registered managers (hedge fund managers are currently not required to be registered), liquidity issues, and fees. A quick checklist developed from the IPS will provide an initial framework as to whether a given hedge fund will qualify for further scrutiny. Figure 1.2 shows the basic information that will give you the foundation of the work that must be completed to meet the goals and objectives of the IPS (see Appendix A).

Fund Name:	
Manager Name:	
Contact:	
Address:	
Phone:	
Fax:	
E-Mail:	

Contact Information	

Private Placement Memorandum
    Onshore
    Offshore	

Subscription Documents
    Onshore
    Offshore	

Fund Summary	
LP Agreement (onshore)	
Memorandum/Articles of Association (offshore)	
Due Diligence Questionnaire	
FO Due Diligence Write-Up	
Audited Financials (Year ____)	
Presentation	
Historical Returns/$AUM	
Newsletters	
Side Letters	
Form ADV	
Risk Management Update	

FIGURE 1.2 Due Diligence Checklist

Use of Leverage

One of the inherent characteristics of hedge funds is the ability to leverage investments, which provides an efficient use of capital that can then be allocated to produce multiple sources of alphas. Unlike traditional or long-only strategies, since the capital is not leveraged, only one source of alpha is possible. Through the use of leverage, multiple sources of alpha are available. The most basic form of leverage is through Regulation "T," which is determined by the broker-dealers financing the strategy. For U.S. equity strategies, "Reg T" defines leverage maximum at 50 percent, or 2:1—one long and one short for one dollar of capital. This is the simplest form of leverage. In other instruments such as fixed income, foreign equities, futures, and options, lines of credit or bank borrowing might be used to take leverage up from the rather mundane level of 2:1 to 10 or 20:1. As the leverage increases, the risk of the fund also increases. Leverage can be a good source of alpha in a market that is experiencing low volatility; however. the dual edged sword of leverage is that returns can be amplified on the downside as well.

The lessons of the Long-Term Capital Management (LTCM) fund should not be lost on investors. The principals at LTCM, through the mathematical modeling work of their PhDs and Nobel Prize winners, developed sophisticated trading systems to allow them, as they quaintly put it, "to scoop up nickels." Well, as most investors know, it is not highly profitable under normal investing conditions to score outsize returns by scooping up small change. However, if one applies a moderate amount of leverage, the profitability rises exponentially. After applying an enormous amount of leverage, the investor might expect an enormous amount of profit.

The LTCM fund was leveraged on the order of 100:1. The LTCM sophisticated models churned through thousands of data points with a reversion to the mean outlook, which meant they leveraged up positions of outliers to their mean reversion model. Leverage can give the illusion of a successful strategy, when in reality it only increases the risk profile (and fees) of the investor. As investors painfully learned, mean reversion works over a long period of time. In the short run they rarely cooperate, and the market movement can leave the portfolio manager facing margin calls. The size of the leveraged trades in turn suffers from a liquidity squeeze as the margin calls need to be met. Most risk models test for 100 year events. When these 100-year events hit, models are of no use, and many times the correlation of all asset classes goes to 1.00.

Another example of misunderstood or misused leverage that gives investors a false sense of safe risk/return profiles can occur in some municipal bond arbitrage funds. The pitch is an 8 percent return in a low volatility investment. A quick review showed these 8 percent returns came primarily as the result of six times leverage. Similarly, fixed income arbitrage at typically 10 times leverage has long term performance that closely tracks the returns of the long term bond indexes (see Table 1.2). The final result brings into question whether investors are fairly compensated for the level of risk they incur.

For a fund of hedge fund investors, leverage is a bit more complicated but must be understood. A fund of hedge funds (FOHF) is an investment vehicle that typically invests in single strategy hedge funds—essentially a limited partnership owning several individual limited partnerships. FOHF investors must understand whether leverage is applied at the individual hedge fund and/or the FOFH level, and what the limits are to that leverage. This information is typically found in the Private Placement Memorandum (PPM) of the fund. Leverage at the FOHF level increases the cost of the

TABLE 1.2 Fixed Income Leveraged Returns

	Fixed Income Arbitrage	Lehman Gov/Corp Index
2002	7.1%	9.8%
2003	10.0%	4.3%
2004	7.1%	3.1%
2005	4.7%	1.6%
2006	6.1%	4.1%
2007	−0.6%	7.4%
3 Yr	3.4%	4.3%
5 Yr	5.4%	4.1%
2002–07	5.7%	5.0%

FOHF and effectively lowers the net returns of the FOF. In effect, if the annual interest cost of the leverage is 4 percent, that is the break even point for the FOHF, and that does not include the other fees associated with the operation of the FOHF.

Generally speaking, it is preferable for any leverage in a FOHF to be applied at the individual HF rather than at the FOHF level. The policies and limits for leverage must be clearly outlined and documented in the IPS. One of the great maxims of short investing is that many times the markets can stay illogical longer than an investor can stay solvent.

Employing the Right Strategy

In addition to the level of leverage risk the investor is able to tolerate, the other main issue is the type of hedge fund strategy the investor wishes to employ. There are many variations of a theme, but the alternative investment industry generally falls into a number of broad major categories, which can then be further subcategorized. Investment strategies employed by a hedge fund can be viewed as: arbitrage strategies, event-driven strategies, fixed income strategies, long-short strategies, macro strategies, multi-fund strategies, sector strategies, and trading strategies. These major strategies may be further identified by investment selection methodology, investment style, geographic focus, and industry focus. Investors need to identify these characteristics and understand the impact on the overall investment portfolio in terms of risk, diversification, and possible sources of leverage exposure.

The issue of benchmarks, which is quite important in tracking how effectively a manager is functioning, also requires different metrics from those of traditional managers. In traditional investments classes, the use of relative return comparison is common. The move to investment vehicles, such as hedge funds, puts an emphasis on absolute returns or Minimum Acceptable Returns (MAR). Also, benchmarking a hedge fund manager can be done through several methods, each providing a further slice of information. The most common would be against the manager's target. For instance, a small-cap long/short manager is typically compared to the Russell 2000 (or a version of it). Secondly, the manager can then be compared to the sub-hedge fund index or against the strategy, that is, long/short hedge funds. The final way is more cumbersome but can be revealing. As you screen managers and gain a further understanding of their style, you can build your own composite of managers that invest in similar ways in similar strategies. The selection and use of benchmarks will be discussed at length in Chapter 7.

THE RISE OF SOCIALLY RESPONSIBLE INVESTING

In recent years we have seen a surge of what is usually described as Socially Responsible Investing (SRI). In the 1970s and 1980s, SRI was chiefly concerned with not investing in weapons, tobacco, alcohol, or gambling. Since then, the definition of SRI has expanded as new investment vehicles appeared. Now, SRI considers not only the traditional "sin industries" but also diversity and workplace issues, environmental or political concerns, and ethical constraints. Hedge funds have sprung up that focus on alternative energy and other environmentally friendly industries.

Funds with an objective of shareholder activism try to get companies and management to make changes that benefit or serve society and shareholders. The IPS must spell out any restrictions or expectations for the investment manager. Those charged with portfolio construction must also account for the various factors that may impact returns, risks, and correlation to other investments held in the portfolio. The impact on the portfolio may need to be quantitatively characterized to inform the fiduciaries in order for them to make reasoned assumptions about their objectives and expected outcomes.

FIDUCIARY RESPONSIBILITY

A fiduciary is someone charged with the legal responsibility for managing investments or investment decisions. Existing ERISA law and the Pension Protection Act of 2006 make it quite clear that the interests of the beneficiaries must be paramount to the administration of pension funds. Those who function as trustees understand that they are governed by similar guidelines under the Prudent Man Rule. The Prudent Man Rule can be best understood by a statement Judge Samuel Putnam made back in 1830: All that is required of a trustee is that he conduct himself faithfully and exercise sound discretion. He is to observe how men of prudence, discretion, and intelligence manage their own affairs, not in regard to speculation but in regard to the permanent disposition of their funds, considering the probable income as well as the probable safety of the capital to be invested. This is the "do no harm" rule for investors. Fiduciaries can be further divided into investments stewards, investment advisors, and investment managers—all of whom have different prospective and legal duties but similar goals in providing a reasonable result for the beneficiaries.

Investment stewards have a legal responsibility to manage the investment process. Stewards can be trustees and investment committee members. The steward is charged with developing the overall investment strategy, deciding on asset allocations, defining the details to execute the strategy, implementing the strategy with the appropriate investment manager, and monitoring the activity and results of the entire process. Many times these stewards are untrained and, while they may be well-meaning, they are generally unprepared for the increasingly complicated task that lies before them. To help them in their stewardship, these people may rely on an outside consultant or advisor.

The investment advisor is a professional who is responsible for advising and managing the comprehensive and ongoing investment decisions. Advisors include wealth managers, trust officers, consultants. and financial planners. The vast majority of stewards are heavily reliant on advisors to assist in executing and managing the stewards' fiduciary duties. An advisor can never delegate his or her responsibility away, but can be a co-fiduciary with investment managers. By following prudent investment practices, the advisor can reduce or limit any liability in his role.

The investment manager is the professional who makes the actual investment decision about which securities or funds to select in order to implement the specific mandate of the IPS. The investment manager, in most cases, is given discretion to buy or sell a security or fund within the guidelines set forth in the IPS. All three fiduciaries must work together using well founded guidance and prudence to discharge their responsibilities to the beneficiaries of the funds.

Pension Protection Act of 2006

The IPS should spell out any fiduciary duty and conflicts of interest that may arise in using these instruments. These are of prime importance to

ERISA plans. The passing of the Pension Protection Act of 2006 (PPA) has given plan beneficiaries a basis from which to sue the plan and trustees over poor performance, high fees, and inadequate diversification. Although this threat has always concerned trustees, the panic over plan underfunding is now taking center stage as the Baby Boomer population is heading toward retirement.

The establishment of a written IPS will provide ongoing guideposts to an investor—a structured view of risk tolerance, return expectations, and manager and benchmark criteria that can be used to more effectively choose managers who will be closely aligned with the goals of the IPS. The asset policy table provides guidance and breakdowns as to the types and ranges of investment in the different hedge fund categories. A working document used by those charged with manager/fund selection may also include screening criteria, minimum requirements, monitoring guidelines, and criteria for terminating a manager.

The passage of the PPA has also put the issue concerning fees on the regulators' to-do list for the coming years. Fiduciaries must now pay closer attention to their selection of hedge funds and the criteria they use to evaluate those funds. Over the years, Congress and the press have tried to drum up pressure against hedge fund managers because of their perception that fees are too high. The response from the hedge fund community has been that no one is holding a gun to the investor's head, forcing him or her to invest. Now, the new regulations, mediocre hedge fund performance, and 2 percent/20 percent fee structures may lead to a rise in litigation.

Tips for Fiduciaries

The Department of Labor and the SEC target several key points as they relate to fiduciaries. Both regulators encourage disclosure and review of information to insure objectivity and avoid any potential conflicts of interest. Any use of affiliates or financial arrangements between any of the involved parties must not only be disclosed but also analyzed to protect the interest of the beneficiaries, in order to make sure they are not being subjugated to the financial benefit of any of the involved fiduciaries. Even what seems to be harmless on the surface must be fully vetted and openly disclosed. Other issues, such as soft dollar commission arrangements and trading, must be studied for best execution and price. Regulators will look kindly on all parties executing a signed document that outlines duties and acknowledges fiduciary obligations.

A growing number of services are being offered to help a fiduciary execute his duties in the hedge fund area. Moody's and Morningstar are providing ratings of hedge funds. I do not intend to disparage the workings of any organization; however, I would caution fiduciaries not to hang their hats on these products. For instance, Moody's ratings are geared to be similar to its credit ratings for corporations and the probability of default. Many times bonds retain a nondefault rating until after the company has in fact defaulted, which only serves to give investors a rating in hindsight. Recently this has led Congress to begin examining the method and validity of the these ratings. Now consider that the speed at which hedge funds can go from a viable business to hanging out a "Room for Rent" sign is light years faster than such an event typically happens to a corporate bond. Relying on these largely quantitative reports could prove problematical for a hedge fund investor. It was only a period of weeks and months before the likes of LTCM, MotherRock, and Amaranth went from the penthouse to the outhouse.

Morningstar uses a system similar to its mutual ranking system. As you will see in Chapter 5, the use of analysis that is helpful in reviewing traditional assets has little value in pointing out telltale signs in troubled hedge funds. The lack of transparency that is characteristic in the hedge fund world will do nothing to help the analysis. During the tech bubble the number of mutual funds that had five-star rankings was enormous. As a result Morningstar did in fact revise its mutual fund rating system in 2003, albeit too late for investors.

It is probably worthwhile to provide a brief description of the Morningstar system for rating hedge funds. Morningstar goes through several calculations to arrive at a Morningstar Risk-Adjusted Return (MRAR), which is used to provide an overall rank. Morningstar applies a statistical unsmoothing procedure to remove the first order serial correlation and uses the result to estimate risk-adjusted returns. Noting that investors are risk-averse and dislike downside deviation, Morningstar gives more weight to downside variation when calculating MRAR and does not make any assumption about the distribution of excess returns:

In the MRAR, when funds are graded, return is rewarded and risk is penalized in all cases. MRAR is expressed as an annual return and therefore can be decomposed in the return component MRAR (0) and the risk component MRAR(0)−MRAR(2) or MR−MRAR.

The results of the universe of hedge funds for 3, 5, and 10 years are put into a bell curve with the scores and weighted total score.

Score	Percent	Label
5	Top 10%	High
4	Next 22.5%	Above Average
3	Next 35%	Average
2	Next 22.5%	Below Average
1	Bottom 10%	Low

Period	Rating	Weight	Multiples
10 Yr	3	50	1.5
5 Yr.	2	30	0.6
3 Yr.	2	20	0.4
Total			2.5 = Rating 3 Stars (rounds up)

The end product derives a rating ostensibly from length of service and performance. No attention is given to the qualitative factor that can greatly impact the fund.

Again, I do not wish to disparage or single out the products or services of either of these companies. My only concern is to point out the rise in companies that will try to provide some service for a fee, but it may not be sufficient to discharge anyone's duty as a fiduciary. Moody's and Morningstar are quite well known and provide a useful service, but of course there are many others that also provide different levels of analysis. It is also worth noting that the number of folks with the ability to understand, analyze, and interpret the activities of hedge funds is limited. The ability to recognize warning signs or pick the wheat from the chaff does not begin and end with sophisticated quantitative tactics, but rather also makes use of good old fashioned qualitative factors that may not fill a spread sheet. One such service that does combine extensive quantitative and qualitative research in its product is Albourne. Albourne can help fill in gaps in one's own work, but the price tag may be steep for mere mortals. Reports are voluminous but they should not replace an investor's old-fashioned work.

WHERE DO I START?

With a sound investment policy in hand, the next step toward finding a successful investment is to plan the search and selection process. The sourcing of hedge fund managers is key. Narrowing down the thousands of hedge fund managers is the first step in a long journey. The IPS will set criteria for asset size, risk/return, and qualifications of the managers, length in business, and other measures. How you search and get access to those prime managers is your next worry. Whether you are a small pension plan, an endowment, or a wealthy individual, getting a peek into the opaque world of hedge funds may not be easy. One of the main reasons Yale, Harvard, and Duke have been able to expertly execute their hedge fund strategy is that they are constantly hounded by new, old, and yet to be launched hedge funds. The search, in effect, comes to them. Using different databases and developing a network will become important assets in helping an investor execute a successful strategy.

It is crucial to remember that regardless of whether you are looking at a single fund or building an entire portfolio, you need to follow a consistent process that provides you (or your board) with a level of confidence that the due diligence process was extensive and rigorous. No one wants to read about his or her hedge fund selection on the front page of the financial pages for spurious reasons.

CHAPTER 2

Large versus Small Funds

Good Things in Small Packages

One question that is continually being asked is how one can obtain alpha in hedge funds. The most common response is to find a manager that has a unique style or edge. Fair enough. Unfortunately the uniqueness that provides that edge is in many instances quickly duplicated. As money flows to a particular style or fund, the law of large numbers takes over. That is, the difficulty of finding the same advantage in large quantities is greatly reduced. There is a growing body of research suggesting that the elusive alpha can be obtained by focusing on small emerging hedge funds. The logic is similar in the more traditional markets. For example, the inefficiencies are more prevalent and better exploited in the small cap market than the large cap market. Why? Small companies are under-followed by Street research, which means that lots of money is not driving up prices, or in the case of hedge funds is driving out alpha. Additionally, the small cap companies have more focused business plans and the opportunities offer greater rewards.

This growing body of research unfortunately is having only a minor impact on how many investors allocate their capital to emerging hedge fund managers. The situation is quite similar to the old investment philosophy that many trust departments followed in the 1980s: no one ever got fired for buying IBM. Despite its relatively uninspiring performance, compared to several other technology rivals IBM was a perennial favorite on many trust department buy lists. It was perceived as safe, despite its sometimes meager returns. Like the upstart technology firms, new emerging hedge fund managers are viewed as "risky."

This questionable logic still exists today in the hedge fund world. Many consultants and wealth management asset allocators use investing in hedge funds as a means to retain business and not to truly provide a value-add to the clients. The recommended hedge fund is typically a billion-dollar fund with a 5- to 10-year track record and generally average results. That by no means implies that all large funds are average. Several—SAC, Tudor, and Moore Capital among others come to mind—are mega-sized funds that year in and year out produce above average results. However many of these require a large initial investment or are simply closed to new investors. In that case the only way to obtain exposure is through a Hedge Fund of Funds (HFOF) that has prior access or carved out capacity. The end result may be the inclusion of possibly other average funds with strong funds. It is true that the majority of hedge funds that close do so in the first couple of years of operations. The closings are due in large part to underfunded operations, poor infrastructure, and an unrealistic business plan.

The parallels to the small cap equity markets are stunning. Start-ups come and go, but if you compare the long-term returns of the capital markets it is quite apparent that the small emerging companies have better growth prospects on an earnings basis and on a stock appreciation basis. In Table 2.1, long term outperformance by small cap over large cap stocks can be seen as measured by the Russell Indexes for the period ending December 31, 2007. The trend is fairly consistent over many periods of time. Those of you who are fans of the classic Ibbotson studies (stocks, bonds, and cash) already understand that equities outperform bonds and that small cap equities have outperformed large cap. The recent results of the Russell indexes also demonstrate how styles come in and out of favor. As always, in the short run periods of outperformance can swing dramatically.

It therefore may not be a real stretch of reason to apply the same logic to hedge funds. Over the years several organizations, have made attempts to implement a strategy of investing in small, emerging managers. The work over the years was usually done by the enormous public pension

TABLE 2.1 Large Cap versus Small Cap Returns: 1998–2007

Period	Russell 1000	Russell 2000
1 Yr.	5.77%	−1.57%
3 Yr.	9.08%	6.80%
5 Yr.	13.43%	16.24%
10 Yr.	6.20%	7.08%

funds like CalPERS (California Public Employees Retirement Systems) or PSERS (Pennsylvania Public School Employee Retirement System). These "farm" teams, as they have been called, were constructed for a slightly different purpose. Due to the enormous size of these plans and the competition in finding new investment talent, CalPERS and PSERS apportion funds from the overall plans to fund new and emerging managers of traditional asset classes. They are typically monitored over a period of two to three years with the end goal of giving them a full allocation if they meet certain performance standards and growth of assets under management (AUM). At the small levels of allocations, a large upside or downside tends not to move the overall dial of fund performance. When the concept was formed, no one conceived that any exceptional performance would be the result of size but thought that it was just an exercise to find a new source to allocate funds. Over the years, this farm team concept evolved to include alternative asset managers. Similarly, the function was not to enhance the risk/return profile of the funds but to find unknown sources of investment talent.

Sometime in this period family offices and large endowments became heavy users of hedge funds in their asset allocation process. Family offices took a slightly different approach; they not only invested in various hedge fund strategies but also became seed investors in general partnerships, thereby making money in the fund and from the fund. This is a somewhat roundabout way of getting to the point that performance is higher in smaller funds.

Duke, Harvard, Stanford, and of course Yale had taken this unorthodox approach of investing in emerging hedge funds. To them, small emerging managers were a good source of alpha for several reasons: (1) they get direct access to the hedge fund investment team and improved transparency, (2) fee structures to early investors may be more favorable, and (3) the search for these funds became easier as they became the first call for many of the new funds seeking new investors. It should come as no surprise that these top endowment funds have had exceptional returns over the last 5 to 10 years while many other investors struggled.

In a field where a search for the next best thing continues to draw attention, scrutiny research studies began to pick up steam and provide guidance in the small versus long debate.

RESEARCH CONFIRMS SMALL FUND ADVANTAGE

Research into hedge funds is a relatively new venture. A lot of good work has come from academia and practitioners. Some of it is quite interesting and I believe has led to some crystallized thinking about investing in hedge funds. So how do we get to thinking about small hedge funds and alpha generation?

Back a few years I was attending a hedge fund conference sponsored by the CFA Institute. One of the speakers was Dr. David A. Hsieh, a professor of finance at Duke University's Fuqua School of Business, whose topic was "The Search for Alpha." During his presentation he made an interesting observation that stoked my inquisitive fires. Dr. Hsieh rather casually remarked that he thought there was a finite source of alpha. I have no recollection of the quantity that was mentioned because, to me, the absolute level paled in comparison to the fact that the search for this elusive beast called alpha was not only difficult but came in limited quantities. Remember the discussion of small cap outperformance? The alpha generation was the result of market efficiencies, or the lack of them in the case of small cap. As more money flows to the inefficient market or stocks, the probabilities of outperformance or alpha decreases. Makes sense! This is not to say that there is no alpha to be gained in large cap, or in large funds for that matter. If the large versus small argument applies, it may tell us that the probability of alpha generation may be higher in small funds.

Crestmont Research was one firm that noticed there was a bifurcation of institutional quality funds and entrepreneurial funds. Most of the capital flows in the industry were going to the larger funds from the large HFOF and institutional investors. It was noted that institutional funds tend to be large funds with relatively modest return objectives (T-Bills plus 3 to 6 percent). Entrepreneurial funds tend to be smaller and have more aggressive return targets (T-Bill plus 5 to 10 percent).

Several studies have taken the next logical step to see if the theory that alpha generation is related to size was applicable to the growing hedge fund market. One of the most interesting studies was conducted by Meredith Jones of PerTrac Financial Solutions.

The study was done by creating three size-based hedge fund indices: less than $100 million in AUM (Small), $100 to $500 million in AUM (Medium), and over $500 million in AUM (Large). Performance records from Hedge Fund Research (HFRI), HedgeFund.net, Altvest (from Investor-Force), and Barclays Global HedgeSource databases were combined into a single database. Monthly performance data from January 1996 to July 2006 were collected and duplicate records were eliminated. Adjustments to the database were also made to eliminate confusion or impact from funds that were denominated in a non-U.S. currency with a very different value from the U.S. dollar. The results are broken out in Tables 2.2 through 2.4.

TABLE 2.2 Small HF Index (<$100 m)

	Month	Quarter	Annualized
Compound returns	1.20%	3.66%	15.46%
Arithmetic mean	1.22%	3.76%	N/A
Standard deviation	1.82%	3.92%	6.31%
Semi deviation	1.87%	2.90%	6.49%
Down deviation (5%)	0.90%	1.41%	3.13%
Sharpe (2%)	0.58	0.88	2.01
Sortino (5%)	0.88	1.73	3.06

Source: Pertrac Financial Solutions, Meredith Jones.

The results show a pattern quite consistent with the results that Ibbotson discovered in measuring returns of large, mid, and small cap stocks; the small hedge funds index provided an annualized return of 15.46 percent, medium-sized hedge funds produced an annualized return of 12.50 percent, and the large hedge fund index produced the lowest annualized return of 11.93 percent. One of the truly great investors of all time, Peter Lynch, may have had some insight into what the results of this test might be. Mr. Lynch, after 13 successful years at the Magellan Fund, retired at a very early age. As the fund grew to $14 billion in size it became increasingly difficult to provide high levels of outperformance. In his 13-year career, Lynch's Magellan Fund returned an unbelievable 29.2 percent per annum to investors, beating the market by 13.4 percent annually. Outperforming a benchmark with large pools of capital can be an uphill struggle. Recently, after the fund had been closed for a decade, Fidelity reopened it. Prior to

TABLE 2.3 Medium HF Index ($100–$500 m)

	Month	Quarter	Annualized
Compound returns	0.99%	2.99%	12.50%
Arithmetic mean	1.00%	3.07%	N/A
Standard deviation	1.70%	3.26%	5.98%
Semi deviation	1.50%	2.93%	5.20%
Down deviation (5%)	0.78%	1.18%	2.70%
Sharpe (2%)	0.49	0.79	1.7
Sortino (5%)	0.74	1.49	2.56

Source: Pertrac Financial Solutions, Meredith Jones.

TABLE 2.4 Large HF Index (>$500 m)

	Month	Quarter	Annualized
Compound returns	0.94%	2.86%	11.93%
Arithmetic mean	0.96%	2.92%	N/A
Standard deviation	1.65%	2.88%	5.72%
Semi deviation	1.48%	2.74%	5.14%
Down deviation (5%)	0.79%	1.12%	2.75%
Sharpe (2%)	0.48	0.84	1.66
Sortino (5%)	0.68	1.46	2.34

Source: Pertrac Financial Solutions, Meredith Jones.

closure the fund underperformed for seven years. Julian Robertson, of Tiger Fund fame, came to a similar conclusion several years back when he closed his famous hedge fund after the outsized returns he had produced for years became more difficult as the fund grew to an enormous size. Unlike some other fund managers, Mr. Robertson made the correct decision to shut the fund rather than keep producing what he perceived as mediocre returns for the sake of continuing to receive management fees.

There also have been some misperceptions about size as it applies to money managers and hedge funds in particular. Many trustees and consultants take the approach that there is enormous risk in choosing small hedge funds while tending to ignore the risk in large hedge funds, such as poor performance or illiquid positions to pursue added alpha There are some levels of risk present in investing in small hedge funds. These risks can be mitigated by a sound due diligence process. This is not for the faint of heart or casual investor. It is very time and resource intensive and involves not only deep quantitative analysis but an inquisitive mind to understand the rather gray areas. The risk that gets overwhelmed by these perceived risks of instability in all small hedge funds is that of investment returns. Headline risk to trustees and consultants continually outweighs the inferior performance of the large hedge funds that are chosen. The question is, should this risk be so important? So far, many remain unconvinced by the above research or quite possibly just ignore it.

Several other studies have examined the relative outperformance of smaller funds. As seen in Table 2.5, there is a decline of 706 basis points from Year 1 returns to Year 7 returns. Also, the return per unit risk (risk as measured by standard deviation.) shows a slight deterioration as the fund ages from Year 1 to Year 7. The progression is not as clear; however, the trend shown indicates that although more analysis needs to be done, the

TABLE 2.5 Annual Returns vs. Return per Unit Risk

Year of Fund Life	Annual Return	Return/Unit Risk
1	22.40%	4.53
2	18.25%	4.09
3	17.37%	4.07
4	17.39%	4.17
5	14.59%	3.54
6	15.61%	3.44
7	15.34%	3.26

Source: The Investor's Guide to Hedge Funds, by Sam Kirschner, Eldon C. Mayer, and Lee Kessler (John Wiley & Sons, 2006). Reprinted with permission from John Wiley & Sons, Inc.

results of previous studies confirm that the relationship between performance and fund aging seems intact.

One of the major factors that affect the analysis of these results is survivor bias, which is also the warning siren of many folks who comment on the sustainability and level of performance of hedge funds. Survivor bias is a factor in the analysis of any theory in the investment world. Several studies have examined the effect of survivor bias. A study by Cross Border Capital demonstrated that after adjusting for survivor bias, funds in the early years outperformed older funds by approximately 1000 basis points.

On a smaller scale, in 2005 I examined the literature to analyze the thesis as it might relate to the perceived risk related to investing in smaller funds, those defined as being <$1 billion in AUM. Combing through the databases, I discovered that the median age for single strategy hedge funds was 44 months and 52 months for HFOF. This takes into account live and dead funds (funds no longer reporting). The data point to a life cycle of funds. More than 17 years of data on the survivor bias, or funds that are no longer in existence, is twice as high for single strategy funds: 1.52 percent versus 0.70 percent for funds of funds, on an annual basis.

This led to an examination of the life cycle of funds as it related to performance and fund flows as they relate to optimal fund size. Studies revealed performance across underlying hedge fund strategies were strongest in the early years of their life and at asset levels much lower than where the fund choose to either close or liquidate. Overall, large single strategy hedge funds underperform small ones as the level of assets grows. The conclusion was scale, while preferable for expenses, was a disadvantage as it related to performance.

PERFORMANCE OF NEW SMALL FUNDS

In recent years, 800 to 1,200 new funds have been launched annually. The amount of funds invested when the doors open varies widely; some are launched with a mere few million from family and friends, while others open and close the same day with several billion from an A-list of prospects. A study of newly launched funds by Sam Kirschner, of Mayercap LLC, provides a convincing argument that larger funds may be more profitable for managers than they are for investors. (*The Investor's Guide to Hedge Funds*, by Sam Kirschner, Eldon C. Mayer, and Lee Kessler, John Wiley & Sons, 2006).

The study examined funds that began their operations in calendar year 2003 and compared the results to relevant benchmarks in 2004 and 2005. The study selected a sample of 167 managers who were selected primarily on the basis of strategy and AUM. According to HFRI, there were about 900 funds launched in 2003. About 15 percent were eliminated for being long only funds (equity and fixed income), short only, multi-strategy, or unclassified. Managers with less than $30 million in AUM were eliminated, since they are seen as having insufficient infrastructure and operational shortcomings. This was about 50 percent of the funds. The remaining 15 percent eliminated from this study were funds that had assets under management in excess of $250 million. The final sample represented approximately 15 percent of the 2003 class. Table 2.6 provides details of the sample that was analyzed for performance.

TABLE 2.6 Hedge Fund Class of 2003 Sample (Strategy and Fund Size)

Strategy	Average Assets Under Management (millions)	# of Funds
Convertible Arbitrage	$103.9	9
Managed Futures	$74.5	18
Distressed	$93.1	20
Equity Market Neutral	$97.7	10
Fixed Income Arbitrage	$88.0	19
Global Macro	$101.6	12
Equity Long/Short	$91.4	59
Event Driven	$128.5	20
Average $AUM/Total Funds	**$97.3**	**167**

Source: The Investor's Guide to Hedge Funds, by Sam Kirschner, Eldon C. Mayer, and Lee Kessler (John Wiley & Sons, 2006). Reprinted with permission from John Wiley & Sons, Inc.

TABLE 2.7 Performance 2004–2005 (Class 2003 vs. MSCI & CS/Tremont Indexes)

Hedge Funds and Indexes	Performance
Class 2003 Equal Weighted	22.03%
Class 2003 Asset Weighted	25.34%
MSCI HF Equal Weighted	15.29%
MSCI HF Index Asset Weighted	15.51%
CS/Tremont Investable HF Index	9.10%

Source: The Investor's Guide to Hedge Funds, by Sam Kirschner, Eldon C. Mayer, and Lee Kessler (John Wiley & Sons, 2006). Reprinted with permission from John Wiley & Sons, Inc.

The research study then calculated the performance over the following two-year period for the Class of 2003. The funds and the indexes had the performance results compared on an equal weighted and asset weighted basis. Table 2.7 lists the performance results.

The study performed a similar study in 2005 using the Class of 2004. In addition to the categories used in the first study, the Class of 2004 study included Emerging Markets as a separate category. The sample represented about 25 percent of the Class of 2004, as hedge funds were eliminated in a fashion similar to that of the Class of 2003 study. Table 2.8 lists the strategies, AUM, and number of funds.

TABLE 2.8 Hedge Fund Class of 2004 Sample (Strategy and Fund Size)

Strategy	Average Assets Under Management (millions)	# of Funds
Convertible Arbitrage	$90.5	7
Distressed	$122.2	16
Equity Market Neutral	$84.0	11
Fixed Income Arbitrage	$92.5	17
Global Macro	$92.4	14
Equity Long/Short	$93.5	88
Event Driven	$95.9	22
Managed Futures	$83.3	21
Emerging Markets	$85.4	23
Average $AUM/Total Funds	$93.3	219

Source: The Investor's Guide to Hedge Funds, by Sam Kirschner, Eldon C. Mayer, and Lee Kessler (John Wiley & Sons, 2006). Reprinted with permission from John Wiley & Sons, Inc.

TABLE 2.9 Performance 2005 (Class 2004 vs. MSCI &
CS/Tremont Indexes)

Hedge Funds and Indexes	Performance
Class 2004 Equal Weighted	11.51%
Class 2004 Asset Weighted	13.28%
Class 2003 Equal Weighted	9.55%
Class 2003 Asset Weighted	12.67%
MSCI HF Index Equal Weighted	8.20%
MSCI HF Index Asset Weighted	7.67%
CS/Tremont Investable HF Index	4.70%

Source: The Investor's Guide to Hedge Funds, by Sam
Kirschner, Eldon C. Mayer, and Lee Kessler (John Wiley &
Sons, 2006). Reprinted with permission from John Wiley &
Sons, Inc.

The investment returns were then calculated in a fashion similar to the
analysis of the Class of 2003 (see Table 2.9). The analysis produced results
that were identical in trend to the Class of 2003. One interesting discovery
was that the Class of 2004, on an equal weighted and asset weighted basis,
outperformed the Class of 2003. Also of interest was the fact that the Class
of 2003 outperformed the indexes for that period.

ATTRITION RATES

As we discussed earlier, survivor bias is a key factor in the analysis of
performance figures. The study by Kirschner, Mayer, and Kessler revealed
that of the 167 funds in the Class of 2003, none closed in 2004, two closed
and liquidated at year-end 2004, and another closed by year-end 2005. This
equates to a failure rate of 1.2 percent in 2004 and 7.3 percent in 2005.
Studies of the various databases have estimated attrition rates for the hedge
fund universe in 2005 in the range of 3.9 percent to 11.4 percent, with the
mean from the four databases at 8.1 percent.

For the Class of 2004, of the 219 funds selected, none closed during
2004, one liquidated by year-end, and another 15 closed by the year-end of
2005. The total failure rate for the group was 7.3 percent, lower than the
mean attrition rate for 2005 of 8.1 percent.

To even the most skeptical of critics viewing these results, the study
conducted by Dr. Kirschner and his associates at Mayercap demonstrated
that the outperformance of new funds is an investment strategy to profitably
pursue.

DRIVERS OF OUTPERFORMANCE

How do we explain this pattern of outperformance by the small funds? The answer quickly supplied by many is that these funds take on higher levels of risk. A quick review of the tables presented in this chapter shows that small funds and small cap funds do have a higher risk profile, although not significantly higher. As measured by an aging process, those funds also have higher risk profiles but again not significantly higher.

We need to examine some other areas to explain this outperformance. One possible source may lie in the ability to exploit niche activities or opportunities. Managers that invest smaller pools of capital are able to find opportunities that are less liquid or would be of insufficient size for larger funds. For example, a stock spin-off might result in an outstanding stock float of two hundred thousand shares or a convertible bond issue of $200 million. If a several hundred million dollar or billion dollar fund takes a position that will provide a meaningful result in investment return, on a risk/return profile it will not be within parameters of the fund. The time and effort that is required to research the investment idea may not provide enough return to show any marginal increase in overall performance. A $3 to $5 million position in a $100 million fund is quite different from a $3 to $5 million position in a $1 billion fund. Not only is this a difficult trade to execute on the buy side, it could be even more difficult when the time or need to sell is reached. Liquidity in small issues has a way of drying up quickly, and as liquidity shrinks so does the market price or, more precisely, the investment return.

One way to assess the perceived level of risk is to examine the alignment of interests in a fund. This is as true of a hedge fund as it is of a mutual fund or even company stock. For an investor to have its fund manager or management team see substantial ownership or investment by the principals alongside normal investors typically produces different actions and results.

INVESTED INTERESTS

One of the key factors in performing due diligence is to analyze whether the interests of the manager are on the same side as those of other investors. Is the manager willing to invest a substantial portion of his own net worth in the fund? When a manager puts 50 percent of his net worth into a fund and this is a significant portion of that fund, there is some level of comfort that the risk profile will not be one to make your heart stop. That is not to say that the risk has evaporated, but a manager that is heavily vested in a fund he owns and runs has a high probability of not wanting to blow up the fund for two simple reasons: 1) he stands a great chance to lose a substantial amount of his money, and 2) he will need to find a new job, and the first line on his resume will read that his last position was as an explosives expert on a hedge fund. Serious managers do not want to be in either position.

ALIGNED INTERESTS

A manager who has just started a new fund has two real goals. The first is to provide exceptional risk-adjusted returns. The second is to attract new capital into the fund.

With 800 to 1,200 new funds starting every year, the competition to attract new investors is stiff. There are few investors, if any, looking for mediocre performance. To attract the attention and interest of new investors the manager must not only compete with other new funds, he must also compete with established well-known funds. It is a clear choice, if the performance is so-so, to choose the well-established firm where operational risk is likely to be of less concern. A manager that has his own capital on the line is in all probability not charging a management fee on his own investment. The cash flow of a new fund is then almost entirely dependent on the performance fee. The mathematics is simple:

$$\$50,000,000 * 1.1931 = \$59,655,000 \quad \text{Year-end value}$$
$$\$59,655,000 - \$50,000,000 = 9,655,000 \quad \text{Performance gain}$$
$$\$9,655,000 * 20\% = \$1,931,000 \quad \text{Performance fee}$$

A $50 million fund (excluding the manager's stake) will collect, on average, 1 percent in a management fee or $500,000 annually. It may seem like a substantial amount, but that must pay for the operation of the fund, which includes computers, data, legal, accounting, administrative fees, marketing, office space, and employee salaries. In many of the high-rent districts of the financial world (New York, London, or Singapore), $500,000 will not go very far. But now let's assume, that a manager's investment strategy produced an annual return of 19.31 percent (average of the Class of 2003 and 2004 asset weighted returns). The performance fee is typically 20 percent, or a cash flow of $1,931,000, or nearly four times the amount of the management fee. The hedge fund manager has a very high vested interest in providing the best return, since it will be highly profitable to the hedge fund manager and the investors. Concern that the manager will take undue risk is mitigated to a large extent if the manager has indeed a significant amount of his own net worth tied up in the fund.

Compare this now to the $1 billion hedge fund. Using the results of the Class of 2003 and 2004 again, the average gain of the asset weighted returns for the indexes was 11.59 percent. This translates into a management fee of $10 million and performance fee of $23.2 million. This is quite substantial; however. the ratio to the management fee is barely over two times. The point is rapidly approaching when the manager wishes to protect the stability of the business and the risk profile of the fund starts to be lower. Succinctly stated, the manager is now trying to preserve the management fee and is willing to accept a lower risk/return profile in order not to blow up the entire business. This may be a sound strategy for the manager but it is not to the advantage of the investor. As these funds get larger, they begin to float across the radar screen of institutions and consultants. The focus of the firm shifts in many cases to asset accumulation and retention. Large firms provide institutions and consultants with a sense of stability and safety. Outsize returns become secondary or even tertiary.

POINT OF DIMINISHING RETURNS

It is difficult to predict a precise ideal size for each hedge fund strategy. From the studies discussed in this chapter, the sweet spot appears to be managers with $30 to $250 million assets under management. One must remember that the due diligence required at this level is substantially higher. The time and effort to do this will be well-spent, as the performance results indicate. The returns out of this fund asset range may still be attractive, but the returns and costs must be compared to other investments (indexing) that provide similar returns without the issues of transparency, liquidity, and others.

This is not to say that all large funds will be underperformers; however, the probability of underperformance seems to be higher. A profile of successful large hedge funds shows a management that instills a highly entrepreneurial atmosphere that incentivizes and provides focus and drive to its employees. Ideas get developed by highly motivated intelligent people who hone their ideas and processes many times while safely ensconced in the comfortable confines of a large firm. They can mimic state-of-the-art risk management and trading operations without spending hundred of millions of dollars. Direct lending, bridge financing, pollution control credits, and alternative energy trading are many of the new ideas that have begun to spring up in the small hedge fund space.

The idea of using smaller funds needs to be carefully reviewed by any investor. There is a growing body of evidence showing that those with the ability to find emerging managers who can consistently provide alpha will find ongoing sources of new edge. However, even with the ongoing research, it is not advisable to jump blindly into the small emerging manager pool.

MASTER OF TREND LINE ANALYSIS

Whether this strategy is applicable is unclear and further research is needed. There are many more factors that need to be understood or adjusted before any true conclusion can be formulated. Some results appear to show similar conclusions, but effects of leverage at the fund and fund of funds levels, plus a better understanding of the underlying strategies, need to be explored. The lack of transparency at the fund level offers a challenge to understanding allocation and strategies of the underlying funds. Starting with a fund of funds dedicated to one type of underlying strategy does offer some positive results.

CHAPTER 3

The Search for an Honest Man

Finding Your Manager

During the times of ancient Greece, there was a beggar who made his home in a large tub on the streets of Athens. His name was Diogenes. Diogenes spent his days walking the streets, holding a lighted lantern and looking for an honest man. He never found one. In the process he did, however, expose many lawyers, and he became known as a member of the philosophical School of Cynics.

The search to find a good hedge fund manager may seem remarkably similar to the quest of Diogenes. I do believe there are many honest folks in the hedge fund business. Finding one will, however, require a set of tools similar to those involved in Diogenes's search: a lighted lantern (deep insights) and a healthy amount of cynicism. A prospective investor has already undergone a lengthy process of defining his investment guidelines and parameters now he must make a definitive decision to allocate a target level of capital to hedge funds. This involves the arduous task of sourcing the managers, which is more complex than a search to locate and analyze traditional long-only managers.

Hedge funds, unlike mutual funds and traditional investment advisers, are not required to be registered with the Securities and Exchange Commission (SEC) or to report performance to a central source. SEC rules governing "accredited investors" and advertising keep information flow to a minimum. Accredited investors are those with an excess of $200,000 of gross annual income ($300,000 for couples), net worth (assets minus liabilities) in excess of $1 million, or who own more than $5 million in securities, real estate (exclusive of personal residence), or cash equivalents. Hedge funds are banned from advertising or speaking to the general public in what might be deemed marketing. As the hedge fund business has grown, so have the supporting vendors. The discreet nature of hedge funds and

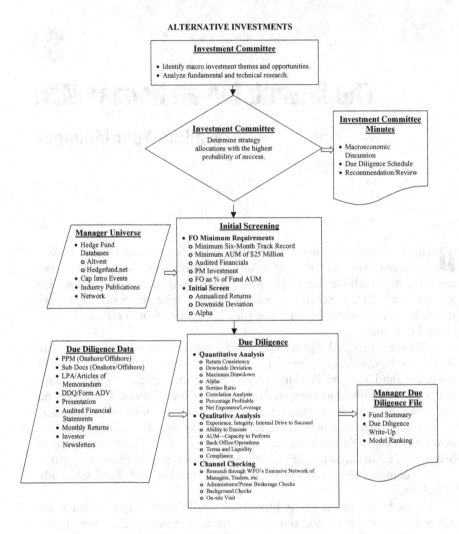

- For Internal Use Only -

FIGURE 3.1   Manager Search and Due Diligence Flowchart

their managers has led to a network of publications, databases, web sites, conferences, and old fashioned word of mouth through high level introductions that start with the hedge funds themselves. In order to establish a sense of consistency in the process, Figure 3.1 serves as an outline for a typical hedge fund selection and as a roadmap for the remaining chapters of this book.

PRIME BROKERS

As managers launch new single strategy hedge funds, they engage the service of prime brokers. Prime brokerage has been a major beneficiary of the explosion of hedge funds. It has been estimated that the prime brokerage business accounts for 15 to 20 percent of sales and revenues, including 40 percent of equity trading and 20 percent of fixed income trading. The major investment banks (listed below) have been aggressively building out their prime brokerage arms. The new hedge funds engage the prime broker to provide many services that make the start-up of small funds possible.

Largest Prime Brokerage Firms
Bank of America
Barclays Capital
Credit Suisse
Goldman Sachs
JPMorgan Chase
Morgan Stanley
UBS

The list is by no means exhaustive. The prime brokers provide trading, portfolio accounting, research, leverage, gross and net exposure calculations, and in some instances computers and office space. The theory behind this aid is that the hedge fund will use the prime broker's trading desk and that will provide a large stream of commissions. One may ask, "What does this have to do with manager selection?" Plenty! Investors, as part of their due diligence, should be very aware of the arrangement between any prime broker and a hedge fund. We will discuss in a later chapter additional roles prime brokers play in the due diligence process.

Many prime brokers require a fund to have a minimum level of assets under management (AUM) or it requires all trading to go through their desk. Several prime brokers may also require a minimum level of AUM. This requirement is not unreasonable, given the history that many funds under $25 million in AUM close within the first couple of years. This is not necessarily a negative—many provide an electronic trading system with up-to-date pricing, profit, and loss calculations. The execution in most instances is quite good. There is even a desk that will find stock to borrow for shorts and handle less liquid trades. This prime broker with an almost seemingly captive source of commission flow now has a somewhat vested interest in seeing this hedge fund succeed. Success in this instance means a steady increase in AUM. In order to help these funds get access to accredited investors, the prime brokerage firms organize events to which they invite accredited investors, consultants, pension plans, funds of funds, and other decision makers to a forum where the hedge fund can give a 15- or 20-minute pitch to a somewhat willing audience. This is the hedge fund equivalent of speed dating.

There are many options in the hedge fund business and seasoned analysts and investors can assess pretty quickly whether they want a second date. These short presentations are typically followed by one-on-one meetings or informal chats, allowing for more direct contact and questioning of the aspiring hedge funds.

There are several advantages for the investor at these meetings. One of the biggest is discovering new and fresh talent. New studies have shown that hedge funds have better performance in the early stages of raising assets, since the fund managers are highly motivated and more reliant on performance fees than management fees. The managers may also be more forthcoming about the internal workings of their investment process, and in some instances may be more flexible on fee structure and lock-ups. These one-off deals, referred to as side pockets, are becoming rarer as the SEC has taken a position that the ability of one investor to receive preferential treatment from a fund should not differ from that of any other investor.

At these gatherings, investors also get exposed to numerous individuals with various levels of experience, who can then provide insight and perspective on strategies and other managers. In addition to the range of fund of fund investors, chief investment officers of endowments and foundations, and consultants and family offices, there are third-party marketers, software vendors, audit firms, law firms, and various other vendors that have cropped up to service the hedge fund market. The referral chain can extend your list of managers to several dozen. Moreover, many of the attendees at these prime broker events have attended similar events with other prime brokers. If you multiply the number of prime brokers by the number of strategies, sectors, or geographic exposure of hedge funds, and the number of funds, you'll get a compendium of several hundred hedge funds.

Remember, there are approximately 800 to 1,000 single strategy hedge funds being launched every year (2 to 3 per day). Uncovering the new rising stars from this could be a yeoman's task. It can also save you time, money, and possibly embarrassment. Each of these vendors brings a different perspective as to the expected success or failure of these newly launched businesses. For instance, a new hedge fund describes the experience of one of its top analysts and his contributions at another firm, yet when you speak to a software vendor and a performance verification specialist, they casually remember being surprised that he was hired, since they recall his contributions as being much less impressive. A court of law would call this hearsay, but it is definitely cause for concern. As you develop relationships with various people in the hedge fund space you will develop reliable sources.

Now, while this process may be a very time-efficient way to evaluate hedge fund managers, the level of efficiency falls dramatically as many of the funds are true start-ups with little in the way of an organization and assets. The risk level is high and you must remember that the prime brokers sponsoring the event are trying to help their own business grow. If by chance the hedge fund manager succeeds and you have a profitable investment, you both will have beaten steep odds.

CONFERENCES AND INDUSTRY EVENTS

Another convenient and efficient source of finding new hedge funds is the myriad of conferences and industry events that take place throughout the year. The conferences are typically held in warm exotic locations with good food and quite often some intellectually stimulating presentations. On a more regular basis there is a rotating forum that makes stops in most major financial centers. Frequent organizers of these events include GAIM, MarHedge (now Institutional Investor), Opal, Infovest21, Terrapin (Europe), HedgeFund.net, and Lipper.

The conferences in attractive locales such as Bermuda, Grand Cayman, Geneva, and various spots in Florida are usually multi-day events with the focus on daily presentations that can offer insights into the hedge fund business. As for speaking with a new star hedge fund manager, the odds here are a bit low. These conferences are heavily attended by third-party service vendors that sell their wares to hedge funds. Trading systems, analytical software, portfolio accounting systems, administrators, and legal counsel make up a solid portion of the attendees.

These venues, while fun, are rather expensive, and one needs to be quite innovative to uncover a new hedge fund in this atmosphere. However, innovative does not necessarily imply impossible. One of the lost skills in this day of gee-whiz quantitative systems and electronic communications is interacting with industry people. They know more about the functioning of hedge funds than many due diligence teams. They move in and about firms and have a strong sense of the firms that are succeeding and those that may be struggling. They religiously attend industry events and are versed in where the money, personnel, and performance are flowing. These folks can quickly provide volumes of insight into funds that may interest you, and they can tell you which funds you should not waste much time in pursuing. As I discuss later, they can also serve as a solid channel check when you may be further into the due diligence process to provide background and color on the operations and workings of the fund.

The industry also offers one- and two-day events that are much more practical and timely. You have an opportunity to meet with some fund managers and discuss some of the new strategies on the horizon. The venues in many financial centers have packed schedules and the interaction is limited to short breaks, lunch, and a later cocktail hour.

This rather long and detailed discussion of hedge fund events may seem laborious in description; however, it is offered to demonstrate that the truly successful investor is very innovative and dogmatic in his quest to find unknown alpha generators. Unless you happen to be on the same call list as the large institutional investors like Yale, Harvard, or CalPERS, which have new hedge funds racing to their doors, you will need to be quite inventive in sourcing managers. These events offer you an environment that is packed with people who have varied views of the hedge fund world and can offer direction, caution, and the names of some yet unknown manager.

INDUSTRY PUBLICATIONS

For someone trying to dig up a list of hedge funds, industry publications are a good source of information. The publications may be daily in electronic format or printed as weekly or monthly magazines. These will include features on new strategies, job movement of professionals, regulatory warnings, manager searches and assignments, and start-up and spin-off funds. These sources can be reviewed at your leisure. However, keep in mind that, in most circumstances, mass produced information does not usually reveal any secrets. It becomes incumbent on the investor to cobble together the flow of information to unearth a solid investment idea.

Some of the distributors of industry publications also have affiliated hedge fund businesses. The investor needs to always be cognizant of the source of information and the possibility of conflicts of interest (as covered by your IPS). Following is a list of some of the more prominent hedge fund publications.

> **Hedge Fund Publications**
> *Hedge Fund Alert*
> *Hedge Fund Intelligence*
> *Hedge Week*
> *Hedge Manager Review*
> *Hedge World*
> *Hedge Fund Daily*

Fierce Finance
Alpha Institutional Investor
FundFire
Absolute Return
The Hedge Fund Journal
Alternative Investment News
Albourne Village
Brighton House

INCUBATORS AND PLATFORMS

Some of the biggest competition for capacity to new managers comes from a variety of incubators, hedge fund platforms, and other seed capital organizations.

Hedge Fund Incubators, Platforms, and Other Notable Sources
Asset Alliance
BNP Paribas
BRI Partners
CalPERS
Capital Z
Decision Capital
Fairfield Greenwich
Fleming Family & Partners
Focus Investment
Frontpoint
Harcourt
HF Ventures
IXIS CIB
Larch Lane
Liberty Ermitage
Man Global
New Alpha Advisors
Protégé Partners
Putnam Lovell
RBC
Skybridge/MSD Capital
Société Générale
Thomas H. Lee
Weston Capital

Incubators are the simplest form of start-ups. New hedge fund managers trade their own capital and the incubator form provides things such as accounting and tax returns for the fund. It allows cost savings for the start-up and allows a vehicle for the manager to establish a track record.

A further extension of an incubator is a seed capital firm. A growing business in the hedge fund world is various seed capital organizations. These organizations review hundreds of new hedge fund business plans every year. In certain instances, they will provide funding in several different forms. Depending on their own organizational goals, they may provide capital to fund the early stage of the business, in return for a substantial percentage ownership in the General Partnership (GP). They may also provide investable assets in return for special fee arrangements and possibly a smaller stake in the GP. Finally, they may also offer something as simple as office space and computer services, which reduce the overhead of the fund while it launches the new venture. For those searching for emerging managers they can serve as an additional source of new names, as well as a channel check on a particular fund.

Some firms, primarily investment banks will build a hedge fund platform. This is an offering of hedge fund managers that typically will carve out capacity for the investment bank's client. The fund undergoes extensive due diligence before being placed on this platform and offers investors some level of confidence that the manager has cleared some scrutiny and is under an ongoing watchful eye.

INDUSTRY WEB SITES AND DATABASES

The largest source of manager sourcing is still hedge fund web sites and accompanying databases. These offer listings of managers along with investment returns, peer comparisons, research, and industry news. Some have searchable features that can provide an easy source of manager information. Some of the most widely used web sites are named in the following list.

Hedge Fund Information Database and Web Sites
AIMA (www.aima.org)
Altvest (www.investorforce.com)
Albourne Village (http://village.albourne.com)
Barclays Global Hedge Source (www.globalhedgesource.com)
CISDM (http://cisdm.som.umass.edu)
CogentHedge (www.cogenthedge.com)
EurekaHedge (www.eurekahedge.com)
Greenwich-Van (www.vanhedge.com)

HedgeFund.net (www.hedgefund.net)
Hedge Fund Research (www.hfr.net)
Hennessee Group (www.hennessee.com)
HF Intelligence (www.hedgefundintelligence.com)
Tass Tremont (www.tassresearch.com)
Strategic Financial Solutions (www.pertrac.com)
U.S. Offshore Funds Directory (www.hedgefundnews.com)

The use of databases allows for some easy screening across strategy, geography, AUM, and geography among others. Referring back to Figure 3.1, you can see the initial screening criteria that can be used. The database has an enormous amount of quantitative and qualitative data on each fund that has chosen to report. The criteria that an investor picks should conform to the goals, objectives, and restrictions outlined in the IPS. As mentioned in the Introduction, some measures are better suited than others in the hedge fund space. Some of the statistical measures we focus on are described here.

Alpha—This is the risk adjusted measure of excess return on an investment. It is the most common measure of assessing an active manager's performance in excess of some benchmark adjusted for risk. This is sometimes referred to as "skill-based" returns of a manager. The calculation is as follows:

$$\text{Alpha} = (R_i - R_f) - \text{Beta}(R_m - R_f)$$

where: $R_i =$ Return of the fund
$R_f =$ Risk free rate
$R_m =$ Return of the benchmark

Average Return (Mean)—This is the simple average return or arithmetic mean, which is calculated by taking the sum of returns for all periods and dividing by the total number of periods. This calculation does not take into account the effect of compounding of investment returns.

$$\text{Average Return} = \left(\sum_{I=1}^{N} R_I \right) \div N$$

where: $N =$ Number of Periods
$RI =$ Return for Period I

Downside Deviation—This measures returns that fall below a defined Minimum Acceptable Return (MAR) rather than the arithmetic mean. The investor can set the MAR at a risk free rate or hurdle rate.

$$\text{Downside Deviation} = \left[\left(\sum_{I=1}^{N} (L_I)^2 \right) \div N \right]^{1/2}$$

where: R_I = Return for Period I
N = Number of Periods
R_{MAR} = Period Minimum Acceptable Return
$L_I = R_I - R_{MAR}$ (If $R_I - R_{MAR} < 0$) or 0 (If $R_I - R_{MAR} \geq 0$)

Sharpe Ratio—A return/risk ratio, developed by Nobel Laureate William Sharpe. The return is the incremental average return minus a risk free rate, typically a Treasury security divided by the standard deviations of the returns. This measure can be misleading in analyzing hedge funds because the Sharpe ratio penalizes funds for positive upside returns as much as negative downside returns; however, it is still frequently used.

$$M_R = \left(\sum_{I=1}^{N} R_I \right) \div N \quad SD = \left(\sum_{I=1}^{N} (R_I - M_R)^2 \right) \div (N-1)^{1/2}$$

$$\text{Sharpe Ratio} = (M_R - R_{RF}) \div SD$$

where: R_I = Return for Period I
M_R = Mean of return set R
N = Number of Periods
SD = Period Standard Deviation
R_F = Period Risk Free Return

Standard Deviation—This is often used as a measure of investment risk. Mathematically it measures the dispersal or uncertainty in a random variable (i.e., investment returns). Or it measures the degree of variation of returns around the mean (average) return.

$$\text{Standard Deviation} = \left[\sum (R_I - M_R)^2 \div (N-1) \right]$$

where: R_I = Return of Fund
M_R = Mean Return
N = Number of Periods

Sortino Ratio—This is a return/risk ratio developed by Frank Sortino. It measures excess return per unit of risk based on downside semivariance. Since this ratio takes into account only the downside size and frequency of returns, it measures the reward to negative volatility trade-off. This is a useful calculation when returns are not normally distributed, as in the case of hedge funds.

where: R_I = Return for Period I
N = Number of Periods
R_{MAR} = Period of Minimum Acceptable Returns
DD_{MAR} = Downside Deviation
$L_I = R_I - R_{MAR}$ (If $R_I - R_{MAR} < 0$) or 0 (If $R_I - R_{MAR} \geq 0$)

$$DD_{MAR} = \left[\left(\sum (L_I)^2 \right) N \right]^{1/2}$$

$$\text{Sortino Ratio} = (R_I - R_{MAR}) \div DD_{MAR}$$

$$\text{Annualized Sortino} = \text{Monthly Sortino} \times (12)^{1/2}$$

$$\text{Annualized Sortino} = \text{Quarterly Sortino} \times (4)^{1/2}$$

Skewness—This is the degree of asymmetry of a distribution around its mean. Positive skewness indicates a distribution with an asymmetric tail extending toward positive values. This is a good characteristic for a hedge fund.

where: N = Number of Periods
R_I = Return for Period I
M_R = Mean of return set R
SD = Period Standard Deviation

$$M_R = \left(\sum_{I=1}^{N} R_I \right) \div N \quad SD = \left[\sum_{I=1}^{N} (R_I - M_R)^2 \div (N-1) \right]^{1/2}$$

$$\text{Skewness} = \{N \div [(N-1)(N-2)]\} \left[\sum_{I=1}^{N} (R_I - M_R) \div SD \right]^3$$

Sterling Ratio—This is another view of return/risk. The return used is the Compound Annualized Rate of Return over the last three years. The risk is defined as the Average Yearly Maximum Drawdown over the last three years less an arbitrary percent (10 percent).

where: D_1 = Maximum Drawdown for first 12 months
D_2 = Maximum Drawdown for the next 12 months
D_3 = Maximum Drawdown for the latest 12 months

$$\text{Average Drawdown} = (D_1 + D_2 + D_3) \div 3$$

$$\text{Sterling Ratio} = \text{Compounded Annualized ROR}$$
$$\div (\text{Average Drawdown} - 10\%)$$

Down Capture—This measures how much of a down market the fund participates in. The smaller the value, the more positive for the fund; the down capture of the investment's compound return when the benchmark was down divided by the benchmark's compounded return when the benchmark was down.

where: R_I = Return for Period I
RD_I = Benchmark Return for Period I
N = Number of Periods
R_p = Return of Investment for Period Measured
RD_p = Return of Benchmark for Period Measured

$$R_I = [(1 + R_0) \times (1 + R_1) \times \ldots \times (1 + R_N)] - 1$$

$$RD_I = [(1 + RD_0) \times (1 + RD_1) \times \ldots \times (1 + RD_N)] - 1$$

$$\text{Down Capture} = R_p \div RD_p$$

Drawdown—A Drawdown is any losing period during an investment record. It is defined as the percent retrenchment from an equity peak to an equity valley. In terms of time, a drawdown encompasses both the period from equity peak to equity valley (length) and the time from the equity valley to a new equity high (recovery).

Maximum Drawdown—Is the largest percentage drawdown that has occurred in any investment data record.

Gain to Loss Ratio—This is a simple ratio of the average gain in a gain period divided by the average loss in a losing period. Periods can be monthly or quarterly depending on the data frequency.

The statistics described above give the screener a starting point from which to launch a search. The decision as to what statistics to use should be dictated by the philosophy of the investor and driven by the investment mandate. It should be remembered that the statistics alone will be insufficient to render a decision and are only the first step in a long process. It should also be remembered that the managers should be screened against a relevant peer group and not against hedge fund benchmarks. The benchmarks tend to be broad in nature and may not provide insight into the fund's ability to meet the investor's goals. For example, an investor is searching for a large cap long/short equity fund and sorts through an analytical database for a fund with a three-year performance track record. Unfortunately, the databases categorize funds in broad terms and the output will list over 100 long/short equity funds. Included in that list will be every long/short equity fund with a three-year track record regardless of style. In the mix will be long/short energy funds, utility funds, health care funds, small cap, and even international and emerging markets funds. It would hardly be a fair comparison to use the long/short equity composite from any of the leading databases. The range of returns is long and wide and not very useful.

One other note of caution in using statistics: Mathematics is a precise science; measuring certain characteristics of investment portfolios is not. In a mean-variance world, standard deviation is used to measure risk. This is deceptive in a few ways. First, standard deviation is measured in relation to an average, a figure that has little meaning to investors. Second, all risk of variation around the mean is given equal weight. This means above-average annual returns is given an equal weight or risk rating as below-average returns. High above-average returns actually add to the overall risk of the portfolio. Finally, standard deviation assumes returns are normally distributed or bell-shaped. Hedge fund results are typically not normally distributed.

BUILDING YOUR OWN DATABASE

It will require more work, but it will be more effective to dig deep and develop a substantial list of manager candidates that are similar in style, sector, and geographic characteristics. It can be as simple as an Excel spreadsheet or, if you have the time and sophistication, a database program such as Access.

Memories tend to blur and papers end up falling behind a file cabinet that will never be moved. Making the effort to memorialize your work can save time and provide a quick refresher on earlier work. As you review hedge funds you can grade and rank the various portions of the firm that you have examined. The components that you rank will depend on which aspect of the fund is most important to your process. The important thing is to develop your own consistent format by which to evaluate each fund.

UNCONVENTIONAL SOURCES

The growth of the hedge fund business has added an unwitting and a rather unused source of hedge fund leads—the media. The upswing in cable TV and the Internet has opened an easy access, highly available source of hedge fund information. In addition to the growth of publications dealing with handling wealth, the development of search engines like Google provides current and historic information on investments, asset classes, and other areas of the Internet dealing with the hedge fund section of the investment business. Common but unlikely sources such as the *Wall Street Journal*, *Financial Times*, Bloomberg.com, Fox Financial, and CNBC may present you with an unknown fund or strategy.

It is also useful at this point to remind readers of the hazards that accompany the technology advances of cable TV and the Internet. As news is now made and reported in nanoseconds, sometimes the truth is lacking and sensationalism is the order of the day. The true thrust of due diligence is to never take anything at face value. Being a cynic (Diogenes), while not making you a hit at social outings, will typically serve you well as you slosh through the opaque world of hedge funds.

SIX STEPS TO KEVIN BACON

In the early 1990s, the fun loving pop culture crowd came up with what seemed to be a rather mindless and pointless game called "six degrees of Kevin Bacon." The premise behind this parlor game was that it was possible to tie any Hollywood actor or actress to Kevin Bacon through six or fewer connections from other actors and actresses in related movies or television series. For example, let us take Marilu Henner. Marilu Henner starred in *Perfect* with Lorraine Newman, who starred in *Saturday Night Live* with John Belushi, who starred in *Animal House* with—you guessed it— Kevin Bacon. The connection from Marilu Henner to Kevin Bacon took only three steps.

By now you're probably wondering if I've lost my mind, but one of the most valuable and most underutilized sources of managers and due diligence is developing a powerful network of Kevin Bacons. Visit any business section of your local bookstore and you will come across many volumes dedicated to developing professional networks. I would offer that there is one key difference between what I'm suggesting and what most of those books prescribe. You should make every effort to be helpful and pass on information and insight to others. You should also remember that you do not want to be part of a gossipy, whisper-down-the-lane kind of scheme. Being professional and honest in providing information and assessments will pay handsome dividends in your efforts. In effect, when you begin a search or need background information on a fund or portfolio manager, you will possibly be less than six phone calls away from your Kevin Bacon.

Once you have established yourself as a reliable professional, folks will seek your opinion and will be more than happy to provide you with leads and insights in the hope that they will be able to count on you to return the favor. It does take effort and honesty to build your network, but your ability to be out front with emerging managers and to form reliable judgments about their abilities is something you can never find in complicated, quantitative models, or by pouring over due diligence questionnaires for hours, or spending countless dollars on buying information drawn from credit agencies, court filings, and news headlines. The science is helpful but the art (thanks to Kevin Bacon) is the edge that can provide handsome returns.

One experience of mine really drove this point home to me. A firm I was previously associated with was considering an allocation to a hedge fund that was referred to us by a third party marketer. The performance numbers were good but not great. As I reviewed all the relevant information, I was not confident that this was a firm that we should be locked into for the next year. I placed a call to someone I knew who was working in the same city as the hedge fund. It wasn't a major financial city, so information overall was light. This conversation led me to discover my contact and the hedge fund manager had in fact worked together previously, but the lead portfolio manager of the fund had been asked to leave for several reasons.

As I mentioned earlier, if something does not feel right—run. We decided to delay our investment in the fund until our Investment Committee could properly weigh the information I received. It turns out we did not have to wait long. A news blurb from one of the trade magazines revealed that the lead portfolio manager, about whom we had reservations, had been arrested on a variety of charges (unrelated to the hedge fund). I have always subscribed to the adage that I would rather be lucky than smart. In this case it was especially true.

There is one final point I would like you to consider. In dealing with this vast network of people, you need to remember that many of these folks are in sales and marketing and their main job is to sell. I do not wish to condemn sales people, as they provide a valuable service to this industry. However, one should never lose sight that by the very nature of their position they have conflicts of interest. Their job is to sell, and while out-and-out deception (or as the SEC refers to it—fraud) is certainly not an acceptable practice, they will put sufficient spin on a product to make sure it is viewed in a positive light. It's important to remember, though, that if they intend to have a long career they must execute their position with a certain level of integrity.

Again, a first-hand example hammered home the concept when I was dealing with a new marketer. He was quite excited to present to me the firm's flagship fund. The brief overview convinced me that the fund warranted some further investigation. Several weeks passed after our first meeting and

I received a call from this marketing person, who informed me that he had left the hedge fund and was going to represent a couple of other hedge funds as a third party marketer. I asked him point blank why he had a sudden change of heart. He could have lied or made up some story, but he did not. He responded quite candidly—he was preparing some new marketing material, but was having trouble squaring off all of the historical performance numbers. When he had repeatedly asked the portfolio manager for the appropriate back-up documents, he received mumbled answers and no documents. He quickly reached the conclusion that the data was inaccurate, and confronted the portfolio manager to inform him he was quitting. I told him I appreciated his forthrightness, and when he was ready I would gladly review the new funds he was representing.

After I hung up the phone, I went back and reviewed my notes and the data I received from that first meeting. With the new pieces of information, I wanted to review the material and try to analyze the data to see if there was any way I could have picked up the discrepancies. This is a practice that I continue to use to this day. Any time I receive news or information that negatively impacts the view of a given fund, I try to conduct some analysis to see if the problem was detectable, and therefore avoidable. Hindsight can sometimes give you great foresight.

No matter how long you are in this business or how many funds you review, there will come a time when a mistake is made. The key is to hope that the mistake has a minor impact on your funds, but more importantly, to learn and apply. In the hedge fund world you always need to reevaluate what and how you do things. Everyone makes mistakes; the objective is to learn from them so as to avoid future pitfalls.

SIZING UP THE FLOCK

After you have given a cursory review of the new hedge fund's performance, process, and people, you would typically begin a more formal and comprehensive documentation of the hedge fund's business model and activity. Enter the Due Diligence Questionnaire (DDQ). This document, used for reviewing a Fund of Funds, comes in various versions and you can customize one to target your concerns more directly. So common is this practice of using a DDQ, many hedge funds have written one to cover their own firm and funds. For many investors this is sufficient, although it may have some gaps. Those issues are easily covered with a follow-up telephone call or e-mail. Accepting a fund's DDQ quickens the pace of your undertaking.

See Appendix C for a sample DDQ.

WHAT'S IN THE DDQ?

The first section of the DDQ includes general information (name, address, telephone and fax numbers, and web site), as well as more specific information about the ownership structure, organizational chart, and employee background and history. Section II asks the manager to give detailed information about the fund's investment process, strategy, and philosophy. Section III asks for details involving the business plan, such as plans for growth and capacity restraints.

One important issue that is not covered in many DDQs is that of capacity restraints. Capacity restraints will delve into the thought process of the manager as to where his comfort level is if the fund is to have an edge or produce alpha. If a small cap manager says he has a capacity for AUM to be $5 billion, this should raise alarms about the manager's knowledge of the small cap space. This figure will also be useful later on as new managers may tend to target a low AUM capacity. When assets do start rolling in, it will be informative to observe whether they maintain their initial assumption. For example, a small cap long/short hedge fund makes an initial assumption of its capacity to be at $500 million. Two years later the fund is approaching that level. However, instead of closing the fund to new investors, the manager raises his capacity target to $1 billion. There needs to be a detailed explanation as to why the target has changed; the logic will give you insight into what your expectations from this fund should be. Going from $500 million to $1 billion is not outrageous, but it does fundamentally change the type of investing a manager may choose. In Chapter 8, which discusses monitoring managers, we will delve more deeply into the impact of such decisions.

Section V in this version of the DDQ deals specifically with manager search and selection as it relates to a HFOF. In a single strategy hedge fund this section would ask some additional questions about the process of buying or selling an investment idea.

Section V, also specific to a HFOF, gives the manager a closer look at risk management of the fund. The same thought process is applicable to single fund strategies. How each manager, whether a FOF or Single Strategy, manages the risk of the portfolio is quite important to the investor. Pricing, leverage, position size, liquidity, credit risk, and fraud are all relevant to the risk profile of hedge fund managers.

Risk management is one area that reminds one of the weather: many talk about it but no one ever does anything about it. The fund's responses about the level of leverage applied, position limits, transparency, and derivative exposure are key to understanding where and how a liquidity squeeze may hit the fund. Once you have an understanding of how leverage is applied, a follow-up question would be to ask for historical data on ongoing levels of leverage. This is helpful in determining whether the fund is producing true alpha or is leveraged to the full extent of its limits.

Section VI deals with the fund's performance reporting and fees. Most funds tend to produce performance estimates by around the fifth business day of the month. Once you are an investor in a fund, you may receive a "flash" estimate from the fund at mid-month. This is useful to provide some insight of how a fund may be reacting to certain market conditions. They manager is also asked to describe all fees associated with the fund. If you have ever read through a fund's private placement memorandum and other documents, you are acutely aware of the sometimes mind-numbing legalese that permeates all the paperwork. Investors, when they think in terms of fees, usually focus on the 1/20 or 2/20 framework. Unfortunately, there are other costs that are not necessarily obvious. Of course, in the operations of a fund certain marketing, legal, and accounting fees are charged back directly to the fund. Leverage or line of credit costs may also filter into the fund. There are others that may be buried deep in the documents, such as bonuses for the fund's traders, computer costs, and believe it or not, health club memberships.

This section can generate a great deal of debate. A wise New Englander was once asked what was his greatest source of revenue and he replied "low overhead." This is especially true of investment funs. Fees, unchecked, can easily eat away any excess returns. There are constant calls for clearer disclosure and limits to fees. The main argument, and I wholeheartedly agree, is: analyze what the true fee structure is, and if you are uncomfortable with the level of fees—don't invest. One of the joys of capitalism is that no one is holding a gun to anyone's head to make him invest. Ask the questions, review the answer, verify the numbers, then decide.

Section VII deals with compliance and client reporting of the partnership. The questions are concerned with SEC registration, other regulatory issues, and the results of any audit by those regulatory bodies. This segment can provide some further insight into the compliance culture of the firm that may not be apparent in the Form ADV. SEC audits or regulatory exams and their frequency offer a window into the regulator's view of the risk profile of the fund. Many investors will be interested in the timing and delivery of tax documents, primarily the K-1s. Prompt delivery of K-1s is a good sign that the fund values its investors. Slow delivery of tax documents always plants questions about why is it taking so long and are they manipulating the numbers (Diogenes the cynic).

Section VIII asks questions about the principals, key personnel, and pay policies. Questions of criminal or civil offenses can be answered here. These are not necessarily deal breakers, but it is important to remember that you want the fund to be forthcoming. Remember, if they are not honest about details, you can search and find out whether they are likely to be candid about investment problems when they arise.

Employee turnover and pay policies are also important. Low turnover can be a key sign that the managers understand how to run a business and that consistency is important to them. One of the unfortunate sides of the financial services industry is that a majority of your assets in the business go down in the elevator every night. Unhappy employees are disruptive and can depress performance results.

The next and highly important part of the DDQ is Section IX, which addresses operations and administration of the fund. In the history of hedge funds, the overwhelming majority of fund meltdowns have not been investment blow-ups but issues related to the operations of the fund. Here you will need to analyze whether the firm has sufficient infrastructure to meet the demands of a growing business. You will also gain insight into the firm's valuation policies and learn whether the firm has the ability to continue to operate in the event of a disaster. It would be distressing to most investors if, in the event of some crisis, they lose the ability to communicate with funds holding their investment capital.

Section X deals with taxes broadly. One issue that is important to high net-worth investors is the tax efficiency of their investment managers. A historical look at the gain and loss record will provide some idea of tax efficiency. This is also another check against the manager's investment process. If the marketing presentation leads you to believe that the management is a deep value with a 3- to 5-year outlook for its holdings, but the tax structure is 90 percent short-term gains, you would have what stock specialists call an order imbalance. Consistency of answers and process provide comfort that you are investing with someone who has a passion for the business and is not receiving market spin.

The balance of the DDQ (Section XI) deals with a detailed performance record. These are quite relevant, but they can also be revealed to you in several other forms, such as the marketing material, product sheets, and in the Private Offering Memorandum (PPM) and offering documents. The DDQ will be useful in two ways by providing that information. First, if and when a visit to the manager is contemplated, the DDQ is a fairly comprehensive document on the firm to have on hand. Second, it can serve as a check against any other published material on the fund. This is an important point to remember, and is especially true as it relates to assets and performance.

Over the years I have seen assets reported in several different ways. One example was a firm that included the amount of leverage (bank loans) in AUM. It gave the impression that AUM was higher, but also hid a potential source of risk to a new investor, since it would effectively give the new investor a higher percentage of the fund's allocation than he might be comfortable with. Additionally, depending on the source, funds may be reporting a gross performance number in one source and net in another. Cross matching the different responses will give an investor a better understanding of the fund's sophistication as well as insight into how they deal with investors. In this process you want to find a manager who treats you as a potential valued partner and not purely a source of additional fees.

SUMMARY

The process of finding a list of managers to search is an ongoing one. The sources are varied, and it is important to build a network of reliable people. When you begin to collect information on a manager it is vital to dig deeply into what is being said. Also, you must look for consistency in the responses. The Due Diligence Questionnaire allows for a broad discussion of important issues that are not otherwise conveniently available. You can customize the DDQ to suit your style and needs. Managers, in the interest of time, may produce their own generic DDQ. It may not be as robust as you hope, but it will generally be sufficient. With this already prepared, the managers can then focus on their main business of running the hedge fund. If you still have some gaps, you can easily bridge those gaps with a follow-up call or wait until you do an on-site visit.

CHAPTER 4

Performance Analysis
Torturing the Numbers Until They Confess

The use and misuse of performance numbers is quite legendary in the investment world. Those in the business of marketing investment products always try to put their best face on all the numbers. For example, if the five-year number is not beating the benchmark, then the focus will become the three-year number. If that fails they can always resort to changing the benchmark. The regulators take a dim view of misusing performance data. Unfortunately for investors there is nothing particularly illegal about the above changes, although the ethical lines in the sand experience a strong windstorm.

This abuse is even more apparent in the dark recesses of the hedge fund world. Although it is one of the most-quoted statistics, how well or poorly a fund is doing as measured over a discrete time period is the subject of ongoing and sometimes heated discussion. This discrete series of numbers undergoes extensive slicing and dicing in an attempt to more fully understand how they truly perform. Maybe the most important truths being sought in the torture of performance numbers is: As an investor, are you being paid a sufficient premium for the risks you are incurring? Performance of hedge funds is typically discussed in absolute terms. Investors will measure their returns against a desired benchmark and appropriate peer groups. The performance numbers serve as the guiding light for hiring (or firing) a manager, and in many cases at the most inopportune time. For the moment let us consider the simple dollar and time-weighted returns of an investor over a period of time.

The simplest performance calculation is the Dollar Weighted Return (DWR). The calculation is nothing more than the profit or gain for the period divided by the amount of the investment. The total return (as opposed to price) approach assumes all interest and dividends are included. The calculation is shown here.

$$DWR = \frac{(EMV - BMV)}{BMV}$$

EMV = Ending Market Value
BMV = Beginning Market Value

Hedge fund investors may also see this reported on a Net Asset Value (NAV) basis. This is similar to the reporting of daily mutual fund prices. Hedge funds, on a monthly basis, monetized the limited partnership. The calculation remains the same except that the NAV values for the periods measured are substituted for the beginning and ending values.

$$DWR = \frac{(NAV_1 - NAV_0)}{NAV_0}$$

NAV_1 = Ending Net Asset Value
NAV_0 = Beginning Net Asset Value

These monthly returns can then be linked together to obtain Chained-Linked Returns (CLR) in order to obtain the compounded rate of return.

$$CLR = [(1 + R_1) \times (1 + R_2) \times \ldots \times (1 + R_N)] - 1$$

R_1 = Return for Period 1 (in decimal form)
R_2 = Return for Period 2 (in decimal form)
R_N = Return for the final period (in decimal form)

We can calculate not only the absolute return but the portfolio's annual returns.

Hedge funds will report performance over several yearly periods as well. This calculation is the annualized return (AR).

$$AR = [(1 + DWR) \times (1 + Yrs.)] - 1$$

DWR = Dollar Weighted Return (in decimal form)
$Yrs.$ = Total number of years in period
$\times$ = Raised to the () power

The final performance calculation is the Time Weighted Return (TWR). This essentially uses many of the concepts in the previous methods but provides a more accurate picture of performance, which accounts for cash flows (in and out) for a review period. Hedge funds typically only allow cash flows, contributions, and redemptions to occur on specific days of the months, typically the first day. The general partner of a hedge fund typically reserves the right to allow cash flows in or out at his discretion during other periods. During those occurrences, a more accurate calculation of performance would be as follows.

$$TWR = [(1 + R1) \times (1 + R_2) \times \ldots \times (1 + R_N)] - 1$$

$R_1 =$ Return for period 1 from start date to date of previous initial cash flow.

$R_2 =$ Return for period 2 from end of day previous to initial cash flow to date before second cash flow.

$R_N =$ Return for the final period from date of last cash flow to end of period. (Returns are in decimal form.)

It is a good idea to collect all of this data and important to understand how it is calculated; the question then becomes "what do I do with this information?"

This chapter discusses the many facets of performance, which is not merely reporting the fund's performance. As is true of any numerical or statistical calculation, the questions become: Is this relevant, or is this significant? Is this compilation of figures telling me everything I need to know to make an informed decision? Before you spend significant calories in answering this question, the quick answer is no! The review and analysis of performance numbers is only a basis on which to begin the next part of your fund analysis.

Before we get into a discussion of benchmarks and peer groups, let's first examine the information you can extract just from a simple analysis of the performance numbers themselves. Remember, despite the fact that hedge fund analysis is highly quantitative, some of the most insightful information comes from very simple and mundane facts.

THE FIRST STEP: UNDERSTAND WHAT IS BEING MEASURED

In Table 4.1, you can see the annual returns for a fund and also its annualized returns. The performance shows an annualized number of 17.8 percent—impressive! The average return is even higher. If you glance at the annual returns you can quickly surmise the issue. What on the surface looks like a spectacular performer shows that three of the five years

TABLE 4.1 Fund XYZ Performance 2003–2007

2003	2004	2005	2006	2007	Average Annual %	Cpd 5 Yr Return %
36.8%	6.8%	7.9%	34.2%	7.4%	18.6%	17.8%

had middling performance being masked by a couple of years of outsized performance. Is the fund a bad choice? Not necessarily, depending on your risk parameters, but it certainly raises some eyebrows and warrants further analysis.

There are two other interesting charts that you may want to examine before deciding if a fund is worth pursuing or is quickly headed for the shredder. The first is distribution of returns (shown later in Table 4.2). The distribution of returns graphically displays the tendency of the manager's performance around given returns. This chart will also give you a visual display of the manager's consistency of returns, if that is important, and point to spotty or outlier return frequency. The manager's distribution of returns will possibly give further evidence as to whether the long-term performance is real or is being unfairly skewed upward (or downward) by a couple of outlier years.

We can make several observations about Figure 4.1. First, the number of monthly periods where performance is negative is higher than the positive months on a frequency basis. Second, the fund had a number of months where the performance was abnormally high. Third, the volatility of this fund is quite high. The chart does provide us with a number of questions to be answered. (Remember: Quantitative analysis provides the questions, not the answers.) The questions presented here are what caused the spikes in performance? How did the manager react to each? Has the manager reached

TABLE 4.2 Long and Short Hedge Fund Performance

Fund ABC	Yr 1	Yr 2	Yr 3	Cpd Return %
Long	3%	3%	2%	9.2%
Short	2%	3%	2%	7.2%
			Net Total Return	7.7%

Fund XYZ	Yr 1	Yr 2	Yr 3	Cpd Return %
Long	6%	6%	7%	19.1%
Short	−3%	1%	−2%	−4.0%
			Net Total Return	7.6%

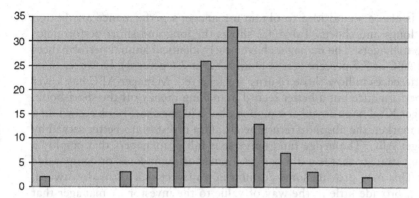

FIGURE 4.1 Frequency Distribution of Hedge Fund Monthly Returns

capacity or does his "edge" not work above a certain level of Assets Under Management (AUM)?

TWO SIDES TO HEDGE FUND PERFORMANCE: LONG AND SHORT

The manager's ability to react quickly in volatile markets is key to his long-term strategies being successful. If the manager has concentrated positions in his portfolio and is heavily leveraged, he will look brilliant in an up market. In fact, nearly everyone is a bull market genius. It is when the markets begin to go bump into the night that a hedge fund manager earns his fees.

The fund manager needs to manage around his large positions and be able to make money on the short side of the market. The impact of leverage is a dual-edged sword. It can give a fund outsized returns in an up market but outsized negative returns as well. When you begin to analyze hedge funds it is important to keep in mind the amount of leverage a fund uses. Comparing an unleveraged fund and a leveraged fund without making a deleveraging portfolio may lead to a false choice. One final point on leverage and performance: It is essential to know the amount of capital a fund has and the leveraged amount, since this does affect the skew performance. Additionally, it is important to determine whether the fund is charging its management fee to the notational amount managed. This will also give you an indication that the hurdle rate of a heavily leveraged fund is higher, and performance and risk may have to increase to meet the hurdle rate.

It is also a sound idea to obtain a manager's performance attribution of his longs and shorts. Table 4.2 shows the long and short performance of two managers. The managers have nearly identical annual performances (Fund ABC at 7.7 percent versus Fund XYZ at 7.6 percent). However, note the differences in how those returns are achieved. Manager ABC has lower long performance but a better record in making money off the short book. Manager XYZ has a stronger long book but a losing short book record. In a rough market, the absolute return needs of an investor are better served by Manager ABC. The hedge fund universe is full of managers that employ a shorting strategy that is nothing more than shorting indexes or comparable ETFs. This may provide some cushion in a market that turns downward, but will provide little in the way of value to the investor. A manager that has 30 to 40 small cap longs in his portfolio will then short the Russell 2000 ETF to hedge the portfolio. From a practical standpoint, the upside value of the fund is diminished, and this action provides little protection on the downside unless its long stock picks have a low tracking error in relation to the ETF they shorted.

Every manager will hit rough patches, so an investor must have comfort with the manager's experience and know how he will react in given situations. A knee-jerk reaction to short term market movements can exacerbate a bad position. By having an extreme leverage position or being poorly hedged, a manager that tries to counteract those positions when the market becomes highly volatile increases the possibility of being whipsawed. By examining the manager's performance at all of these different levels—gross, net, versus market benchmarks, hedge fund benchmarks, peer groups, and long and short attributions—an investor can better understand how managers might react to different market conditions. Remember, the past is not indicative of future performance, but it does give a better idea, given similar conditions, of how that manager is likely to position the portfolio.

PERFORMANCE STANDARDS

So far, we haven't discussed whether the performance figures are gross or net of fees. I will leave aside a discussion of the regulatory requirements of the Securities and Exchange Commission (SEC) and standards for GIPS verification (Global Investment Performance Standards). The SEC sets guidelines as to when numbers should be reported gross or net, and the GIPS has requirements that allow an apple-to-apple comparison of performance. The GIPS is the newer, more comprehensive update to the AIMR-PPS (AIMR-Performance Presentation Standards). Both are products of work from the same organization, which has recently been updated. AIMR, or the Association for Investment Management and Research, has been re-named the CFA Institute. You will occasionally see references to both standards. We examine the use of performance verification standards in the chapter on due diligence. The point is that you should examine both gross and net performance numbers.

The gross performance provides a glance into each manager's raw ability to produce investment returns. In the comparison of gross returns, Manager #1 has generally underperformed Manager #2. When you glance down to the net performance numbers, the difference maybe less convincing. If you assume that both managers are charging a 1 percent management fee and a 20 percent performance fee, what could account for the difference? Although we will discuss this in further detail in upcoming chapters, the management fee of 1 percent may not be telling the whole story as to what expenses the LP's investors are footing. The accrual of the performance fee may also be different between the two funds.

CHECK THE ENTRY

Managers report performance numbers through different sources. The first introduction that many investors get to a particular fund's performance is through its marketing brochure. The presentation form of various brochures may be different in style, but the substance should be the same: fund, benchmark on a monthly basis, plus annual numbers if applicable. Other information such as net exposure may also be nearby.

Another medium whereby a manager's hedge fund performance number gets distributed is through a reportable database, such as HedgeFund.net or eVestment. These databases are then fed into some application software that allows for extended analysis.

The third way that an investor receives performance reporting is from the fund administrator, who is providing fund investors with monthly statements on the calculated NAV of the fund.

It is a sound idea to cross check the veracity of the numbers. Wide spreads between the three sources of numbers should be met with deep skepticism, especially if they differ from the report by the administrator (assuming the administrator is indeed independent). Numbers in marketing material and provided to databases are often quick estimates; however, depending on the date of the estimates, they should not vary greatly. Of course one needs to be certain that comparison is done for the same share class and domiciled fund.

FINDING A BENCHMARK

The next performance comparison should be against a suitable benchmark. Some providers of hedge fund indexes try to show an overall snapshot of performance of the hedge fund industry regardless of strategy such as the HFRI Fund Weighted Composite Index. The range of strategies and substrategies employed by hedge funds is broad, and many indexes focus on individual strategies such as the CSFB/Tremont Global Macro Index or the HFRI Equity Index (Table 4.3). The use of a hedge fund index will provide a basis as to how hedge funds as a group have performed over time. In Table 4.3, an investor can see a breakdown of some broad strategies on an annual basis over 17 years. It will also shed light onto the historical average of each strategy over time as well as the annual average of hedge funds over time. The average of hedge funds as an asset class is a key measure to follow over long periods. It will provide an indication that hedge funds are worth their fee structures. It will also provide a context for how you can expect a strategy to return and what kind of ride in volatility you can expect.

For example, let's examine the Short Selling sector. Over the entire 17 years, this strategy's average return was a Treasury bill-like 3.0 percent. In fact, short selling had positive years about 53 percent of the time over that period. At first blush 3 percent doesn't seem worthwhile; however, maybe you believe the market is going to go through a very weak economic period similar to 2000–2002 and you need a Short Selling hedge fund. A quick glance at the table shows that the average short seller returned 24.9 percent during the 2000–2002 period. It should also be noted that the average hedge fund strategy returned 4.4 percent during that time. Checking to see how your possible short sellers did in the period will be a good starting point. If you subscribe or have access to the databases, you can break the annual return down by month, providing some further insight and a line of questioning for the manager about how his fund handled difficult times.

There are a couple of rational points of view in determining other benchmarks that are more based on the type of asset the manager invests in, such as international large cap or domestic small cap. The first is to compare the fund against an appropriate traditional benchmark if possible. For example, if the hedge fund manager is a small cap long short hedge fund, the logical benchmark would be the Russell 2000. An additional matrix comparing the hedge fund not only to the Russell 2000 would be to add the NASDAQ index as well. In Table 4.4, you can see how the hedge fund compares to both stock indexes, in addition to the S&P 500 and the HFRX Global Hedge Fund Index. One may logically ask, "Why so many index comparisons?" Great question. From an investor's standpoint, it gives you a quick snapshot that provides information on how the fund performed against its asset

TABLE 4.3 Hedge Fund Strategies Historical Annual Returns

Index	1990	1991	1992	1993	1994	1995	1996	1997	1998	1999	2000	2001	2002	2003	2004	2005	2006	Average '90-'06
Convertible Arbitrage	2.2%	17.6%	16.4%	15.2%	-3.7%	19.9%	14.6%	12.7%	7.8%	14.4%	14.5%	13.4%	9.1%	9.9%	1.2%	-1.9%	12.2%	10.3%
Distressed Securities	6.4%	35.7%	25.2%	32.5%	3.8%	19.7%	20.8%	15.4%	-4.2%	16.9%	2.8%	13.3%	5.3%	29.7%	19.0%	8.3%	18.8%	15.9%
Emerging Markets	-3.4%	45.4%	24.4%	79.2%	3.4%	0.7%	27.1%	16.6%	-33.0%	55.9%	-10.7%	10.4%	3.7%	39.4%	18.4%	21.0%	24.3%	19.0%
Equity Hedge	14.4%	40.2%	21.3%	27.9%	2.6%	31.0%	21.8%	23.4%	16.0%	44.2%	9.1%	0.4%	-4.7%	20.5%	7.7%	10.6%	11.7%	17.5%
Equity Market Neutral	15.5%	15.7%	8.7%	11.1%	2.7%	16.3%	14.2%	13.6%	8.3%	7.1%	14.6%	6.7%	1.0%	2.4%	4.2%	6.2%	7.6%	9.2%
Equity Non-Hedge	-7.2%	57.1%	22.8%	27.4%	5.1%	34.8%	25.5%	17.6%	9.8%	41.8%	-9.0%	1.4%	-8.5%	37.5%	13.3%	9.9%	15.5%	17.3%
Event Driven	-0.5%	27.4%	19.5%	28.2%	6.0%	25.1%	24.8%	21.2%	1.7%	24.3%	6.7%	12.2%	-4.3%	25.3%	15.0%	7.3%	15.3%	15.0%
Fixed Income Arbitrage	10.8%	12.9%	22.1%	16.6%	11.9%	6.1%	11.9%	7.0%	-10.3%	7.4%	4.8%	4.8%	8.8%	9.4%	6.0%	5.6%	7.2%	8.4%
Fixed Income Convertible Bonds	n/a	n/a	n/a	23.6%	-0.6%	19.2%	18.2%	17.6%	7.5%	36.9%	-11.2%	3.3%	-13.1%	17.5%	7.9%	2.5%	24.2%	11.0%
Fixed Income High Yield	-12.1%	41.8%	18.5%	22.7%	1.5%	15.2%	16.2%	12.5%	-5.3%	7.4%	-3.0%	5.4%	5.8%	21.3%	10.5%	5.3%	10.6%	10.3%
Macro Trading	12.6%	46.7%	27.2%	53.3%	-4.3%	29.3%	9.3%	18.8%	6.2%	17.6%	2.0%	6.9%	7.4%	21.4%	4.6%	6.8%	8.5%	16.1%
Market Timing	13.5%	23.2%	7.7%	24.2%	3.5%	12.6%	13.5%	13.6%	24.8%	26.2%	11.8%	4.1%	-3.2%	15.4%	6.4%	14.4%	16.4%	13.4%
Merger Arbitrage	0.4%	17.9%	7.9%	20.2%	8.9%	17.9%	16.6%	16.4%	7.2%	14.3%	18.0%	2.8%	-0.9%	7.5%	4.1%	6.3%	15.7%	10.7%
Regulation D	n/a	n/a	n/a	n/a	n/a	n/a	44.5%	26.9%	26.3%	34.1%	14.5%	-1.7%	-5.5%	20.5%	6.1%	12.4%	6.0%	16.7%
Relative Value Arbitrage	13.4%	14.1%	22.3%	27.1%	4.0%	15.7%	14.5%	15.9%	2.8%	14.7%	13.4%	8.9%	5.4%	9.7%	5.6%	6.0%	12.4%	12.1%
Sectors: Aggregate	32.1%	23.4%	46.5%	33.7%	8.0%	39.7%	30.7%	5.2%	7.6%	67.0%	0.3%	-4.9%	-12.9%	27.9%	11.3%	9.1%	15.7%	20.0%
Short Selling	36.2%	-17.0%	10.1%	-7.5%	18.5%	-17.1%	-4.0%	3.9%	-0.5%	-24.4%	34.6%	9.0%	29.2%	-21.8%	-3.8%	7.3%	-1.5%	3.0%
Statistical Arbitrage	11.2%	17.8%	10.8%	12.6%	4.7%	14.3%	19.6%	19.4%	10.1%	-0.2%	8.9%	1.6%	-3.2%	3.4%	4.0%	5.3%	14.6%	9.1%
Average	*9.1%*	*26.2%*	*19.5%*	*26.4%*	*4.5%*	*17.7%*	*18.9%*	*15.4%*	*4.6%*	*22.5%*	*6.8%*	*5.4%*	*1.1%*	*16.5%*	*7.8%*	*7.9%*	*13.1%*	*13.1%*

TABLE 4.4 Hedge Fund Monthly Return Comparison to Benchmarks

	Jan	Feb	Mar	Apr	May	Jun	Jul	Aug	Sep	Oct	Nov	Dec	Year End
2005													
Oak Street Capital Master Fund, Ltd.							3.87%	1.70%	0.58%	1.47%	1.55%	6.04%	16.10%
Russell 2000 Index							6.34%	−1.86%	0.33%	−3.10%	4.85%	−0.45%	5.91%
S&P 500 Index							3.72%	−0.91%	0.81%	−1.67%	3.78%	0.03%	5.75%
HFRX Global Hedge Fund Index							1.67%	0.43%	1.11%	−1.85%	1.69%	1.48%	4.55%
2006													
Oak Street Capital Master Fund, Ltd.	5.77%	10.39%	1.23%	6.41%	−6.21%	−5.25%	5.05%	−3.21%	−3.39%	2.13%	6.44%	5.17%	25.50%
Russell 2000 Index	8.97%	−0.28%	4.85%	−0.01%	−5.61%	0.67%	−3.25%	2.96%	0.83%	5.76%	2.64%	0.33%	18.37%
S&P 500 Index	2.65%	0.27%	1.25%	1.34%	−2.88%	0.14%	0.62%	2.38%	2.58%	3.26%	1.90%	1.40%	15.79%
HFRX Global Hedge Fund Index	2.45%	0.17%	1.15%	1.15%	−1.31%	−0.49%	−0.57%	0.76%	0.50%	2.02%	1.54%	1.58%	9.26%
2007													
Oak Street Capital Master Fund, Ltd.	2.34%	3.82%	−0.43%	4.10%	3.18%	−3.06%	−0.53%	−0.62%	1.15%	5.56%	0.12%	6.21%	23.63%
Russell 2000 Index	1.67%	−0.79%	1.07%	1.80%	4.10%	−1.46%	−6.84%	2.27%	1.72%	2.87%	−7.18%	−0.06%	−1.57%
S&P 500 Index	1.51%	−1.96%	1.12%	4.43%	3.49%	−1.66%	−3.10%	1.50%	3.74%	1.59%	−4.18%	−0.69%	5.49%
HFRX Global Hedge Fund Index	1.50%	−0.21%	0.28%	2.21%	2.55%	−0.07%	−0.93%	−2.55%	1.28%	2.82%	−2.41%	−0.07%	4.23%
2008													
Oak Street Capital Master Fund, Ltd.	−19.72%	8.23%	−2.97%	0.58%	−9.21%	−2.10%							−24.63%
Russell 2000 Index	−6.82%	−3.71%	0.42%	4.19%	4.59%	−7.70%							−9.35%
S&P 500 Index	−6.00%	−3.25%	−0.43%	4.87%	1.30%	−8.43%							−11.85%
HFRX Global Hedge Fund Index	−2.06%	1.77%	−2.46%	1.20%	1.44%	−0.83%							−1.03%

class, small cap. Also it compares how small cap did in the overall market as measured by the S&P 500. Was it a small cap market or were the equity markets strong in general? Finally, it shows you how all of these indexes compare to the global hedge fund index.

On the surface Table 4.5 gives you the absolute numerical comparison, but if in your due diligence process you can scratch the surface as to the types of holdings (attribution analysis) and sector exposure the fund may have had, that gives some further insight into the source of performance or lack thereof. The next logical comparison would be against an index of Hedge Fund L/S funds. I would caution you that logic may not provide much in the way of useful analytical information. If one takes a quick look through a Long/Short database the types of funds will be mind-boggling. The range of types will be small, mid, large, and all cap by value, growth, and GARP (Growth At a Reasonable Price) styles. Next the database can be separated by sector specific funds—healthcare, biotech, energy, consumer staples, utility, and technology. As you can deduce, the information from the combination of all of these funds will not be very useful.

PEER ANALYSIS

An investor would gain better insight by developing his own peer group of funds for comparative purposes. The best way to develop this peer group is, as you go through your screening process, for you to discover a variety of funds that are interesting and have acceptable performance, but for one reason or another they just don't make the cut. In examining other funds you get a better understanding of how each one invests. The group does not have to be large (four or five), but the funds should use both similar and different investment processes. This will allow you to examine where the performance of the fund will come and how correlated the fund might be to different types of markets. You might ask, why include funds with a different investment process? Since transparency is also a difficult issue, an investor can compare performance by investment process.

Let's say the small cap long short manager tells you that he invests in high quality stocks. You build your peer group with two managers that pick high quality small cap stocks. You also pick two managers who scour the gutter for the dregs of the small cap world. Over a couple of years you notice that when high quality stock performance is mediocre, this fund does quite well (as do the bottom fishers). This may give you a tip to run a correlation of those returns, which may suggest that the manager is playing loose and fast with the fund's investment process. Once again the reoccurring theme is that the quantitative numbers give you questions, not answers.

TABLE 4.5 Hedge Fund Monthly Return Attribution and Exposure Levels

	Jan	Feb	Mar	Apr	May	Jun	Jul	Aug	Sep	Oct	Nov	Dec	YTD
2005													
Long							3.86%	0.21%	-1.00%	1.17%	1.78%	5.94%	
Short							0.01%	1.49%	1.58%	0.30%	-0.23%	0.10%	
Net Return							3.87%	1.70%	0.58%	1.47%	1.55%	6.04%	16.10%
Beta and Delta Net Exposure							4.60%	22.80%	8.50%	14.30%	24.70%	44.40%	
2006													
Long	7.34%	10.47%	2.68%	6.52%	-6.85%	-6.76%	2.92%	-2.63%	-3.51%	2.90%	7.63%	6.15%	
Short	-1.57%	-0.08%	-1.45%	-0.11%	0.64%	1.51%	2.13%	0.58%	0.12%	0.77%	-1.20%	-0.98%	
Net Return	5.77%	10.39%	1.23%	6.41%	-6.21%	-5.25%	5.05%	-3.21%	-3.39%	2.13%	6.44%	5.17%	25.50%
Beta and Delta Net Exposure	40.00%	41.20%	45.10%	43.80%	43.40%	42.10%	47.80%	39.30%	32.90%	45.30%	55.40%	55.00%	
2007													
Long	2.76%	3.63%	-0.48%	4.66%	3.79%	-3.42%	-2.77%	2.70%	1.56%	7.26%	-3.40%	4.42%	
Short	-0.42%	0.19%	0.05%	-0.56%	-0.61%	0.36%	2.24%	-3.32%	-0.41%	-1.70%	3.52%	1.79%	
Net Return	2.34%	3.82%	-0.43%	4.10%	3.18%	-3.06%	-0.53%	-0.62%	1.15%	5.56%	0.12%	6.21%	23.63%
Beta and Delta Net Exposure	49.30%	48.60%	50.30%	45.50%	50.90%	55.10%	52.80%	1.60%	9.30%	53.70%	45.50%	31.10%	
2008													
Long	-24.24%	1.27%	-7.31%	4.50%	-8.61%	-12.37%							
Short	4.52%	6.96%	4.34%	-3.92%	-0.60%	10.27%							
Net Return	-19.72%	8.23%	-2.97%	0.58%	-9.21%	-2.10%							-24.63%
Beta and Delta Net Exposure	26.50%	-3.40%	-7.30%	-5.90%	-3.20%	-0.90%							

CONFUSION FROM THE BEST AND THE BRIGHTEST?

Now it is appropriate to discuss the various databases and the benchmark numbers they provide. The major complaint against these hedge fund indexes is that they do not represent true hedge fund performance and are burdened with survivor bias. The bulk of complaints seem to come from the traditional mutual fund advisors that have seen a lot of assets leave to find better risk/return results in hedge funds. There have also been several academic studies.

One study was conducted by Gaurav S. Amin and Harry M. Kat, both highly respected researchers in hedge funds. They examined data from Tremont Capital Management's TASS database from 1994 to 2001. The data included 1.195 live funds, 526 dead funds, and 291 funds of funds. The "dead funds" are defined as funds that stop reporting to a database. The study showed that the impact of attrition created an overall survivorship bias of around 2 percent. The survivorship bias leads to an overestimation of returns by the indexes. It should be noted that, in this study, the cause of the stoppage (dead funds) was not evaluated and may be the result of other factors than the fund failure.

A more disturbing study was one by Burton G. Malkiel and Atanu Saha (*Financial Analysts Journal*, November/December 2005). The study was an attempt to show that hedge funds were no better in performance and of higher risk than more traditional vehicles such as mutual funds. Both the Amin and Kat study and the Malkiel and Saha study make one fatal assumption about hedge fund databases: that they are similar to the S&P 500 index or the Dow-Jones Industrial Average. The primary use of databases by hedge fund managers is marketing or, more precisely, to raise capital for their fund. The databases provide hedge funds with a viable way to more or less publicly disgorge performance results without running afoul of SEC regulations. What was disturbing about the Malkiel and Saha study is that they make a broad statement that hedge funds are launched and report results "at some later date and only if the results are favorable." If some of the other databases had been examined, the authors would have discovered that other databases and reporting outlets have strict minimum requirements for funds before they accept information such as minimum asset size or length of track record. This leads to the mistake of confusing the database with an index. The various hedge fund indexes are far from a perfect way to reflect the absolute accuracy of any hedge fund strategy. Malkiel and Saha also tried to make the argument that the biases are not found in traditional indexes like the S&P 500 or the Russell indexes. Yet from a practical standpoint the biases in those indexes are as broad, although different, from those in the hedge fund index.

Consider that the S&P 500, which has a group of people huddled in a dark room in lower Manhattan deleting weak and failing companies and adding stronger growing ones into their list of 500. The turnover of companies in the S&P 500 doubled in the 1990s from 4.5 percent to about 9 percent. Coincidently, technology stocks were being added just as the technology bubble was building. Or examine the Russell indexes, where by the mere stroke of an accounting pen by company management, a growth index member becomes a new member of the value index. as its book value has been recalibrated. The Russell rebalance is highly quantitative and is done annually in June. The S&P 500 is rebalanced on an ongoing basis and is much more subjective.

After doing some additional digging, I came across a working paper from Malkiel and Saha dated in late 2004, which no doubt was the basis of their *FAJ* article. The authors, in their working paper, noted the fact that LTCM was not reporting when it lost 92 percent of its value from October 1997 to October 1998. What was also missing from their analysis was that LTCM's outsized returns were not reported once the fund was closed. Many of the highly successful funds stop reporting when they are no longer in the market for additional investors. This is neither good nor bad. Unlike the S&P 500, in which one can always invest, the closed fund is of little use to an investor seeking to place funds.

Some other interesting work has been done by Ed Easterling of Cresmont Holdings LLC. Two of his studies examined fund closings in months leading up to the end of reporting concluded that two-thirds of the funds had positive performance and only one-third had negative performance. The survivorship bias in hedge funds is skewed heavily toward "closings" (to new investors) rather than "closures" (going out of business).

Why is this important? When examining performance of any fund or any study of performance it pays to be skeptical. Given the relatively unstructured nature of the hedge fund industry, it will be difficult to develop a perfect benchmark. The managers start funds for different reasons, not the least of which may be that the manager has made his fortune and is starting a fund to manage his wealth and maybe that of a few family members. Academics who serve on mutual fund boards may not be providing research of value but a marketing edge for the mutual fund. It is best to use any benchmark judiciously and defer to the peer group you have built for purposes in which you have better faith.

A PRACTITIONER'S VIEW

Much of what is written about examining the performance of hedge funds stems from Modern Portfolio Theory (MPT). Unfortunately, hedge fund returns do not mathematically comport with MPT. There is a growing body of study that is referred to as PMPT or Post-Modern Portfolio Theory. The assumptions and calculations are a bit different, but they are more applicable to the study and analysis of hedge funds. In PMPT, the success of an investment portfolio is determined by the individual's or institution's required return or Minimally Acceptable Return (MAR). The MAR determines what returns are needed to meet the goal of the portfolio, and it is not based on implied returns from historical data. Investors view risk in three ways in PMPT.

- Returns below zero.
- Underperformance to a benchmark.
- Failure to meet one's goal.

In viewing hedge funds, it is more useful to analyze the funds by using calculations that are more agreeable to non-normal distributions of returns. The major concern of the investor that uses PMPT is the downside. Downside risk is a concern that is appropriate and useful to a hedge fund investor and it should be examined within the framework of PMPT. To assess the downside risk of a hedge fund, a measure called downside deviation is used. The downside deviation considers only returns that fall below a defined MAR rather than the arithmetic mean. This measure differentiates between risk and uncertainty and incorporates skewness.

Where R_I = Return for Period I
Where N = Number of Periods
Where R_{MAR} = Period Minimum Acceptable Return
Where $L_I = R_I - R_{MAR}$ (If $R_I - R_{MAR} < 0$)

$$\text{Downside Deviation} = \left(\sum (L_I)^2 \div N \right)^{\frac{1}{2}}$$

The more common measure, standard deviation, yields little useful data in the analysis of hedge funds. The standard deviation equates risk with uncertainty. The measure of standard deviation also implies a symmetric, normal return distribution. It also measures risk relative to the mean of returns and assumes the same risk for all goals. Additionally, the standard deviation treats upside volatility on an equal basis with downside volatility. That final concept may be puzzling to investors. From a logical standpoint, investors would accept an unlimited amount of upside volatility and would try to minimize downside volatility. This logic should also drive investors to using downside deviation as a more complete measure to evaluate hedge funds.

The concept of MPT is the performance measure that is used is the Sharpe Ratio. The Sharpe Ratio is the risk adjusted excess return, as measured by the investment return minus the return on a risk-free asset divided by the standard deviation. The comparable calculation for hedge funds is the Sortino Ratio. The Sortino Ratio is the measure of excess return per unit of risk as measured by the reward to negative volatility trade-off.

The Sortino Ratio is the return of the fund minus the MAR divided by the downside deviation. The MAR is set by the client's goal. Unlike the Sharpe Ratio, it does not have to be aimed at some particular target, such as the three-month U.S. Treasury bill. It could be simply a number, such as six. That is the return the client wishes to see consistently. It could also be more complex, say the risk-free rate adjusted for inflation. The Sortino Ratio, unlike the Sharpe Ratio, does not penalize the fund for positive upside returns in equal amounts to the undesirable downside returns. As a simple example, Table 4.6 compares the Sharpe and Sortino ratios between the S&P 500 and the Lehman Aggregate index. Note how the advantage shifts dependent on the level of MAR.

Two other statistical measures that surround performance data are skewness and kurtosis. Skewness measures the degree of asymmetry of a distribution around its mean. Positive skewness indicates a distribution with an asymmetric tail extending toward more positives values. Conversely, negative skewness extends toward more negative values. Since hedge fund returns are not normally distributed, skewness gauges whether a manager has a tendency to perform positively or negatively.

Kurtosis measures the degree to which a distribution is more or less peaked than a normal distribution. Positive kurtosis is a relatively peaked distribution while negative kurtosis is a relatively flat curve. Skewness and kurtosis differ from normal distributions and provide an indication of reliability.

TABLE 4.6 Comparison of Sharpe and Sortino Ratios

	Aggregate	S&P 500	Favors
Sharpe Ratio 5% risk free	0.69	0.64	Lehman
Sortino (10% MAR)	(0.14)	0.37	S&P 500
Sortino (5% MAR)	1.15	0.88	Lehman
Sortino (0% MAR)	3.01	1.48	Lehman

Period from January 1976 to August 2001.

EXAMINE THE BAD

Another component in the analysis of performance numbers is the drawdown. A drawdown analysis can be broken down into three basic parts. The first is to identify the worst performance month. Second is the maximum drawdown, and third is the recovery period. The worst performance should be examined in the context of absolute and relative framework. A return of −2.05 percent on the surface does not seem to be too horrid. Now, suppose the manager experienced that drawdown when its benchmark was +3.5 percent and its peer group was +4.7 percent. Now that low drawdown does not look so innocuous. Questions immediately come to mind about holdings, position sizes, and net exposure. The drawdown may also question how far afield that manager had taken the investment process in light of the large underperformance, not only to its benchmark but to its peer group.

Sometimes the fund drawdown can take place over several months, since market volatility can make for unpleasant stretches in certain sectors or security types. Another insightful measure is maximum drawdown, which is the largest peak to valley performance period. Although the worst performance month may be only −2.05 percent, the maximum drawdown will string several negative months together and may exceed 10 or 20 percent. Depending on the strategy, some highly volatile elements such as futures and commodity strategies can often see significant drawdowns. As a single measure it may not be useful; however, taken in context of overall performance. it can provide insight into whether the downside performance can be attributed to the markets or to the manager's investment style.

The accompanying measure to the maximum drawdown is the number of months to recovery. That is how long it took the investor in a given fund to come back to par from the period of maximum drawdown. In the volatile strategies it is typically a period of a couple of months. If that period extends to five or six months, some warning sirens should be going off. It would appear that the risk/return profile is out of whack and/or the manager has no particular edge in that given strategy. It may also be a sign that the downside returns may be higher than the upside for the strategy.

In the examination of returns, an aspect of behavioral finance comes into play. Investors are most impressed by and remember best the most recent set of returns. If poor performance occurs in the distant past, less weight and analysis is given to that set of numbers. It is always a useful exercise to delve into that period from several different perspectives. Somewhere in the follow-up due diligence, the manager should be questioned about poor periods, how he reacted, and whether his actions resulted in any significant change in their investment process.

EXAMINE THE GOOD

When an investor experiences poor performance, he may begin to spend some time trying to analyze what went wrong. The manager also should do a quick review of the process, models, and other decision tools to verify that the assumptions for that strategy remain intact.

One area that is generally overlooked is periods of good performance. Investors seem to follow the advice not to look a gift horse in the mouth. But the lesson to be learned from the demise of such funds as Amaranth is that good performance should be examined and not taken at face value. The fund's strong performance in the energy sector deflected concerns that the portfolio risk was growing as exposure to energy was becoming more and more unwieldy. The issue of the large sector bets being made by Amaranth should serve as a warning to investors. Performance, regardless of whether it is exceptionally poor or exceptionally good, should be examined. There is much to be learned by analyzing good performance. Investors should keep in mind that blow-ups usually happen to funds that have been reporting good performance. Funds that have strayed from announced strategy, are mispricing assets, or are having trouble operationally will typically report good performance numbers. It is much easier to hide illicit activities and not be subject to any great amount of scrutiny when the investor is at least marginally satisfied with the results.

From the group of numbers shown in Table 4.3, we can do additional quick calculations that will lend further insight. One measure is the fund's batting average. The batting average is simply the percent of times the fund beats the benchmark, which in this case is the Russell 2000. For the fund in Table 4.3, the batting average is 44 percent, or 16 out of 36 periods. Not spectacular by any means, if you this as an isolated factor.

Another quick calculation is the percent or positive months. For that fund the figure was 66.7 percent, or 24 out of 36 months. You now have several pieces of substantial data to review. The fund has handily beat all benchmarks over the period, although its batting average is a bit low. The fund does, however, provide positive performance two-thirds of the time. Some insight is that the fund provides some strong alpha but may be a bit volatile, and its investment holdings are truly long-term oriented.

From this same manager we obtained long and short performance on a monthly basis. In Table 4.4, the breakdown shows that the manager had positive performance in 19 of the 36 months or 53 percent of the time. Being able to be profitable long and short is key to successful hedge fund management.

Investors should as a matter of course scrub numbers good or bad. The tendency is to worry about the bad performance numbers, but history has shown that the largest surprises come from funds that have not been on anyone's radar due to performance numbers.

EXPECT THE IMPROBABLE

When you examine improbable performance there are three attributes that are apparent. The first, it's an outlier. Whenever an outlier appears when examining performance, further analysis is needed. If, for example, performance is much poorer than the benchmark or peer group, all three should be examined to confirm that the benchmark and peer group are still appropriate and determine whether the fund continues to invest according to its PPM. The second is, it carries an extreme impact. If the performance returns are beyond the bands of what is expected, it will have a significant (positive or negative) impact on an investor's overall portfolio. An extreme negative impact can unduly burden a portfolio to the point where a forced liquidation is required at inopportune prices, if there is anything left to price. This brings us to the third attribute, which is that in hindsight, the final outcome can be seen as predictable.

The last attribute may be the most important to remember. By applying a little analysis upfront and asking what can go bad and how quickly, some of the flashing signs from old fashioned performance reporting become clear markers.

I SURRENDER

The title of this chapter was "Torturing the Numbers Until They Surrender." Performance is the first place, and sometimes the last place, that investors examine in hedge fund investing. We walked through the simple time weighted return calculation, which led to the distribution of those returns. The make-up of returns can get spliced further into long and short returns, after which you can check these results against a benchmark and perform some peer analysis. The ultimate test is how the fund stacks against an investor's goals using MAR and the Sortino Ratio.

Even after all of these exhaustive calculations, this is only part of the due diligence that still needs to be completed. There are still countless other quantitative measures, in effect torturing the numbers. In the long run, as we discuss in the upcoming chapters, there are some more productive ways to explore hedge funds that will provide insight into our ultimate decision that cannot be captured even in the most complicated and sophisticated mathematical formulas.

CHAPTER 5

Risk in Hedge Funds

Risk Is like the Weather: Everyone Talks About It, but No One Does Anything about It

Risk and risk management are tricky subjects for the hedge fund industry because risk is typically viewed in mathematical terms, which makes it convenient to view but not always informative or even accurate.

Risk is one of the most overused and misunderstood terms. Factions that wish to have a much higher level of regulation are always cautioning about the risks of hedge funds. If one reviews a 10-year period ending June 30, 2008, for risk/return profile as measured by annual total returns and standard deviation (see Table 5.1), hedge funds have one of the best risk/return profiles of any asset class. Depending on the headline of the moment, risk can be in transparency, leverage, liquidity or investment vehicle, all of which require a separate view of the problem. Members of the media are always wringing their hands over the risks of hedge funds whenever one fund has a spectacular meltdown and is forced to close. The headline grabbing risks are typically limited to investment or operation risk. Yes, Bayou, Long-Term Capital Management, and MotherRock all proved to be risky investments, for different reasons. The actual causes of the meltdowns are not always well defined or understood. What is ignored is that they turned out to be no more risky than common stock blow-ups like Enron, WorldCom, or the multitude of dot-coms, or dot-bombs as they've become known. The end result was investors lost life savings in an area that has some of the most extensive regulations: the public company and securities markets.

So what is risk? To most investors, risk is the probability of permanent impairment of capital. In the end, that is the true definition of investor risk. As Warren Buffett has described it to Berkshire Hathaway's shareholders in his annual reports, investors should be more worried about the return of their capital rather than the return on their capital. Risk is not a monolithic

monster that strikes fear into investors. While risk ultimately can be corro-
sive to the value of investments, it comes in many forms, some of which may
be unrecognizable or simply ignored by investors. Higher risk is associated
with higher returns and conversely lower risk equates to lower returns.

The questions about what is my risk exposure or what is the potential
loss are typically couched in dollar terms or percent decline in value. Besides
the accuracy of these measures, the question arises, do they fully examine all
the risks that an investor may face? As in the overall due diligence process,
risk assumes different faces, some quantitative and some qualitative.

The very nature of the hedge fund structure means that the risks associated with such funds are numerous, complex, and somewhat dependent
upon the strategy each fund undertakes. There is a lot of focus on finding
nifty mathematical formulas for determining the risks in a hedge fund, and
there are a couple of significant issues that make the use of these formulas
misleading. First, hedge funds, by design, do not have normally distributed
return streams, which brings into question the value of standard deviation as
a measure of risk in this asset class. In Modern Portfolio Theory (MPT), risk
is measured in standard deviations. This is not overly useful since investors
describe risk in terms of loss of dollars, whereas MPT describes risk in terms
of deviations around some mean of expected returns.

For example, let's look at return streams for two hypothetical funds
shown in Table 5.1 Over the five-year period, the average annual return for
Fund I is a bit higher than that of Fund II, 5.8 versus 4.6 percent. If we turn
our attention to the risk measure, Fund I has a 26 percent higher standard
deviation than Fund II. The return per unit risk as measured by the standard
deviation is identical, 0.76 for both funds. If we then turn our attention to

TABLE 5.1 Hedge Fund Risk/Return Comparison

	Fund I	Fund II
Returns		
Year 1	18%	9%
Year 2	3%	−2%
Year 3	8%	9%
Year 4	0%	−2%
Year 5	0%	9%
Average Return	5.8%	4.6%
Standard Deviation	7.6%	6.0%
Return per Unit Risk	0.76	0.76
Value of $1,000 at Year 5	$1,312.63	$1,243.74

the one measure that ultimately matters most to clients, the value of the investment, we see that even though Fund I had 0 percent return in the final two years, the final valuation was 6 percent higher than Fund II. The fact is that using the standard deviation as a measure of risk gives equal weight to positive and negative values from the mean of the data set. As I believe most investors would view the situation, they would take all the upside risk they could find. Downside risk is the killer to investment value. Given the higher risk level and the same return per unit risk of Fund I, its higher investment value would suggest that upside volatility and downside deviation are more important factors in the measurement of risk in hedge funds.

Second, the use of historical data has, time and time again, proven to be an extremely unreliable indicator during periods of stress. A prime illustration of this reaction to historical data came during the crisis at MotherRock. Its value was shrinking at an alarming rate, but not once during its demise did it violate its daily VaR (Value at Risk) parameters. The paperwork involved in calculating VaR could have filled a file cabinet, but it did not do anything to protect the return of an investor's capital.

At this point it is useful to discuss VaR, which many view as the Holy Grail of risk management. VaR is a statistic that is defined as a one-sided confidence interval on portfolio losses.

$$\text{Prob}[\Delta P(\Delta t, \ \Delta x) > -\text{VaR}] = 1 - \alpha$$

Where $\Delta P(\Delta t, \Delta x)$ is the change in the market value of a portfolio, expressed as a function of forecast horizon Δt and the vector of changes in the random state variables Δx. The parameter α is the confidence level.

The complete book on VaR has yet to be written. In simple terms, VaR is the worst loss that can happen under normal market conditions over a specified time horizon (one day), at a specific confidence level. VaR was developed to provide a single measure that could capture information about the risk contained in a portfolio. The forecast horizon period (Δt) is referred to as the "orderly liquidation period." As investors experienced the downfall of MotherRock, the liquidation was not orderly but swift and fatal.

The calculation of VaR falls into three categories: parametric, historical simulation, and Monte Carlo. Parametric most closely relates to MPT and standard deviations, and it expresses VaR in terms of a multiple of the standard deviation of the portfolio's return. Monte Carlo expresses hypothetical returns by choosing random data from a distribution of price and rate changes with historical data. Historical simulation calculates a hypothetical return on a portfolio if the day's prices and returns from history were to repeat themselves. All of the methods are subject to large errors, and under certain situations, such as when an option is essentially valueless or as other risks are correlated to market risk.

Regardless of the method used, VaR does not measure market behavioral or event risk in case of a crash, nor does it calculate liquidity differences between instruments. All methods also require a fair amount of computing power and access to an extensive database of historical data and prices. For example, a VaR of $5 million that is calculated daily with a 95 percent confidence level over a one-month period will tell us there is a 95 percent chance that a loss of $5 million will be avoided. Conversely, there is a 5 percent chance of a loss exceeding $5 million.

MAJOR RISK CATEGORIES

Before calculating the risk of a given portfolio, the investor needs to understand the major sources of risk. People picture risk along three broad categories, but it's actually more helpful to break down and analyze risk as it is classified in the hedge fund risk matrix (see Figure 5.1). Labeling risks by these different categories allows investors to evaluate a wide variety of situations that reflect all types of risk. The key point of the matrix is to show that interrelationships between risks should not be overlooked—the culprit in a high risk portfolio is seldom one factor. This is the defining reason why even a complex mathematical calculation may not be sufficient to properly evaluate risk.

In broad terms, risk in hedge funds can be categorized into operational risk, manager risk, and market risk.

- **Operational risk** describes risk inherent with the business and administrative management of fund management companies. Chapter 7 provides a more in-depth look at how operational risk represents one of the biggest risks associated with investing in hedge funds.

Liquidity	High Watermark	Concentration	Operational	Liquidity Mismatch
Transparency	Risk Process	Leverage	Short Selling	Reputational
Submerged	Counterparty	Market	Credit	Model
Intricacy	Key Person	Assumption	Pricing	Derivative

FIGURE 5.1 Hedge Fund Risk Matrix

- **Manager or investment risk** is common to all investments and cannot be completely controlled. No manager can assure future performance, and the drivers of a manager's investment return and exposure levels are a major variable in the underlying attribution of those returns.
- **Market risk** is different but ultimately related to manager or investment risk. There's a common misconception that traditional funds carry a higher level of market risk than hedge funds. An actively managed long only portfolio typically aims to outperform a benchmark. A hedge fund will seek to deliver absolute returns regardless of the direction of the markets. Hedge funds actively hedge their exposures to protect returns from market risk.

To gain a more comprehensive understanding of risk, it is necessary to break down these categories into a more robust matrix of factors that reflect the different types and levels of risk. Figure 5.1 shows such a matrix; it will help the investor create a framework for a disciplined process to examine the risk in a particular opportunity.

The due diligence reviews of managers should not treat risk management as a separate independent function or activity. It is important to understand and identify the risk management process in the fund consistent with the complexity of the strategies used, in addition to the management style in which the fund is operating. Written policies are essential and more effective than leaving it all up to judgment.

The rest of this chapter will examine the other risks that face hedge fund managers and investors. Some are readily apparent while others are not. Each sector of the hedge fund business comes factory equipped with its own risk that, while not necessarily calculable, is certainly palpable.

LIQUIDITY RISK

In its simplest form, liquidity is the ability to exit an investment without severe damage to your capital. As investors exit, the doorway to liquidity is tight, the toll is high, and sometimes the door is slammed shut.

Liquidity risk is probably one of the most threatening of all risk factors. Many of the high profile meltdowns that were blamed on investment risk, in reality, had liquidity as their underlying cause. We have already mentioned the implosion of MotherRock and Amaranth. Both funds saw their demise brought on by liquidity issues in the natural gas markets. The derivatives markets for the energy complex are generally considered to be highly liquid. Thousands of contracts trade daily with little market impact. Unfortunately for MotherRock and Amaranth, because of the sheer number of trades they made in energy markets, they essentially *were* the market. Despite the misperception, the issue that led to the shutdown was not concentration risk, but rather liquidity.

In these cases, liquidity was not helped by the fact that the portfolios were well known on the Street and trading pits. Many firms, both traditional and hedge fund, used some form of liquidity calculation to determine how fast they could revert to cash in the event of some catastrophic event or a surge in redemptions. The calculation typically assumes that the number of trading days at a historical average trading volume rate will be the magical mathematical answer to give the manager some comfort that the portfolio has sufficient liquidity, if needed.

For example, let us look at how this is calculated in a rather simple case that will illustrate the point. Fund X owns First Cash Financial Services (FCFS-NASDAQ*). The fund is a long/short fund with about $300 million in AUM. A recent price for the stock was $13.66/share. If the fund feels the stock is slightly undervalued but they are not extremely bullish, they may take a nominal position size of $1\frac{1}{2}$ percent of the portfolio. The math is as follows:

$$.015\% * \$300,000,000 = \$4,500,000 \quad \$4,500,000 \div \$13.36$$

$$= 336,826 \text{ shares purchased}$$

$$\text{Average Volume (10 day)} = 323,044$$

At $1\frac{1}{2}$ percent, Fund X owns more than the current daily volume. If by practice, Fund X does not want to be more than 20 percent of any day's volume, it will now take 5 days to close out its position. (0.20% * 323,044 = 64,609 shares).

$$336,826 \div 64,609 \text{ shares owned} = 5.2 \text{ days}$$

Now, assume that Fund X is extremely bullish on the stock and takes its ownership level up to the maximum allowed by its investment guidelines of 5 percent at market value. (Assume all trades are done one day and at one price.)

$$0.5\% * \$300,000,000 = \$15,000,000$$
$$\$15,000,000 \div \$13.36 = 1,122,755 \text{ shares}$$

---

*The stock is for illustration purposes only and is not a recommendation to buy or sell.

For now, we will ignore the length of time it would take to actually accumulate a position of that size. Trading volume has not changed. The impact of the larger position has decreased the liquidity of the fund, or increased the time from 12 days, or 234 percent, to 17.3 days to fully liquidate that position.

$$1,122,755 \div 64,609 = 17.3 \text{ days}$$

The problem with this mathematical exercise is that all the trading is taking place in a vacuum. The one piece of the puzzle that's missing and difficult to quantify is how the stock would trade in a crisis, either to the market or to Fund X itself. This is the lesson that MotherRock and Amaranth learned quickly, and the grading was severe. In some cases, an investor takes comfort in the fact that the fund calculates its liquidity, based on recent trading data, and based on never being more than 20 percent of the average daily volume. The reality of a market or fund under duress is that liquidity can instantly dry up and the ability to sell shares at any price becomes compromised. As traders begin to smell blood in the water, the short sellers come out with a vengeance. Concurrently, buyers dry up, and the stock price is under extreme downward pressure. This issue of liquidity is compounded if the Fund has a large concentration of securities in one sector or exchange, as was the case of Amaranth.

This example is not intended to scare investors out of hedge funds, but rather to serve as an illustration of the dark side of liquidity risk. Events such as 9/11 are extremely difficult to forecast and in most cases more difficult to hedge. As part of the due diligence process, an investor needs to fully access, understand, and evaluate how a fund will trade, its position, its position limits, and how they will conduct an orderly liquidation or protect capital during a time of high stress in the markets.

HIGH WATERMARK RISK

The application of a high watermark to an investor's capital means that the manager will receive performance fees on that particular pool of invested money only when its value is greater than its previous greatest value. Should the investment drop in value, then the manager must bring it back above the previous greatest value before the fund can receive performance fees again.

The calculation of a high watermark may vary from fund to fund, but the risk remains the same. The most common difference is whether the mark is set at the highest value ever, or does it simply reset every year.

The fund manager may collect 1 or 2 percent (or more) in the form of management fees, but the true upside of compensation for a hedge fund manager is the performance fee. The risk to the investor may take form in one of two ways. The first is when the drawdown is so severe that, in order to retrace to a level above the high watermark, the fund will begin to take outsized risks. This can be a disaster in the making if the fund continues its losing ways—the manager will need to increase risks at an alarming rate. As an investor you may have been under water by 10 to 15 percent under the original drawdown; however, a continuation of the poor performance can push that figure down to 50 percent or more.

To view this numerically, let's assume your Net Asset Value (NAV) was $100 and suffered a drawdown of 15 percent. Your NAV is now $85. To reach the previous high watermark of $100 in three years, a manager needs to return only 55.7 percent or 17.65 percent in one year. Now assume that the drawdown was more severe and your NAV is now resting at $50. It's not rational to expect the manager to assume the same course as when he was down 15 percent. If the manager assumes a less aggressive stance to return 11 percent per annum, which will essentially double the risk profile of the fund, it will take the manager more than seven years to reach the previous high watermark.

Most managers target risk and return ranges for their fund. If the manager takes a large step away from that risk/return profile, it may compromise the manager's ability to exercise within his core competency. It's not an ideal situation for an investor to assume a risk/return profile that is significantly higher than it might be under normal circumstances, and in actuality the investor may suffer further losses as a result of the aggressive strategy. The other possible outcome that's a component of high watermark risk is if the General Partner chooses to close the fund. From the view of the manager, this makes absolute business sense. From the investors view, however, this is close to disaster. By closing the fund the loss is certain, and returning back to par, so to speak, will not happen. The GP distributes money back to investors, closes the fund, and there is a high probability that the Fund manager reopens the same strategy hedge fund under another name.

This is quite discouraging to investors, although unfortunate timing may have been the only issue that confounded the fund. For example, opening a fund just prior to a severe market correction can kill a fund before it truly starts. Closing and reopening offers a fresh start to this manager. What's of more concern is that the fund managers, who have poorly managed portfolios, have taken outsized risk and experienced sharp drawdown. There are managers who have done this several times. The risk of high watermarks is well worth noting, especially if closing a fund that has run afoul of its high watermark seems to be standard practice for a manager. With a little digging, this fact can typically be uncovered in the background checks of the manager.

CONCENTRATION RISK

Concentration risk relates primarily to the size of positions as it relates to the fund portfolios and markets. Concentration or size of each position in the portfolio, sector, or issue is important as it will impact trading, performance, and volatility. Concentration of the security in the trading environment, such as percent of outstanding float, percent of short volume, and percent of daily trading volume, also needs to be understood and monitored. Monitoring largest position size, sector, performance attribution, number of positions, and sector exposures is a good method for trying to understand this risk.

Transparency is an issue; however, it's good practice for an investor to verify limits that a manager imposes. For example, in the fund documents, the fund manager will discuss limits of holdings by holding or sector. It is a good practice to ask the manager for a prime brokerage statement to check if indeed the math adds up. There will be some managers that balk at providing current statements; however, older statements can suffice if they have been done routinely.

OPERATIONAL RISK

Operational risk is associated with the business and administrative management of fund management companies. Despite the lack of headlines about operational risk, it is the leading cause of hedge fund failures. Fraud (31 percent), financial issues (17 percent), and undisclosed operational issues (6 percent) have accounted for 54 percent of the defaults. Hedge fund managers are in business for a single purpose: generating consistent, excess portfolio returns. Therefore, they may be less versed in an equally important area of running the business. The ability to accomplish non-core activities will determine the ultimate success of a fund. The controls on money flows, trade settlements, managing technology, producing accurate performance and accounting reports, and delivering K-1s on time are all part of the necessary functions that need to be examined before investing. An investor should require that these functions be completed by a competent CFO and not the portfolio manager.

It's quite common to see hedge funds being formed by people who've been highly successful on a "prop" desk at a top tier investment bank. Their job was solely to exploit market inefficiencies to maximize profit. Simple things like confirming trades, paying salaries, dealing with a landlord, or installing computer software, were never a concern. As many people who have launched a money management business know, this side of a business can be distracting and time consuming, but without proper attention it can sink a firm as quickly as a bad investment. Conversely, focus on these can lead to disastrous investment results. The smooth operations and infrastructures of a firm need to be valued and handled with care in order for the business to have a chance at success.

If the fund does not have the financial backing or cash flow to support a person dedicated to the business operations, the once focused money manager quickly realizes that, after the trading day is over, another full-time job is waiting for him. It is very easy for a dedicated, passionate investment manager to give short shrift to these chores. Unfortunately, it is this short-sightedness that can rapidly torpedo an upstart business. The smooth operation of the firm is an important factor, just as much as the generation of alpha.

LIQUIDITY MISMATCH RISK

Liquidity mismatch risk is a bit different from liquidity risk, discussed earlier. This mismatch deals with buying and holding securities without having the ability to convert them into cash, usually through a call or maturity provision. In certain strategies, being forced to liquidate portfolio positions to meet cash flow needs and redemptions will have a negative impact on performance.

This is most typical in a fixed income portfolio whereby a portfolio manager needs to have sufficient liquidity to meet future projected cash needs for additional purchases or to meet distributions or liquidation cash outflows. If the manager understands these future needs, they are most easily met by matching the maturity of some instrument to that date certain. This reduces the risk that the markets may be going against the manager if he is forced to sell an instrument to meet this need.

TRANSPARENCY RISK

One of the largest complaints from investors is the lack of transparency in hedge funds. Lack of transparency can expose investors to a rising level of risk without sufficient warning. Attitudes toward transparency are beginning to change, however. Investors no longer tolerate a blackout on vital fund information, and hedge funds anxious to grow assets are becoming more accommodating. Managers' concerns over proprietary research, short squeezes, and competitors can be more easily managed. Some funds allow more access to investors, either directly or through third party vendors that specialize in producing such calculations. Third party firms sign nondisclosure agreements with managers that give them direct access to portfolio holdings, which allows for significant data manipulation. It is now easy to determine security concentrations, exposures, leverage, and stress tests.

Those investors who are unable to afford third party analysis can negotiate transparency before investing. If a manager refuses a reasonable level of transparency, an investor needs to seriously consider the reasons for these refusals. Is the manager nervous about increased scrutiny, or is the infrastructure inadequate? Both are danger signs.

Building adequate tools for transparency is within the reach of most investors. Separate accounts are one method of ensuring transparency, although manager minimums to run these can be quite high ($25 million or above). Investors need to verify fund balances monthly with custodians. Knowledge of concentration of holdings by sector and gross and net exposure can aid in attribution and volatility. It's also smart for investors to review past blowups and frauds for common threads. As in life, those who ignore history are doomed to repeat it.

RISK PROCESS

The risk process a firm uses is a key factor in how the fund runs. One that is unable to articulate a cohesive, comprehensive risk process that guides the firm should be viewed warily. The simple declaration of a process is insufficient and raises an investor's risk.

A firm that cannot demonstrate and articulate a method by which they protect the assets of the fund does not have a risk process. To say they may be flying by the seat of their pants may sound harsh, it but may in reality be true.

LEVERAGE RISK

The image of hedge funds taking on enormous amounts of risk is misguided at best. The average amount of leverage across the hedge fund universe is around 2 times, although it would not be surprising to see 7 to 10 times leverage for some strategies; global macro and certain fixed income strategies come to mind. That doesn't mean that some funds do not readily engage in leverage. Leverage is actually conducive to improving returns in certain strategies, primarily fixed income whereby narrow returns can be magnified.

Leverage risk does not necessarily refer to traditional leverage covered by Regulation T (Reg T) or the margining of securities. The larger concern over leverage involves a fund increasing funds invested through a borrowing agreement with a lending institution. A global macro fund or fixed income arbitrage fund borrowing $2 or $3 for each $1 of capital allows the fund to take a meaningful position in a certain transaction. There are funds that will lever up 5 to 10 times. If they are correct, the return stream is helped dramatically. If incorrect, leverage is a double-edged sword and will greatly depress returns. The risk of leverage is at its peak here. Once the returns have plummeted, there is a temptation to lever up more in order to quickly recover the losses. This can lead to a death spiral for investors.

SHORT SELLING RISK

Short selling risk is actually a form of leverage. Short selling is defined as borrowing a security (or futures contract) from a broker-dealer and selling it, with the understanding that it must later be bought back (one hopes at a lower price) and returned to the broker. This technique is used by investors in order to profit from the falling price of a security.

For example, consider a fund manager who wants to sell short 1000 shares of a company, believing is the shares are overpriced and the price will fall. The fund's broker will borrow the shares from someone who owns them, with the promise that the fund will return them later. The fund immediately sells the borrowed shares at the current market price. If the price of the shares drops, he/she "covers the short position" by buying back the shares, and his/her broker-dealer returns them to the lender. The profit is the difference between the price at which the stock was sold and the cost to buy it back, minus commissions and expenses for borrowing the stock. But if the price of the shares increases, the potential losses are unlimited. The company's shares may go up and up, but at some point the fund's broker has to replace the 1000 shares he/she sold. In that case, the losses can mount without limit until the short position is covered.

The investor needs to carefully view a manager's process in order to curtail losses in the fund's short book. It would be interesting to know if the manager has a threshold of pain for shorts going against the fund, or does the PM limit exposure to any particular short, and how much non-Reg T leverage may be employed to execute the short strategy.

REPUTATION RISK

One of the most difficult risks to measure is reputation risk, also called headline risk. Investing in hedge funds is not much different from entering into a business partnership; you must feel comfortable with the partner. Integrity of the general partners is imperative. No one wants to wake up one morning to read an embarrassing headline concerning their fund, and then have to deal with the unfortunate consequences.

The troubled fund outfit run by A.R. Thane Ritchie has barred investors from withdrawing money from Ritchie Capital. This action is the imposition of a "gate." Hedge fund managers increasingly impose gates, or redemption limits. A gate of 20 to 30 percent (in the case of annual redemptions) or 10 to 15 percent (in the case of more frequent redemptions) is not uncommon. The gate provision in theory allows the manager to increase exposure to illiquid assets without facing liquidity crises as a redemption date approaches. Many fund managers invoke it when a hedge line event risk causes massive exits from the fund.

In the case of Ritchie Capital, Mr. Ritchie told Reuters and the *Wall Street Journal* that keeping his investors' money in the fund was the best move right now, since the alternative was to sell securities at "fire-sale prices." To some investors a fire-sale might be preferable, since claims against Ritchie Capital seem to be building. In the past year the fund has been involved in a bevy of convoluted scandals that have been heavily reported:

- Ritchie was fined $40 million by the SEC for late-trading. Ritchie had gone as far as forging orders to back-date them to before 4 p.m. (The late trading took place between 2001 and 2003, at least as far as the SEC knows). (http://www.sec.gov/news/press/2008/2008-10.htm)
- Two other fund outfits, Benchmark Plus Management, and Sterling Asset Management sued Ritchie over its management of a fund (Ritchie Multi-Strategy Global fund), in which all three invested. (http://www.finalternatives.com/node/3186)
- Ritchie then countersued Benchmark for various aspects of breach of contract, which prompted the latter fund to drop its own case. (http://www.finalternatives.com/node/4746)
- Ritchie sued Coventry First, an insurer, over fraud in investments undertaken with Ritchie. Claiming $700 million in damages, Ritchie invoked RICO. Coventry was already fending off a suit begun by New York Attorney General Eliot Spitzer. Still, Coventry considered the Ritchie suit "a cheap publicity stunt." (http://www.finalternatives.com/node/1613)

- An investor in the above Coventry deal through Ritchie, Huizenga Managers Fund, sued Ritchie over its management of the insurance fund, saying the fund was misrepresented to them, and may be a total loss (Huizenga is still waiting to get its $10 million back). (http://www.finalternatives.com/node/2673)

SUBMERGED RISK

Submerged risk may be the most dangerous risk in the hedge fund industry. It is not unlike the iceberg that sank the Titanic. The nature of the hedge fund business is that regardless of how much detailed due diligence is done, it is impossible to garner all information. The facts we know peek up at us from the surface, while we remain completely unaware of the pile of information that lurks below.

The presence of this risk should serve as a reminder that we must remain vigilant in assessing all risks. Submerged risk is a reminder to always ask the questions: What can go wrong? How can we protect against this? And what else am I missing?

COUNTERPARTY RISK

Counterparty is the risk that a party to a transaction will fail to fulfill its obligations. This risk is a growing concern in a deteriorating credit environment where financial institutions such as Bear Stearns are literally disappearing overnight. The term is often applied specifically to swap agreements in which no clearinghouse guarantees the performance of the contract, particularly as the transactions relate to options or futures instruments. These instruments typically are purchased to protect or hedge positions; however, they may be an additional form of concern to the fund. The assumption has been that these derivative or synthetic instruments allow investors to lay off risk, but it by no means disappears. As entities evaporate, agreements unravel, and anyone left standing who may have had a passing acquaintance with the instrument may be summoned to make somebody else whole.

MARKET RISK

Securities that are held and have not been adequately hedged give the fund exposure to market risk. The proliferation of derivative instruments such as options or indexes, ETFs and inverse ETFs, allows this risk to be managed.

A manager with exposure to S&P 500 stock holdings has several ways to hedge away that market risk. The most efficient way is to short the S&P 500 in the futures market or buy put options against the index on one of the exchanges like the CBOE (Chicago Board of Option Exchange). If, for some reason of preference or policy, the manager cannot use this type of instrument because of a leverage restriction, the development of inverse ETFs provides an easy answer. These are fairly new and are actually a closed end fund. These closed end funds even come with various levels of leverage built into them. A manager can opt for 1:1, 2:1, or in some cases 3:1 levels of leverage. That is, in the case of 2:1 leverage, for every dollar decline in the designated index the closed end fund rises in value two dollars.

Market risk is one of the most discussed and analyzed risks in hedge funds. Quantitative analysts slice and dice market statistics as they try to determine if a fund is a genuine producer of alpha or a generator of expensive beta. Investors need to understand what level of market risk they are being exposed to by a given manager, and whether they are affectively hedging the portfolio or should add value through their short selections.

CREDIT RISK

Credit risk is typically considered an issue only for fixed income related funds, although it can also impact equities. The impact to investors, however, is most severe in the fixed income markets, where the default risk can be high. In the equity markets, the fund entity may also default, but the second acts of restructured companies typically show that less pain is suffered by the equity holders than by the fixed income holders.

The issue of credit is not limited solely to a security the fund may hold. As recently seen in the mortgage markets, a tightening of credit standards by the Federal Reserve preceded a flight to quality and a liquidity squeeze in the mortgage-back market. As the credit markets tightened, billions of dollars were written off by the holders of those sub-prime mortgage securities. The lack of buyer interest or liquidity led to a free fall of prices. By the end of the first quarter of 2008, financial firms worldwide had written down about $300 billion, and it was estimated that another $100 billion would be written off. (See Table 5.2.) Fannie Mae and Freddie Mac, the two quasi-governmental corporations that guarantee mortgages, are on the hook for nearly $5 trillion. The U.S. Government was forced to open up lines of credit to these entities, although for a *de minimus* amount of about $3 billion. At the same time values of real estate have been plummeting. The full effects of this economic deleveraging may not be known for years.

TABLE 5.2 Mortgage Delinquency

	2008 Q1	2007 Q4	2007 Q1
Started in Qtr, Sub-Prime %	4.06%	3.44%	1.35%

Source: S&P.

Like leverage, credit risk is a dual-edged sword. There are funds that take advantage of credit risk in the markets, go short the securities under fire, and enjoy huge profits. It is important to understand credit risk and how a manager can be properly positioned. Credit risk does not come alone in a portfolio, and the problems compound as liquidity and possible leverage have an exponential negative impact. The potential impact that credit risk may entail is quite evident. As seen in Table 5.2, Mortgage Delinquency, and in Table 5.3, Falling Real Estate Prices, the numbers are just recently being reflected, and financial institutions are just beginning to recognize credit risk as well. The process can be self-repeating as new foreclosures and falling real estate prices will force new write-offs.

MODEL RISK

As in traditional asset management, hedge funds are not spared the issue of model risk. The finance world, and in particular the hedge fund world, have become highly mathematical and quantitative over the year as PhDs from MIT are just as coveted as Wharton MBAs. Academics and practitioners develop models in an effort to forecast price movements, capital returns, arbitrage, and option values. They will stress test the models and vary their assumptions in order to assess the reliability of the models. As many people involved in the development of models discover, the outputs of a model may not always bear a resemblance to the results in real life.

Several major factors directly affect the results of models. The first is the quantity and quality of data chosen to be included in the model. As with any model, the output is only as good as the data input. It is advisable when using 60-year-old interest rates to realize that the possible drivers of rates may have changed over time. The U.S. dollar hasn't been on a gold standard for a long time, and access to tradable information is nearly instantaneous.

The second factor is: Does the model output have any true predictive power? Any model is useful only as long as its output shows some predictive power in its results. The more complex the model, the more imbedded

TABLE 5.3 Falling Real Estate Prices

Year	Quarter	S&P/Case-Shiller U.S. National Home Price Index
2000	Q1	100.00
2000	Q2	103.77
2000	Q3	106.33
2000	Q4	107.90
2001	Q1	109.27
2001	Q2	112.69
2001	Q3	115.50
2001	Q4	116.23
2002	Q1	118.00
2002	Q2	122.24
2002	Q3	126.13
2002	Q4	128.58
2003	Q1	130.48
2003	Q2	134.20
2003	Q3	138.41
2003	Q4	142.29
2004	Q1	146.26
2004	Q2	153.92
2004	Q3	158.53
2004	Q4	163.06
2005	Q1	169.19
2005	Q2	176.70
2005	Q3	183.08
2005	Q4	186.97
2006	Q1	188.66
2006	Q2	189.93
2006	Q3	189.00
2006	Q4	187.31
2007	Q1	185.40
2007	Q2	183.57
2007	Q3	180.28
2007	Q4	170.62
2008	Q1	159.18

moving parts may result in an outsized error. Markowitz was cognizant of this fact when he remarked on the possibility of error in the mean-variance calculation. Even a small error in the input stream will result in a huge output error.

The third factor: Is the model reliable? The last significant factor is human behavior. Economic and financial data, often operating in a vacuum, can somewhat reliably predict possible outcomes. But models have difficulty in assessing the reaction of human behavior to certain economic and financial events. The certainty of mathematics in these models is sometimes overwhelmed by the lack of cooperation from human behavior. Behavior is difficult to quantify. Some of the simplest models use economic data that highly correlates to movement in stock prices. The movement of airline stocks has a high correlation to the inverse price movement of oil. That is, as oil price drops the price of airline stocks rises. A slightly more complex model is one that uses mean reversion. The study of many stock and bond models suggests that many of these instruments trade within some theoretical band and, as the data fluctuates over time, it will eventually revert back to its long-term historic mean. This may prove to be true in general; however, the trigger point to the reversal is subject to factors quantitative and qualitative. This was very much in evidence with LTCM. They plugged tens of thousands of numbers into their SPARC computers and, through science and not art, boldly assumed that investors would experience a loss of 5 percent or more in about one month in five. Only one year in fifty did the model calculate at least a 20 percent loss, and the model did not even entertain a larger loss. The only questions of relevance were: What were the anticipated average returns, and how much did the return vary in a given year? Volatility equaled return. Increased volatility led to higher returns. On the contrary, the results could lead people to conclude that this quantitative model was not a science but simply a blind belief in the power of a model. The human element in any trade was never considered.

Some funds have been successful using highly quantitative models. There are some funds that continuously work to retool and refine their models. Renaissance, with its Medallion Fund (now closed), had a model that was highly successful. That does not infer that there were no bumps along the way. The key to such success is to continually evaluate the assumptions and predicted results. The process should not end with the results of the model's tests, but should include an understanding of how outlier results may impact liquidity and other associated risks. One must have feel sure that the fund is spending sufficient resources in technology and human capital to keep its models sharp.

COMPLEXITY RISK

Complexity risk relates to the almost limitless types of securities that are now available in the financial markets. Financial engineering is now at a level where synthetic securities are being underwritten for a wide variety of purposes. These new instruments do serve a useful purpose, but they are complex in financial and legal terms. A fund manager and an investor must understand the characteristics of these instruments and the impact on the portfolio.

In my early days in the investment business I became acquainted with a fixed income portfolio manager, who explained his approach to investing in the different synthetic securities that were being underwritten. He told me that when a broker called to interest him in purchasing a security hot off their desk, he would tell the caller that for every minute over three it took him to explain the instrument, his required rate of return increased by 10 basis points. This drove the point home that as complexity (risk) increased, the purchaser's understanding and return needed to increase as well.

KEY PERSON RISK

Key person risk is inherent in many hedge funds. Building a successful hedge fund firm that can survive the test of time is very difficult. Is there sufficient intellectual capital in the firm to survive the untimely demise of its founders? That is the major question and the inherent risk to most start-ups. The investment processes of some funds are built around the intuitive research ability of a fundamental analyst, or a trading process that someone learned at a prop desk. One needs to quickly examine the investment team, their backgrounds, and find out long the team has been together. Without the continuity of a team that has general investment experience and is steeped in the philosophy of the fund's investment process, key person risk is palpable.

SENSITIVITY TO ASSUMPTIONS RISK

All investors are wrong from time to time. For many hedge fund investors, the risk in being wrong is how sensitive the success or failure of a strategy is to the assumptions that have been made. Large bets made without the comfort of a margin of safety will make the fund extremely volatile and possibly not suitable to an investor's overall risk parameters.

NAV INSTABILITY RISK

NAV (Net Asset Value) instability risk has a direct bearing on the invested securities, their level of liquidity, and the valuation procedures of the fund. The higher the level of off-the-run, illiquid securities, the higher the level of NAV risk. Transparency and operational risk also play a part in NAV risk for investors. Delving into pricing procedures and process, and agreeing in concept that the proposed method is disciplined and fair, is an essential part of understanding a fund.

Valuation, in general terms, is what a willing buyer will pay to a willing seller to complete a transaction. Finding an independent fair valuation is not always easy. Investors must be able to verify the marks posted by the fund and be aware of any conflicts that may be inherent in the process.

DERIVATIVES RISK

Derivatives have been accused of being the demise of many investors. Ever since the October 1987 market crash, derivatives have been considered a large source of risk for investors (Report of the Presidential Task Force on Market Mechanisms, U.S. Government Printing Office, 1988). Their multiplication and complexity have only added to the mystique of derivative risk. Investors need to understand the use and misuse of these instruments in a portfolio. The derivative instrument adds several interrelated risks of complexity, leverage, and liquidity.

It is quite important to understand the different types of risk that impact a portfolio. An investor's due diligence process should not view each risk in isolation. A proper due diligence process will take heed of any financial and mathematical calculation, but the output from those exercises yields more questions, and not definitive answers. The predictability of any output is only as accurate as the assumptions and conditions that are duplicated in the current situations. There are several risks discussed above that do not lend themselves to quantitative models. Leverage, pricing, and liquidity lend themselves to numerical research. Others, such as reputational, operational, and submerged risks, may need more qualitative or human analysis that will not comport to the precision of numbers that the financial world sometimes demands. Human analysis can, however, lead to a better understanding of a hedge fund and protect capital in the long run.

Once you get a firm grasp as to what risk may be a major factor in a given hedge fund, you can then dig deeper to understand how the fund deals with these issues. Many funds talk about risk management; however, many times it simply means that they limit position, sector, and exposures within certain bands. This has little to do with the risks that investors actually face. The more comfortable you become with each item in the 20-box matrix (Figure 5.1), the easier it will be to determine where you put your attention in ongoing monitoring of a fund. Scratching below the surface is indeed a major necessity for each box, especially if transparency is an issue.

SUMMARY

The concept of risk in hedge funds is a major concern. Risk, however, is not a monolithic problem and it takes many forms. Avoiding all risk is not necessarily essential. In investing you need to establish your tolerance for risk and decide whether you are being properly compensated for those risks. You also need to make sure you know what you are measuring. When considering a hedge fund, you must identify the variety of risks and quantify each one. In the following chapters, as we work through the due diligence process, we will learn how the keys to risk is not fearing it but to identify and quantify risks.

SUMMARY

CHAPTER 6

You Only Find Out Who Is Swimming Naked When the Tide Goes Out

Look Behind the Numbers

T he numbers—or more precisely performance—are what matter in the end; however, many other factors can impact the persistence and consistency of those numbers. Potential investors need to take a look under the towel to see if their fund managers are really wearing Speedos or, as Warren Buffett put it, to see who is swimming naked. The due diligence process will be a large paper trail of regulatory, marketing, and business documents that will begin to build an image of what the manager is all about and how he runs his hedge fund business. In essence, you are gathering information as you would if you were buying a business. If the manager passes your test, you indeed will become a partner, a limited partner in a hedge fund.

At this point, the initial screening of your hedge fund has been completed. You have a solid understanding of the fund's performance, and the logical next step is to obtain some other pertinent, detailed information. This is the heart of the due diligence process. The key point to remember during due diligence is that the numbers provide questions, *not ultimate answers*. It's critical that investors dig deeply into the fund and not become infatuated with the "hot dot" of performance.

FILLING OUT THE DDQ

The Due Diligence Questionnaire (DDQ) is an extensive document that allows you to build a rubric of the fund and manager in depth across all aspects of the firm. Histories and backgrounds on the people, performance, assets, and business plan are probed here in great detail. For a sample DDQ, see Appendix C.

The DDQ, a fairly inclusive document, will encompass most of the vital information concerning the hedge fund you are examining. It includes sections that are devoted to obtaining a deeper understanding of the fund manager's business, from basic facts (contact information and organization) to more in-depth analysis of the investment strategy, process, and portfolio construction. This should include position and sector limits. Also, a breakdown of AUM, growth of assets, and total firm assets, are listed. It is helpful to have a due diligence checklist for each manager; it provides contact information at a glance and a list of the due diligence information and process that is ahead.

The information on the fund should include an in-depth organizational chart. This may seem like a routine exercise, but in large complex organizations it will give you a better understanding of how the resources are allocated as well as how much corporate responsibility may be required from the principals. This may be helpful in a fund that receives a large share of its operational support from a large, well established firm. For example, although CCI Healthcare LP is a small hedge fund organization, it receives an enormous amount of operational and business help from Columbus Circle Investors. Columbus Circle Investors is a multibillion dollar traditional institutional firm that has a long and impressive operational track record. The portfolio team and investment researchers are the key personnel for CCI Healthcare. CCI Healthcare receives additional research support from Columbus Circle Investors' stable of healthcare analysts. It also receives middle and back office support from them in the way of human resources, compliance, accounting, and operations. This is quite possibly the best of both worlds from an investor standpoint; you have a small, strong, alpha-producing fund backed by a solid institutional money management organization.

Other smaller, newer funds will have a flat organizational chart, since the President, Chief Investment Officer, and Chief Compliance Officer may be one and the same. From this you will realize that a different line of questioning will be needed in your due diligence process.

Along with your request for completion of the DDQ, it is now an appropriate time to ask the fund to supply the following information:

- Fund's audited financial statements (three years preferable).
- Access to their website.
- Professional references on fund's principals.
- Copy of fund's code of ethics.

- Compliance manual and annual compliance review.
- Trading procedures.
- Pricing policies.
- A copy of most recent SEC audit with response letter (if applicable).

One key point is that you should not acquire a level of comfort just from size. Some of the largest trading fiascos have happened in exceedingly large. mature firms, such as the Treasury trading scandal at Salomon Brothers; the demise of Baring, the oldest merchant bank in London (1762–1995); and the recent troubles at the French bank, Société Générale. Risk management and control are the key, not size.

Asset Growth

The DDQ should include a matrix that details how the assets grew, how fast they grew, and where the growth came from. This should be more detailed than the information taken from the original performance analysis (see Chapter 4), since the growth can now be reviewed in light of contributions and withdrawals. A deeper analysis comes when you examine performance as an overlay to asset growth. This can be one of the early warning signs in a fund. As asset flows gain in momentum, the strategy and/or the manager may be hard-pressed to earn competitive returns on the new money. Certain niche strategies are capacity restrained and large sums of money will overwhelm returns. This is especially true in markets that are liquidity restrained, such as parts of the energy or commodity markets, or in micro-cap stocks. The fund may have peaked in capacity and returns are being compromised. The fund manager should anticipate a level of assets that he feels can provide a stable stream of returns. Viewing asset returns in light of asset growth can amplify the probability that the shelf life of a manager as an alpha producer is coming to an end.

Third Party Vendors

The DDQ should also ask for all third-party outside vendors that are used by the fund. The information should list the service provider, account contact person, address, e-mail and telephone information. The vendors include auditor, administrator, prime broker, and legal counsel (on-shore and off-shore, if applicable). This information is vital. You need to contact these vendors and confirm that the fund is not only a client but also one in good standing. If the vendors hesitate or refuse to confirm, you need to encourage the fund to have the vendors provide more disclosure. If the stonewalling continues, it may be more than a privacy issue that is involved. If you cannot obtain a level of comfort with the answers to your questions from the fund and vendors concerning their work for the fund, then run. Even in the most nontransparent fund, you should get sufficient assurances that everything is as presented with regard to the relationship between the fund and the vendor.

Audit and Prime Brokerage

The auditing firm should provide a letter verifying that they had been engaged to audit the fund and whether they still are under engagement. The administrator and prime broker should also confirm that they are engaged by the client. It is also a sound practice to do a prime broker check. That is simply to make sure the fund has the prime broker give you a report of holdings from some prior period. This will allow you to verify assets and position size, and it gives you an opportunity to analyze the suitability of the holdings to the fund's investment process as described.

A frightening example of how a simple verification would have saved angst and money is the demise of Wood River Capital Management in 2005. The SEC on October 13, 2005, filed suit in the U.S. Southern District of New York, alleging that Wood River made material misrepresentation on oversight and diversification of its hedge funds. Wood River secretly amassed an enormous position in EndWave (NASDAQ), which comprised over 60 percent of the fund. Concurrently, the fund advertised that it was audited by American Express Tax and Business Services (now known as RSM McGladrey Business Services), which lent credence to the fund. Subsequently, EndWave, which hit a high of around $55, fell to just under $10 per share. Needless to say, this will be settled in the courts, but by asking and searching for confirmation of holdings and audit records the heartache for some investors might have been avoided.

Risk Management

Risk management should not be viewed in isolation from, but rather as an integral part of, fund management. The risk process needs to be consistent with the complexity of strategies being undertaken by the fund. The risks that the fund and investor are exposed to are complex and more widespread than might readily be assumed. There are a variety of risk factors that may impact a given strategy. With each of these risks, the manager should be aware of the relevant risk measures and how they can mitigate some of the risk. Are they aware of the prospective warning signs and what may be the potential blow-up scenarios? The investment world and especially the hedge fund business like to quantify risk in terms of 100-year, or once in a lifetime, events.

Unexpected Financial Shocks
1970: Penn Central
1974: Franklin National
1980: First Pennsylvania
1984: Continental Illinois
1987: Stock Market Crash
1990: S&L Crisis
1995: Latin America
1997: Asia
1998: Russia/LTCM
1999: Brazil
2000: NASDAQ
2001: September 11
2003: Freddie Mac and Fannie Mae
2006: Housing Bubble
2007: Subprime Mortgage
2008: Wall Street Meltdown/Fannie and Freddie Collapse/Washington
    Bailout

Despite much study, investors and policymakers refuse to acknowledge that these events occur fairly often. When the unraveling begins, distinctions between market and credit risks disappear and there is no liquidity in the markets. This loss of liquidity increases volatility and is typically accompanied by a sharp drop in asset prices. The recent government intervention in the financial systems of a capitalistic society has now surfaced as an additional risk.

Quantitative risk calculations such as Value at Risk (VaR) and standard deviation are based on past values. These trends remain fairly intact until investors get a first hand look at Newton's Law of Physics. The law states that an object—in this case a trend—remains at rest or in balance until acted upon by a force that will change its speed or direction. Or to put it in trader's language, a trend is a trend until it bends.

Fund managers should describe in fair detail exactly how money moves, who has the authority to trade, the types of trades, how the trades are confirmed, the people responsible for trade breaks or errors, and valuation methods for illiquid securities. The details should also include how trades are affirmed. A trade blotter should not be reviewed only by the person responsible for generating the transactions. On a larger scale, any risk management tool, whether it is simply position and sector limits, liquidity tests, attribution analysis, or a complex software system such as VaR or Risk-metrics, should be discussed, as well as how the tools are used to ensure that the parameters of the fund are being met. With many funds still slow to grasp the concept of transparency, these risk management tools become quite necessary for investors.

It is always a useful exercise to ask the fund about transparency. In some cases, the fund will give the investor considerable transparency at the fund's offices. There are usually limits to the type of information that can leave the office, and of course the investor will be required to sign a nondisclosure agreement (NDA).

Investors who do not have anything more sophisticated than a spreadsheet can develop sufficient information to determine the level of risk that a manager is taking. For example, a manager who provides the size of the fund's 10 largest positions (long and short) by sector, gross and net exposures, and overall sector weightings can give an investor the framework for developing clues and questions. By using the given information, the puzzle can become a little clearer as the investor reviews performance attribution compared to exposures. If the numbers prove to be an outlier, flags should be raised. I remind investors again that the quantitative measures, no matter how detailed, only provide questions, not answers. It remains incumbent on the investor to ask the questions.

Technology and Business Continuity Plans

Technology is paramount to running most successful businesses and is especially vital for hedge funds. The firm needs adequate portfolio reporting, trading, and analytical systems with which to build a sound base. The need for technology does not stop with a simple desktop or laptop. Back-up systems and off-site data facilities are the minimum required today. Unfortunately, in this day of terror threats, a fund must be able to manage its assets regardless of some external event. Funds that are heavily dependant on short-term trading strategies are especially at risk. An investor does not want a fund to be unable to determine its positions, and or trade out of them when markets may be going against them.

Some firms will duplicate computer systems and trading desks offsite for hedge funds; there are financial bunkers being built. This type of back-up is cost prohibitive to small hedge funds. There are, however, several more affordable solutions that will serve the hedge fund well and provide a level of comfort and security. In a start-up, the fund may use a phone chain and equip its employees with laptops. Backup of data is done nightly and weekly and stored offsite; this is a bit crude and simplistic, but it can be effective if executed properly. There are also companies that have built technology centers in what can only be described as fortresses. These companies will rent desk and computers and back-up systems in the event an unfortunate occurrence does strike. This is the middle of the road solution. Again, this is only as good as the vendor and fund that execute the plan.

There are also firms that for one reason or another find the third-party vendor solution inadequate. One, Wolverine Asset Management, has dedicated an enormous amount of money to build its own off-site state of the art facility to meet certain specifications. They have discovered that they can also use this facility to outsource offsite services to other hedge funds (another profit center for the firm).

Business continuity should also cover the demise of the firm's principals. Funds that have ownership heavily concentrated in a few hands may be vulnerable if the fund is forced to close or seek a transition if one of the principals comes to a sudden departure. The issue of ownership can also be a prime recruiting tool, and how they handle distributing ownership to key employees can serve as a guide to a smooth transition and more focused operations. It can be something as uncomplicated as a formulaic calculation covered by a shareholder agreement, to having an intensive business valuation in order to set an entry price.

FORM ADV PART II

You should also request Form ADV Part II, if applicable, to give you a brief snapshot of the investment structure of the firm. Many funds remain unregistered or have deregistered since the SEC lost the legal battle over registration. Consequently, not all hedge funds will have a Form ADV Part II. You can acquire much of this information from other fund materials or a telephone call to the manager. Under no circumstances should you feel that the Form ADV Part II is equivalent to the SEC's approval of the fund, its business, or even accuracy of information. Appendix B includes a sample Form ADV Part II. The form is also available online for advisors that are federally registered (advisors with more than $25 million in AUM) at: http://www.adviserinfo.sec.gov/IAPD/content/search/iapd_orgsearch.aspx.

The form provides a general description of the advisory services, fee schedules, and client type. Investors should pay particular attention to questions 9–14:

- Questions 9 and 10 deal with an advisor's participation or interest in client transactions and conditions for managing the accounts, This can give a general indication of whether there may be a conflict of interest.
- Question 11 describes how an advisor will manage and review the accounts; this may include hedge fund and separate accounts. It will also describe the nature and frequency of reports to the client.
- Question 12 will describe investment and brokerage discretion. This should also be viewed carefully. There are several hedge funds that are

associated with brokerage firms, which in itself may not be a direct conflict, but investors should fully vet the relationship between the two entities.

- A follow-up to the brokerage question is Question 13, which describes any additional compensation that an advisor may receive in connection with the management of a client's money.

- The final question, Item 14, deals with the applicant (advisor) providing a balance sheet; the advisor may have, by SEC regulations, custody of client assets. This could also be a red flag to investors. If the applicant answers "yes" to these questions, he must provide broader explanations in Form ADV Schedule F.

In Schedule F, the applicant must explain in greater detail its services, investment strategies and analysis, investment instruments used, privacy and proxy voting policies, and fee structures for clients. In addition, the principals of the investment advisory firm must give detailed educational and employment background for the past 10 years. Finally, the applicant must disclose any direct or indirect interests in other financial companies or products. Reviewing all the details in Schedule F is an investor's time well spent.

The SEC has taken a serious stance to insure that advisors disclose any real or perceived conflict of interests. By merely answering "yes" to a question and fully detailing the circumstance does not imply the advisor has a conflict or that you as an investor are in danger of being taken advantage of. The investor should, however, fully understand what is being said and how it may affect the way an advisor operates.

I have mentioned that many hedge fund managers are not registered or have deregistered, so there will not be a Form ADV or Schedule F available. That should not stand in the way of an investor inquiring about those conflicts during a conference call or directly in his own due diligence questionnaire (DDQ), discussed later in this chapter. I would suggest that those questions should be more pointed and targeted. One of the valid complaints from hedge funds is that the Form is too broad and general and does not really provide specific information that will be useful to either regulators or investors.

FUND BROCHURES AND DOCUMENTS

The next request that an investor should make to the fund manager is for a copy of the fund's current offering documents—including the Offering Memorandum, Subscription Documents, and Limited Partnership Agreement. These are legal documents that can be tedious to read, but they define all the terms that will govern the investment and operation of monies in the hedge fund.

You should also request the current marketing material, which provides a snapshot of the firm's investment process and examples of the portfolio construction and constraints. The marketing brochure is the roadmap to how the fund is to be run. Understanding the philosophy and firm structure will allow you to do a better job during your on-site visit. It will also give you a benchmark, since during that visit the investor can find out if the manager truly believes in his firm. The marketing brochure includes basic information such as terms of investing (minimums, lock-ups), fund administrator, auditor, legal counsel, and prime broker. It should also include brief biographies of the firm's principals.

All of this information forms the building blocks for the huge due diligence process that still lies ahead of you. Along with the questions generated by your analysis of performance, you'll have a sufficient number of other questions to justify a telephone interview or face-to-face meeting with the hedge fund principals.

Although reading these documents is a tedious part of the due diligence process, it occasionally yields discovery—and concerns. There may be uncertainty about terms for side pockets or the guidelines for allowing the hedge fund to invest in private equity deals. This may seem unimportant, but you might discover in the documents that you can opt out of the side pocket. Another concern might be the terms and conditions of the fund's expenses and how they are charged, or the true extent to which the fund can be leveraged.

PLANNING THE ON-SITE VISIT

Before you schedule an on-site visit, a telephone interview may be in order. The decision to hold a conference call first is driven by several important factors, the most important of which is how much of the investor's budget is allocated to making on-site visits. Such a visit can be critical, especially if you are searching among emerging managers. During the initial information gathering you may not be gung-ho about a given manager for any number of reasons. The geographic location of the manager and your travel plans will be the deciding factor that will convince you that a conference call may be the quickest way to put you at ease. If you have developed a strong network among administrators and prime brokers, an on-site visit to large well-established funds like Cerebus or SAC will provide little tangible gain for the investor. These will also tend to be large staged presentations. Needless to say, it is imperative to visit newer, younger managers to get first hand knowledge of the fund's operations and infrastructure.

As we will discuss in Chapter 9, the majority of hedge fund failures are due to operational rather than investment failures. The biggest danger in reviewing emerging managers may rest in relying on conference calls because the performance numbers are outstanding. Picture the following: You are having a conversation with a manager thousands of miles away about investing several million dollars. Unbeknownst to you, the manager is sitting in his garage wearing bunny slippers and day trading stocks based on tips he gathers from some blogs. The information from general observations is hard to duplicate on conference calls, even those that may be video cast. It is easy to build illusions of an expansive office while sitting behind an impressive desk wearing a coat and tie—but no pants. Remember that fraud is built on illusion. This is not to say that unless a manager has a penthouse office with expensive furniture and million dollar art, you should avoid investing. I have talked with firms that not only fit that description but also had two corporate jets at their disposal. However, I would not let them invest my money in a passbook account, let alone a hedge fund.

The qualitative factors discussed here are equally as important as the numbers but are much harder to process. Investors with limited budgets may instead wish to have an extended conference call with a list of standard questions, plus others generated by the performance analysis and review of the fund's documents. If possible a web cast meeting is preferable, as it is always good to see people's reactions to pointed questions that may arise. On the plus side, having many general firm questions and procedures covered can make the on-site more productive or alleviate the need for the on-site at all.

SUMMARY

You can customize your DDQ to include whatever areas of concern you have or guidelines that must be met by your IPS. The list of information that can be asked for is enormous. Keep in mind that you should limit the information to things that are relevant and vital to making a sound decision. Funds, especially small emerging ones, have limited manpower and their personnel need to be focused on managing the fund. Unless you are prepared to invest large amounts of money, funds will typically give short shrift to a DDQ asking for detailed information that is not easily deliverable. Your goal, in addition to finding a solid long term investment, is to build a good relationship with the fund so that you may enjoy the benefits of easy and useful information flow.

With the completed DDQ, Form ADV (if it exists), marketing brochure, and vendor information, you now have a full picture from many angles to help you begin to form an opinion of the fund. You need to be mindful to keep your Columbo hat on to assure that the picture is the same from all angles and is not distorted. The distortion can lead to the investor receiving some disastrous results. Consistency may be the hobgoblin of little minds but it's the shield against fraud and disappointment in the hedge fund world.

The information gained should provide you with more data to analyze. It will be a roadmap to the historic and future growth of the firm and provide details on the principals involved and how the firm operates daily as well as under catastrophic conditions. It should all meld quite well with information and data you have already collected and move you a step closer toward making a final selection of a manager.

CHAPTER 7

Let the Games Begin
The Due Diligence Process

Doubt is the vestibule which all must pass before they can enter the temple of wisdom.

—C.C. Colton

For many investors, the search for investment managers—especially hedge fund managers—begins and ends with performance numbers. It is generally accepted that performance is a key metric. Unfortunately, as the SEC states in its required disclosure, past performance is not indicative of future performance.

It is paramount for investors to dig *deeply* into the inner workings of a manager, in order to understand not only his investment strategy and process but also the core and character of the business operations.

As you examine a hedge fund, the methodology and process you follow should be consistent with each manager. The strategy may differ, but how you review each fund should be quite similar. The process begins with the Investment Committee and works through document and data collection, then the analysis of all. You will then prepare a memo for posterity that describes the firm and your findings. Finally, you will rank the manager against a peer group. These steps will allow you to make a rational judgment and evaluate these funds in a consistent manner.

THE PROCESS

Figure 7.1 shows a typical flow chart of how a hedge fund works its way through a due diligence process. In this due diligence process we have now

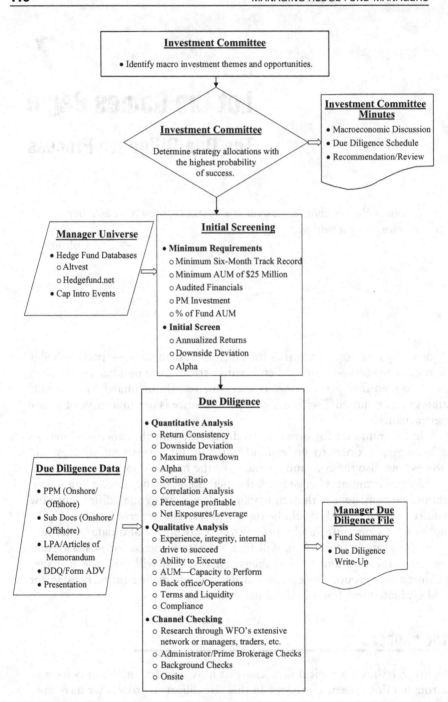

FIGURE 7.1 Alternative Investments Process

screened a database or our referral sources for several possible hedge funds in which to invest. We have given the numbers an initial scrubbing and have accumulated a fair amount of information about the manager and operations from our review of the Private Placement Memorandum (PPM), Form ADV, and the Due Diligence Questionnaire (DDQ). We must now assimilate the data and cast a wary eye on all.

We begin with the organizational structure of the investment firm, which is a key place to focus. In order to understand a firm, one must ascertain its business structure (partnership/LP, Limited Liability Corporation/LLC, or Limited Corporation/Ltd.), its place of incorporation and its legal domicile. Due to the state's favorable legal environment for business, most funds are incorporated in Delaware. Although the legal system is quite favorable to the corporate filer, the investor can also derive comfort from the fact that filing requirements in Delaware are consistent and the fund must retain a business agent in the state to maintain the fund's legal status. If perhaps an investor receives information from a fund incorporated in, say, Idaho (with no disrespect to the fine state), it should set off some warning bells to the investor. Offshore funds (Ltd.) become a bit more complicated. A fund can be located in a tax neutral jurisdiction such as Bermuda, the Cayman Islands, or even Ireland. The laws governing these locales often require legal counsel and fund administrators to be located in those jurisdictions. Such offshore firms may not be as well known or recognizable as U.S. firms.

The Internal Revenue Service also plays a role in the structure of the hedge funds. Pursuant to the U.S. Internal Revenue Code of 1986, the hedge fund, depending on its organizational and investment, l present advantages and disadvantages to investors which they must be keenly aware.

The master-feeder structure is one form used to invest money from taxable U.S. investors and U.S. tax-exempt and non-U.S. investors in one common vehicle. The use of the master fund increases the critical mass of the tradable assets which help to increase the operational efficiencies. The typical master feeder structure is shown in Figure 7.2. The Domestic feeder, for purposes of the U.S. income tax code, is treated as a pass through entity thus avoiding the double taxation. The offshore feeder set up as a corporation allows offshore investors to retain anonymity with regard to the IRS and avoid U.S. estate taxes that offshore investors may be subject to as they invest in U.S. partnerships. (Please check with your own tax advisors for specific guidance on the U.S. Tax Code). Additionally, only one set of books need to be maintained for the investments of both the Domestic Feeder and the Offshore Feeder. Management and performance fees are usually payable at the feeder fund level.

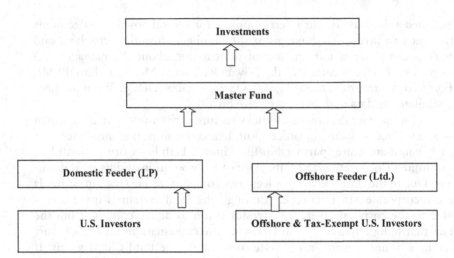

FIGURE 7.2 Master Feeder Structure

There are several disadvantages to the master-feeder structure. There is a loss of U.S. income tax treaty benefits for the Domestic Feeder. Also, Regulation T (Federal Reserve Board credit requirements) may limit the leverage which is generally available to Offshore Investors. Finally, the operating costs of the master-feeder structure are generally higher than a side-by-side structure.

The side-by-side structure is quite similar to the master feeder structure. The main difference is the absence of the Master fund and the investments are allocated, typically by the prime broker directly into the U.S. limited partnership and the offshore corporation. Without going into a mind numbing discussion of the U.S. Tax Code, the side-by-side structure relieves the hedge fund manager's concern about generating unwelcome "effectively connected taxable income." On the negative side, once again due to Tax Code issues, the returns of offshore funds may be different due to the negative impact of withholding taxes on dividends and certain interest payments.

Investors must therefore determine the suitability of the hedge fund's structure to the needs and concerns of the investor. The disadvantages of one structure may more than outweigh the expected return stream of the fund. In addition to the suitability, the actual fund structure will require slightly different ongoing due diligence as the investor is faced with a more complex structure in the Master Feeder and possibly less well known regulations and third party vendors. These aspects will require more work and disclosure before each investor can find his level of comfort with the manager and the hedge fund.

EXAMINING THE ORGANIZATION

Once the investor understands the structure of the fund, he needs to examine the people that make up the organization. (See Figure 7.3.) Hedge funds typically are formed for fairly simple reasons. Individuals who have been successful in proprietary trading environments (prop desks) or larger, established hedge funds decide to spring out on their own, hoping to garner higher percentages of income relating to their work or to escape some of the perceived formalities of bigger firms. These newly launched funds in some instances receive seed capital from their old cohorts. Despite this vote of confidence from former employers and colleagues, the track record and anticipation of future performance are unknown. This freedom of overseeing a new venture can easily distract focus and energy from the investment function. The ability to lead a business may not be a core competency to someone who was a stellar investor. Tasks such as operations, facility management, IT, Human resources, and normal business banking can be a full-time job. These functions that may have been taken for granted are now layered on top of the investment function that was the driving force leading to the launch of this new venture.

There is a lot of time and energy spent on determining the depth of a manager's pedigree. A quick read of the biography provided in the DDQ will give a summary as to the manager's background and possible sources of background checks. Approach the biography with the same skepticism

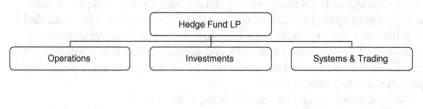

Operations	Investments	Systems & Trading
Client Service	Research & Analytics	Prime Brokerage
Fund Accounting	Idea Sharing & Process	Best Execution
Compliance	Industry Coverage	Monitoring
Back Office	Decision Making	

FIGURE 7.3   Hedge Fund Organization

that you would in reviewing the resume of a possible new hire to your firm. In hiring a manager you are effectively doing the same. The common discussion usually revolves around the fact that Mr. HF Superstar was one of the youngest managing partners at a Bulge Bracket firm. Or John Trader worked at All World Hedge Fund. Many believe such attributes to be a strong recommendation, and they might very well be. But there are several issues with this superficial analysis. First, Mr. Superstar may have been a wonderful performer at Bulge Bracket. The correct follow-up questions are: Did he manage money in the strategy he is now employing? Can he manage a business? Mr. Trader may have in fact been a trader. What were his daily functions? How successful was he and what did he contribute to the fund's performance. Is the performance verifiable?

Here is another way to think about this: Every year the top medical schools in the United States graduate hundreds of new doctors. Every year many of these doctors graduate near the bottom of their class. They have all survived a competitive entrance process, a rigorous curriculum, and top notch training, but if given a choice, would you pick someone at the top or the bottom of the class at Johns Hopkins or Harvard Medical School? The same standards should be applied to the pedigree analysis of your hedge fund manager.

PREPARING FOR THE ON-SITE VISIT

All of the questions from the screening, DDQ, and possible telephone interview are leading up to the requisite on-site visit. The visit should be scheduled with sufficient notice to enable you to completely review all the documents, responses, and analyses that you have completed to date and prepare a list of questions that may have been generated as follow-ups in areas where the responses were less than robust.

The visit should focus on the following critical areas:

- How well does the manager articulate the investment process?
- Are the logic and approach consistent?
- How does the manager generate ideas (alpha) for the portfolio?
- Is the investment team a cohesive unit?
- How is the infrastructure being managed?
- What are the goals of the firm?
- What are the sources of return?
- Does the manager value its investors?
- What are your risk parameters and who monitors them?
- Who has operational access to trades and cash?
- What are the pricing and valuation policies?

- Does the firm have a code of ethics?
- What are the disaster recovery plans?

Understanding the investment process, how it is implemented, and the underlying fundamentals that drive investment decisions are the real key points to a successful manager. The manager's understanding and his ability to help you understand are vitally important. A lack of conviction from either party at this point typically leads to an unsuccessful relationship and poor investment results.

How Well Does the Manager Articulate the Investment Process?

This may seem to be a straightforward subject, but after speaking with several hundred hedge fund managers it becomes quite clear that some of them are true believers and others are just repeating marketing brochures. The need for the investment team to articulate a detailed description of their approach can give an investor some comfort that the approach may be consistent. You should remember that if you cannot understand the approach at this stage of the relationship it will be difficult to weather adverse market conditions with this manager. Many managers have a firm conviction in the investment process of their firm and how and why it will be successful at providing a consistent stream of alpha to its investors. If the manager and the firm's analysts have difficulty walking through a typical investment selection, it certainly raises the doubt that the process may be ineffective or that they are not true believers.

It is always useful to have the investment team walk through a recent buy/sell or short. At each point in the process the team should articulate clearly the valuations and trigger points that moved the idea to the next step. If they are unclear and conviction is lacking, it could lead you to the perfectly logical conclusion that the process may be more theme- or emotion-based than following a tried and true philosophy. Getting information from firms on its investment process is sometimes difficult and the results can be sketchy. Depending on the securities that a fund invests in, the level of detail in the process becomes more important.

For a large cap long/short manager, the investment process should become clear quickly. A manager using complex derivatives, tranches of securitized loans, or straddle options, the explanation may be more detailed and tortured. No matter how long one has been in the business of analyzing hedge fund strategies, an analyst sometimes comes across a fund that makes him stop and say Whoa! Investment and trading strategies have become more and more complex as the search for "edge" or alpha grows increasingly competitive. The ability to distill a manager's investment process becomes paramount in the due diligence process. If you do not have the ability to understand the process as a snapshot in time, your odds of clarity decrease exponentially when the forces of the market take over. Having people on the due diligence team who have experience in the actual management of investment strategies becomes a definite plus in your selection process. It is clear that the market and investment strategies do not always comport with quantitative analysis and numbers.

Are the Logic and Approach Consistent?

Once you have a solid understanding of the process, seek to have the manager explain, provide examples, and generally demonstrate about different market occurrences how they reacted and why. Remember the performance outliers and return distributions from your screening process? Did one or two positions have a disproportionate impact on performance? Have the manager defend or propose why the process held up, worked, or failed. The manager's response to how the portfolio performed under times of stress will give you insights into his approach and consistency and how the team responded. This will help you be able to project the manager's ability to replicate past results.

It is useful to obtain portfolio holdings or portfolio characteristics from previous months or quarters. (See Table 7.1.) Examining the historical data and holdings allows you to form questions about the process and determine

TABLE 7.1 Fundamental Data of Hedge Fund

	Long/Short Hedge Fund	S&P 500
Market Capitalization		
Weighted Average	62,414.503	88,542.969
Weighted Median	26,460.934	52,498.863
Median	25,920.470	12,091.400
Minimum	701.993	817.702
Maximum	368,222.750	368,222.750
Dividend Yield	1.63	1.85
Price/Earnings	20.13	19.31
P/E Using FY1 Estimates	17.83	16.92
Price/Cash Flow	14.39	13.71
Price/Book	3.82	3.40
Est 3–5 Year EPS Growth	12.32	12.27
Beta	0.81	0.93
ROE	20.39	19.52
Long-Term Debt/Stockholder Equity	0.47	0.90

whether the manager was consistent in his approach. The easiest funds to view are those with very tight or limited investment criteria. For example, in a small cap fund or a value fund, the fundamental holdings statistics over time can confirm whether a manager has consistently applied his craft. Median and mean market capitalization, P/E ratios, and earnings growth characteristics go a long way to fill in the puzzle. Similarly for fixed income strategies, portfolio attribution, sector weights, duration, and yield curve positioning provide some guidance about past portfolio management decisions. Unfortunately, hedge funds are set up giving the fund manager the flexibility to invest with the broadest mandate possible in the hope of generating alpha. You need to look at additional measures to insure that the approach is indeed consistently applied.

How Does the Manager Generate Ideas (Alpha) for the Portfolio?

You should have prospective managers articulate their proprietary process or "edge" in generating ideas to the portfolio that will produce alpha. This is especially important for those managers that may have spun out of brokerage firms or "prop desks" (proprietary trading desks). Overreliance on Street research or ideas from brokerage firms can be a warning sign.

Many funds use technical analysis and quantitative models. The growing use of quantitative models is a mixed blessing for investors. Data and information about the reality of markets are in short supply for properly testing theory. The models are used to employ theory and produce profits. Failure to understand the underlying theory of models can lead to enormous risk and a dangerous assumption that volatility is greatly understated. The Street is becoming increasing littered with models that failed to get market cooperation in confirming their assumptions. The solid fund manager can articulate and demonstrate a proprietary process for delivering ideas that will generate persistent alpha.

Is the Investment Team a Cohesive Unit?

It is desirable to have a team that worked together in the past and focused on areas that served them well. Teams that have worked together can provide a level of confidence that the process and idea generation are consistent and follow a tested method. Understanding how the team members are compensated and their responsibilities in the overall process is essential as well. The process can break down if one or more of the team members feel they are being slighted in any way.

One of the major drivers of professionals in the investment business is their desire to enjoy a high level of compensation for providing successful ideas. If the professional is not happy with the compensation and possibly with ownership levels, this dissatisfaction can lead to dissention, a lagging work ethic, and less desire to unearth the next big idea. It can also lead to staff turnover (and the possible new launch of yet another hedger fund). The challenge that must be addressed is whether the fund has identified these risks, and do they have future plans to expand opportunities to keep the cohesive unit happy and intact.

How Is the Infrastructure Being Managed?

The main business of a hedge fund is to produce alpha. When looking at smaller firms it is essential to look at noncore activities. For emerging managers, the breakdown of operations or infrastructure presents the greatest risk of failure. Operational items such as accurate performance reporting, managing technology, timely distributions, and on-time delivery of K-1s are a necessary part of a successful business. For small firms, handling these factors successfully will help them stand out.

The valuation procedures should be well constructed, and a disciplined pricing policy should be adhered to and examined by auditors. There is an urgent requirement for an independent and reliable pricing of securities at month-end; it should not be one based solely on the manager's best efforts.

What Are the Goals of the Firm?

Passion for investments is the driving force for successful investing, and ambition to lead their own ship is a required desire for those leaving the comfy confines of a larger firm. This drive to grow can be a blessing and a curse. An investor needs to ascertain the maximum size of assets that the hedge fund manager thinks is ideal for their given strategy. Too much ambition, which can also be confused with greed, will eventually drive down returns, while too little leads to complacency throughout the organization. Have the goals changed substantially over time? A small cap manager that planned to close at $250 million in AUM, and is now over $500 million and still open, should raise concerns. It is sound analysis to review how the return stream performed during times of high cash inflows.

What Are the Sources of Returns?

The investor needs to determine the sources of returns. Is it superior, consistent security selection, or did the manager make an outsized one-time return? It is important to examine large deviations from the normal performance of the fund and how it performed relative to its markets. Analyzing

TABLE 7.2 Top Ten Holdings

Position	% of Portfolio	Sector	Price ($)	12-month Target ($)	% Upside	Prc/FCF (Current Year)	Prc/FCF (Next Year)
A	10%	Water	9.0	18.0	100.0%	15.0	11.0
B	4%	Financial	7.0	25.0	257.1%	10.0	5.0
C	8%	Restaurants	7.0	24.0	242.9%	7.0	5.5
D	6%	Industrial	14.0	30.0	114.3%	12.0	10.0
E	9%	Commodity	7.0	12.0	71.4%	3.5	2.1
F	9%	Alternative Energy	26.0	75.0	188.5%	16.0	9.0
G	5%	Tech	15.0	45.0	200.0%	15.0	10.0
H	7%	Packaging	8.0	18.0	125.0%	6.1	4.9
I	4%	Retail	15.0	24.0	60.0%	9.0	8.0
J	6%	Software	10.5	20.0	90.5%	15.3	10.5
	68%		Median		119.60%	11.0x	8.5x

past holdings (Table 7.2) will shed light on the consistency of the manager's approach and his ability to navigate markets. Hedge funds are sometimes criticized for not truly being hedged at all. You need to determine whether the manager has the ability to make money on the fund's long picks as well as short picks. The ability of a fund manager to be profitable in all markets (Table 7.3) will weigh heavily in the portfolio construction process. If the manager only implements shorts through derivatives or ETFs (Exchange Traded Funds), the true source of returns will be heavily dependent on the long selection. This type of hedging, while it will reduce some of the market risk in the portfolio, will also increase the fund's correlation to the markets.

Some additional quantitative measures can be helpful to achieve a better understanding of how a fund manager performs in various markets. Remember, under the PMPT the MAR is an important benchmark. To achieve the client's MAR consistently the portfolio needs to participate in up markets and, more importantly, protect capital in down markets. A Capture ratio provides a snapshot of how the manager performs in up and down markets. The Up Capture Ratio is a measure of an investment's compound return when its benchmark, let's assume the Russell 2000, was up. Conversely, the Down Capture ratio is a measure of the investment's compound return when the Russell 2000 was down. Mathematically, a negative result indicates that an investment's compound return was positive when the Russell 2000 was down. In a Lake Wobegone scenario where every manager is above average, the Up Capture ratio would be +100 percent and the Down Capture would

TABLE 7.3 Net Fund Return Analysis

	Jan	Feb	Mar	Apr	May	Jun	Jul	Aug	Sep	Oct	Nov	Dec	YTD
2006													
Long	7.3	10.5	2.7	6.5	(6.9)	(6.8)	2.9	(2.6)	(3.5)	2.9	7.6	6.2	
Short	(1.6)	(0.1)	(1.5)	(0.1)	0.6	1.5	2.1	0.6	0.1	(0.8)	(1.2)	(1.0)	
Net Return	5.8	10.9	1.2	6.4	(6.2)	(5.3)	5.1	(3.2)	(3.4)	2.1	6.4	5.2	25.5%
Russell 2000	9.0	(0.3)	4.9	(0.0)	(5.6)	(0.7)	(3.3)	3.0	0.8	5.8	2.6	0.3	18.4
2007													
Long	2.8	3.6	(0.5)	4.7	3.8	(3.4)	(2.8)	(2.7)	1.6	7.3	(3.4)	4.4	
Short	(0.4)	0.2	0.1	(0.6)	(0.6)	0.4	2.2	(3.3)	(0.4)	(1.7)	3.5	1.8	
Net Return	2.3	3.8	(0.4)	4.1	3.2	(3.1)	(0.5)	(0.6)	1.2	5.6	0.1	6.2	23.6%
Russell 2000	1.7	(0.8)	1.1	1.8	4.1	(1.5)	(6.8)	2.3	1.7	2.9	(7.2)	(0.1)	(1.6)

be −100 percent. Since we live in a different world, an Up Capture ratio of 85 to 95 percent is excellent. The Down Capture with a range of +50 percent to negative number shows that the manager does well at capital preservation.

Does the Manager Value His Investors?

How the manager treats you as an investor is important. Are your questions answered honestly and quickly? A manager who allows a reasonable amount of transparency on the portfolio and fees provides a window to the fund but also to the ethics of the firm. This is not to say that a firm without significant disclosure is unethical, but it does leave you to wonder what may lie beneath the surface. Given the lock-ups, gates, and other criteria for withdrawing your money, it is imperative to have a strong relationship and level of trust with the manager.

PREPARING THE FINAL EVALUATION

The sources of answers on your on-site visit will be the Chief Investment Officer, portfolio manager, analysts, traders, Chief Compliance Officer, Chief Operating Officer, and other investment and operations personnel. On-site visits are extensive and time-consuming for both the manager and the investor. Being prepared will aid you in quickly reaching a conclusion. In Figure 7.4 you can see the various segments that must be reviewed in order

- **Third Party Service Providers**
  - ○ Analyst will request a list of service providers and gain an understanding of the role they play in the operations of a hedge fund manager. In the case of service providers that are not well known, Analyst will perform additional due diligence at its discretion to assess a firm's competence and gauge its industry reputation.
  - ○ Each manager should have written service agreements with third party service providers clearly defining their roles, responsibilities, and liabilities. In addition, Analyst may, at its discretion, request additional information inclusive of the following:
    - Administrator
      - Confirm nature and duration of relationship to manager.
      - Review NAV calculation and valuation process.
      - Discuss pricing discrepancies and resolution.
      - Conduct cash movement authentication.
      - Confirm AUM (if applicable).
    - Accountants
      - Confirm nature and duration of relationship to manager.
      - Review NAV calculation and valuation process.
      - Discuss any pricing discrepancies and resolution.
      - Confirm AUM (if applicable).
    - Auditor
      - Confirm nature and duration of relationship to manager.
      - Review any concerns or questions on previous audit (if applicable).
      - Discuss any potential roadblocks for issuing a qualified opinion and their resolution.
    - Legal Counsel
      - Confirm nature and duration of relationship to manager.
      - Review any past or current litigation on behalf of or against the manager.
    - Prime Broker(s)
      - Confirm nature and duration of relationship to manager.
      - Confirm AUM (if applicable).
      - With approval of manager, request to view a prime brokerage statement.
  - ○ Conflicts of Interest: Analyst will assess whether a manager has disclosed significant conflicts of interest that may arise from:
    - Relationships with brokers and service providers.
    - Use of Soft Dollar arrangements.
    - Side-by-side management of multiple accounts and allocation of investment opportunities.
    - Side Letters offering preferred fee structures and enhanced liquidity such as waiver of lock-ups.
- **Valuation Policies and Procedures**
  - ○ A Hedge Fund manager should establish pricing policies and procedures that assure that NAV is marked at fair value. Such policies, typically based upon GAAP, should be fair, consistent, and verifiable. Analyst prefers that valuations are done independently (typically by an administrator) and incorporate the concept of "fair value," defined as follows.

(Continued)

FIGURE 7.4 Operational Due Diligence

- Fair Value: In situations where a manager does not believe the application of fair value (as required by GAAP), will produce an accurate or fair valuation for a given instrument, the manager may employ alternative means to value an instrument as permitted by agreement. Exceptions of this nature should be resolved based on coherent and consistent policies determined by the manager and accepted by the administrator or independent accountant. For such exceptions, Analyst will request a copy of pricing policies and procedures. Analyst will also validate other valuation procedures such as:
  - Pricing Sources: What are the fund's pricing sources and what is the manager's policy with respect to verification of the accuracy of prices and under which circumstances (if any) it may override a pricing service's recommendation?
  - Where market prices do not exist or are not indicative of fair value, a manager should clearly establish the valuation methods to be used for NAV purposes. For positions traded over the counter or derivative instruments, where the only external source of fair value may be quotes from relevant market makers, what is the number of quotes sought by the manager to gain comfort with the fair value and how are such quotes utilized?
  - In instances where transactions are one of a kind (such as exotic options, MBS, ABS) and a pricing model is used to determine fair value, the manager may be asked to explain and support the model parameters used in determining the valuation.
- Illiquid and Hard to Value Investment Instruments
  - A manager may use alternative approaches for valuing illiquid, or otherwise hard-to-value, securities, such as "side pockets." Under side pocket methodology, investment instruments that are removed from the valuation process that applies to the rest of the portfolio are held either at cost or at fair value (depending on the manager's valuation policies).
- **Risk Monitoring**
  - Analyst may assess each manager's risk monitoring procedures with respect to quantifying market risk, credit risk, and liquidity risk (both funding and asset liquidity risk). Each manager should employ a consistent framework for measuring the risk of loss for a portfolio (as a result of any of the aforementioned risks) such as a Value-at-Risk (VaR) model. Whatever model(s) are utilized by a manager should be subject to stress testing.
    - Market Risk: Market risk relates to losses that could be incurred due to changes in market factors such as prices, volatilities, and correlations and encompasses interest rate risk, foreign exchange rate risk, equity price risk, and commodity price risk. Analyst will review each manager's market risk monitoring procedures in the context of portfolio construction and suitability for the fund's strategy.
    - Credit Risk: Credit risk relates to losses that could be incurred due to declines in the creditworthiness of entities in which the fund invests or with which the fund deals as a counterparty.
      - Obtain a list of credit counterparties. For counterparties that are not well known, Analyst will perform additional inquiries to assess a firm's competence and gauge industry reputation.
    - Liquidity Risk: Asset liquidity risk, or portfolio liquidity risk, will be scrutinized as part of WFO's review of portfolio risk monitoring. With respect to funding liquidity, Analyst will review each fund's investor base, side letters, and other agreements that can impact the fund's ability to provide investors with liquidity in the case of redemptions.

FIGURE 7.4 (*Continued*)

- **Regulatory Controls**
  - Analyst may verify that each manager actively monitors and manages its regulatory responsibilities to ensure compliance with all applicable rules and regulations. For managers that are registered investment advisors, the designation of chief compliance officer to administer its policies and procedures is required by the Advisers Act. Analyst will review each manager's compliance procedures, Schedule ADV Part II, and Code of Ethics.
  - For managers choosing not to register with the SEC, Analyst will review what internal controls are in place and whether they are sufficient to merit an investment from WFO.
- **Transactional Practices**
  - Analyst will review each manager's transactional practices to determine consistency of bilateral terms across numerous counterparties.
- **Business Continuity and Disaster Recovery**
  - Analyst will request from each manager a copy of their Business Continuity and Disaster Recovery (BC/DR) plan. In addition, Analyst may request contingency plans for responding to the failure of a third party administrator, credit provider, or other mission-critical party with which the fund conducts business.
- **Supplemental Documents to Request from Managers**
  - ADV Part II and Schedule F
    - Check each ADV via IARD on SEC web site.
    - Reconcile AUM from ADV versus audit and other fund materials.
    - Perform background check on other investment advisors related to the manager.
  - Code of Ethics
  - BC/DR Plan

FIGURE 7.4 (*Continued*)

to complete a thorough operational due diligence on a manager. Studying the performance and portfolio of a fund is a much easier task to tackle than studying the operational side. The operational aspect involves the infrastructure of the fund along with its third party service providers.

Third Party Vendors

During the on-site visit you should request extensive information about the fund's service providers, including the nature and length of the relationship. The most important fact is to verify any and all information. When examining the administrator, it is necessary to confirm how NAVs are calculated, the input into determining that value, pricing issues, cash movements, and confirming AUM. It is also a sound idea to identify whether any of the interested parties to the fund, a general partner or a third party vendor, have a beneficial interest in any other part or activity of the fund.

Ask for and review, at minimum, the most recent annual audit. Determine whether the values listed in the audit square up with the report from the administrator and published information from the fund itself. Above all, verify that the auditor is independent and real. In 2005 the Bayou Group had a hedge fund that raised $400 million in assets. Due to what was later determined as fraud, the fund lost $300 million. After the dust settled, it was discovered that the fund's chief financial officer owned the "independent" auditor who misrepresented NAVs to investors. One of the co-founders was later sentenced to 20 years for fraud. Justice was served, but it was little comfort to investors whose angst could have been avoided just by asking a few questions about the auditor.

Trading

In addition to some accounting issues with Bayou, it was also discovered that the fund had paid around $50 million in commissions to an affiliated broker, a sum equal to nearly 13 percent of the fund's value. Trading and brokerage are important services that need to be examined. The starting point is the prime broker(s) relationships. Have the prime broker confirm the asset level the manager claims to be under management. Also ask to receive copies of some past brokerage statements. This will serve as a check on money flows, AUM, and trading efficiency, and it will offer a peek into whether the investment style pitch matches the reality of running the fund. During the on-site visit you can quiz the traders of the fund as to how trades get executed, authority for trading, interaction with the back office, and whether the firm is seeking best execution. At this time an explanation of a Soft Dollar policy would be useful. An investor's stance on a Soft Dollar policy varies. Some believe it is full of conflicts and is a misuse of a client's funds. Still, many small start-up firms rely heavily on Soft Dollars to launch their business, using Soft Dollars as a method to afford needed research services. The SEC takes a dim view of Soft Dollars and has taken steps to tighten or limit their use. Using Soft Dollars does not have to be a deal breaker for an investor; however, more care and diligence must be exercised to insure that the fund is make judicious use of the invested monies.

Background Checks

Upon review of the fund's Form ADV Parts I & II, if applicable, the investor should spend time with the Chief Compliance Officer to determine the compliance culture of the firm and discuss any SEC audit or other regulatory body exams in addition to any legal complaints filed. There will be plenty of papers to collect and review: valuation policies, risk policies, compliance manuals, ethics policies, personal trading policies, business continuity and disaster recovery plans, and possibly succession plans. Any filed document can be used to cross-check any information that may be stated in marketing brochures or web sites. This seems to be a simple and almost silly exercise. Unfortunately, many investors would be surprised to see the number of discrepancies between the marketing documents and the legal documents. In all probability legal documents such as ADVs will contain correct information, and some exaggeration or fabrication will arise in the marketing material. Technically that is equally fraudulent; however, since someone attests to the accuracy of the ADV, the probability shrinks but does not disappear.

It is also a good practice to perform an Internet search of the fund's principals. This is quite a simple thing, not overly quantifiable, but it can lead to interesting information and save some headaches. For example, a quick Internet search may show a securities lawsuit filed years ago, a bankruptcy claim, a drunk driving conviction, or a previously failed hedge fund. Some of these facts may turn out to be nonissues, but it is always comforting to know what you are dealing with before investing. Remember, there are more than 10,000 hedge funds. If you are uncomfortable with any aspect of one, there are always more to review.

Depending on the complexity of the strategy and the organization, the on-site may take more than one visit. Once you complete your work, you may consider two additional steps to memorialize your work and provide some documentation.

Manager Summary

It is a sound idea to generate a short report that reconfirms the findings of your intensive due diligence process. The brief summary (Figure 7.5) will be a formulation of your understanding of the investment strategy and process, position sizing, risk management, performance, and fund terms. This should synthesize the proposed new investment, and reviewing the highlights should confirm your conviction (or not).

Model Ranking

The final step is a method whereby you assign and rank quantitative and qualitative measures. This benchmarking exercise allows you to rank the fund independently but also against your customized peer group for all factors. Early in the process, we developed a customized peer group to compare performance measures. If after the ranking the fund does not compare favorably to the peer group, more work may be warranted. The Manager

Fund Name	Hedge Fund LP
Investment Manager	Chief Investment Officer
Address	Financial Street, Big Town, AL
Phone	
Person(s) Met at Fund	CIO, COO
Person(s) from WFO	
Visit Date / Type	September 27, 2007/Follow-up

Strategy

HF is a long/short small cap equity fund. The investment team seeks to identify mispriced securities relative to assets or free cash flow. The process begins by running over 2500 small cap companies (U.S. and international) through a proprietary screening process for valuation and price movement (1 week, 1 month, 3 month, 6 month). This portion accounts for 70–80 of the portfolio. The second process done weekly (Fridays) has 10 screening factors for events and includes items such as share repurchases, new guidance, new management, acquisitions or divestitures, name changes, as well as technical items like price and volume and options volume. Produces a list of about 100 companies which is then reduced to 5 to 10 companies that will be researched that week. Investment team uses extensive industry contact and buy-side analysts (third party due diligence) in addition to a review of public filings, financial models (CF, balance sheet, income statement), and discussion with management, which then serve to develop risk/reward pricing and expected catalysts. Regardless of the end decision of the company research, a "2 Note" is written (a two-page summary Word.doc that describes the research, documents, meetings, and contacts). This intellectual capital contains information and modeling on over 2,500 companies (long only) and over 400 companies (short only). Short ideas, typically soon-to-be-broken growth stocks, are selected from bad business models, declining industries, or after good news. This allows Oak Street to act quickly when an opportunity arises. Investment selections are bottom-up and thematic.

Portfolio Overview

Style—Sectors—Instrument Types—Geography

The portfolio is typical structured with about 25 longs and 25 shorts. The long positions are typically 3–10% (cost) in size. Position are typically waded in with 1% and built up. Top 5 positions in the portfolio accounts for about 50% of the fund. Short positions start at 0.5% and may be as high as 4%. Longs as a percent of market value as they approach 12% are pruned back to 10%. The top 5 long positions are in the market cap range of $300 million to $1.5 billion. The shorts range from $200 million to $2 billion. Sectors are constrained to +/–25% of the Bloomberg sector baskets. Oak Street makes no allocation to biotech or financials (banks, insurance) where they feel they have no edge. Fund may own warrants and options. International names make up about 20% of the portfolio with 90% in Canada. Fund buys local shares in Canada and ADRs elsewhere. Currency is hedged. Shorts are 60% single names and 40% in options and ETFs. Turnover is two times/year for shorts and one time/year for longs.

Exposure Profile

	# Long Positions	Gross Long %	# Short Positions	Gross Short %	Net Exposure
Current	25	116%	25	86%	30%
Average	23	95%	20	52%	43%

FIGURE 7.5 Manager Summary

Position Sizing

	Long		Short	
	Cost	MTM	Cost	MTM
Average	3%	5%	1%	2%
Maximum	10%	15%	2%	4%

Leverage

n/a

Risk Management

Risk is controlled by tightly monitored gross and net market exposures, and sector and size limitations. Risk/reward ratios are calculated to identify issues that may be volatile. Portfolio is 90% liquid in 10 days. Capacity is expected to be $250–$300 million.

Investor Base

HNW/Family Office 45% (24 investors)

FOF 50% (8 investors)

Principals 5% (2 investors)

Strategic Outlook— Return Drivers

HF uses an intensive research process combined with extensive knowledge on a broad company base that allows them to act quickly as mispricings occur. Look for solid values based on assets and free cash flow that protects downside while catalysts are able to grow sales and earnings get resolved. Have become more adept at trading around positions and markets (net short for the first time in August). Consistently make money in longs and shorts. Longs positive 70% of months and shorts 50%. Generate about 80% of gains when market is down.

Fund Assets	$62 million	Lock-up	1 Yr.	Prime Broker	Goldman Sachs
Firm Assets	$62 million	Penalty	—	Legal Council	Drinker Biddle & Reath
Minimum	$1,000,000	Management Fee	1.5%	Auditor	Rothstein Kass
Redemption Terms	Quarterly	Incentive Fee	20%	Administrator	Goldman Sachs
Notice	60 days	On / Offshore	Y/Y—Cayman		
Gate	No	Domicile	DE		

FIGURE 7.5 (*Continued*)

Organizational Overview

CIO makes all portfolio decisions. COO runs operations. Most services are outsourced. SEC registered when the law was first passed. Subsequent to court ruling they have deregistered after consultation with all clients. Will be adding a second analyst within the next month—B-school grad with investment banking experience at a bulge bracket firm. Have followed this fund from its start-up stage with around $10 million in AUM. They have continued to rationally build and grow the firm with a focus on pure alpha and have no delusions of running a $1 billion AUM firm.

Performance/Benchmark

	Jan	Feb	Mar	Apr	May	Jun	Jul	Aug	Sep	Oct	Nov	Dec
2007	2.34	3.82	(0.43)	4.10	3.18	(3.06)	(0.53)	(0.48)	1.20			
2006	5.77	10.39	1.23	6.41	(6.21)	(6.26)	5.05	(3.21)	(3.39)	2.13	6.44	5.17
2005							3.87	1.70	0.58	1.47	1.55	6.04

	Fund	R2000V	R2000			
					Annualized Alpha	20.97
					Sharpe Ratio (3%)	1.28
Cumulative Return Since Inception	61%	25%	29%		Sortino Ratio (5%)	2.2
Net of Fees					Downside Dev. (5%)	7.2

Updates

Date/Type	
Attendees from Fund	
Attendees from FO	

Date/Type	
Attendees from Fund	
Attendees from FO	

Date/Type	
Attendees from Fund	
Attendees from FO	

FIGURE 7.5 (*Continued*)

Ranking Model in Figure 7.6 separates the fund into four important components:

1. People
2. Process
3. Performance
4. Organization

The subcomponents and weightings are subjective and should reflect the factors that are most important in your search. What this ranking does is allow you to compare managers under different asset classes in a similar fashion.

Manager:	XXXXX
Asset Class:	Equity
Style:	Large Cap
AUM$:	$125

Wt%	Factors	Breakout Variable%	Maximum Points	Manager Score
20%	People		20	
	Manager/Team Skill	30%	6.0	3.00
	Direct Product Experience	15%	3.0	2.50
	Portfolio Knowledge	20%	4.0	3.00
	Depth	15%	3.0	2.00
	Research Capability	20%	4.0	2.50
				Subtotal 13.00
40%	Process		40	
	Consistency	16%	6.4	3.00
	Discipline	10%	4.0	3.00
	Portfolio Construction	12%	4.8	3.00
	Diversification	8%	3.2	3.00
	Style/Process Drift	5%	2.0	3.00
	Liquidity	10%	4.0	3.00
	Sell Discipline	7%	2.8	2.00
	Capacity	12%	4.8	1.50
	Portfolio Review	8%	3.2	2.00
	Proprietary Research	12%	4.8	2.00
				Subtotal 25.50
20%	Performance		20	
	Performance Absolute	15%	3.0	2.00
	Performance Relative Peers	5%	1.0	1.50
	Performance Relative Benchmark	5%	1.0	1.00
	Sortino Ratio	20%	4.0	1.00
	Information Ratio	8%	1.6	1.00
	Correlation	8%	1.6	0.25
	Downside Deviation	15%	3.0	2.00
	Up/Down Capture	10%	2.0	1.00
	Persistence	10%	2.0	2.00
	Rolling Performance	4%	0.8	1.00
				Subtotal 12.75

FIGURE 7.6 Manager Ranking Model

20%	Organization/Operations		20	
	Succession Plan	10%	2.0	1.00
	Ownership/Incentives	10%	2.0	2.00
	Turnover	10%	2.0	1.00
	Accommodation of Growth	12%	8.4	1.00
	Systems	13%	2.6	2.00
	Compliance	10%	2.0	1.00
	Reconciliation/Administration	10%	2.0	1.50
	Reporting	7%	1.4	1.25
	Client Service	8%	1.6	1.50
	Quality of People	10%	2.0	1.50

Subtotal   13.75

Analyst
Adjustment   +/–3%   (1.00)

Total   64.00

Peer Group
Average   60.00

FIGURE 7.6   (*Continued*)

At this point we should consider some of the vehicles for investing. A comfort level with limited transparency and K-1s from the LP may not be forthcoming no matter how attractive the risk-return prospect is. An available alternative is a separately managed account (SAM). Not all hedge fund managers are open to this possibility since it adds another layer of trading and reporting separate from the LP. However, the fund may be willing, providing the proposed invested amount is large enough. Typical amounts for a SAM are around $25 to $50 million. For many ordinary (if that term applies) hedge fund investors, that amount is a much higher commitment than they can make.

Another alternative is investable indexes. These are not to be confused with hedge fund indexes, the reporting databases. These are investment vehicles that replicate a hedge fund index in terms of constituents and weightings. They may be strategy specific. Their performance is dependent upon the quality of funds on which they are based. They are constrained by including funds that have capacity for new money. These investable indexes are usually produced by a separate firm. Their ability to produce hedge fund-like returns is still an open question.

IN CONCLUSION

The due diligence process is intensive and you need to take a cynical approach. Believe in nothing if you cannot verify the numbers or the source of any document. It is human nature to believe the best of people. It is less hazardous to your wealth to assume that everything can go wrong or that you do not have all the information you think you do. Once you have turned over every stick and stone in your search for a hedge fund, you must take the next step and configure your portfolio.

The next chapter will show you how to construct your portfolio in a way that makes the most use of your top-flight due diligence.

CHAPTER 8

Getting Ready Is the Secret of Success

Portfolio Construction

Now that we have walked through an extensive process to research and select a hedge fund manager, the final test for the fund selected is how it fits into your current portfolio. All of the cumulative work, if done properly, will increase your probability of success. As we discussed in Chapter 1, the process began by outlining the goals and objectives in an investor's Investment Policy Statement (IPS). The IPS gives the particular client's investment criteria for risk and return, which leads to the manager selection. After that, you still need to perform three steps:

1. Top-down strategy analysis.
2. Bottom-up manager analysis.
3. Modeling and testing of the final portfolio.

After the due diligence process is complete, an investor needs to make a portfolio decision as to what effect or impact a particular hedge fund will have on the current exposures in his overall portfolio. The obvious temptation is to put the highest performance fund into the portfolio. You should resist that temptation until you can quantify the expected strategy returns and the correlations of the fund, not only to its peers (your other holdings), but also to general market benchmarks. You also need to be comfortable with the risk exposures of possible short positions and leverage in the fund. Now we look at how to quantify those exposures. The key to successful portfolio construction, whether you are picking stocks or picking managers, remains essentially the same: Identify an investment that matches your risk/return profile and has low correlation to the markets to which you may be exposed in your pursuit of alpha.

TOP-DOWN STRATEGY ANALYSIS

The IPS is the beginning of the process, but how an investor starts to approach the due diligence process goes beyond the mere search for high performance. Remember that one of the features of hedge funds is a lock-up period, typically one to three years. If an investor has to have his money locked for an extended period, the type of strategy he chooses must have some staying power. You cannot day-trade hedge funds. The investor must undertake a top-down strategy analysis by reviewing the macro-economic and strategy-specific factors that are the primary drivers of performance and risk for a given strategy.

A simple example is the convertible arbitrage space in the mid-2000s, which is shown in Table 8.1. You can see that convertible arbitrage funds underperformed the average of all hedge fund returns in each of the years from 2003 to 2006. The strategy also underperformed its own long-term average of 10.3 percent in 3 of the 4 years. A note of caution is warranted

TABLE 8.1 Hedge Fund Indexes Annual Net Returns 2003 1/n 2006

Index	2003	2004	2005	2006
Convertible Arbitrage	9.9%	1.2%	−1.9%	12.2%
Distressed Securities	29.7%	19.0%	8.3%	18.8%
Emerging Markets	39.4%	18.4%	21.0%	24.3%
Equity Hedge	20.5%	7.7%	10.6%	11.7%
Equity Market Neutral	2.4%	4.2%	6.2%	7.6%
Equity Non-Hedge	37.5%	13.3%	9.9%	15.5%
Event Driven	25.3%	15.0%	7.3%	15.3%
Fixed Income Arbitrage	9.4%	6.0%	5.6%	7.2%
Fixed Income Convert Bonds	17.5%	7.9%	2.5%	24.2%
Fixed Income High Yield	21.3%	10.5%	5.3%	10.6%
Macro Trading	21.4%	4.6%	6.8%	8.5%
Market Timing	15.4%	6.4%	14.4%	16.4%
Merger Arbitrage	7.5%	4.1%	6.3%	15.7%
Regulation D	20.5%	6.1%	12.4%	6.0%
Relative Value Arbitrage	9.7%	5.6%	6.0%	12.4%
Sectors: Aggregate	27.9%	11.3%	9.1%	15.7%
Short Selling	−21.8%	−3.8%	7.3%	−1.5%
Statistical Arbitrage	3.4%	4.0%	5.3%	14.6%
Average	16.5%	7.8%	7.9%	13.1%

Source: Hedge Fund Research, Inc.

here in using the sole parameter of performance as the beacon for investing. In viewing performance in isolation, a contrarian might draw the conclusion that this out-of-favor sector may be ripe for new investment. Convert. Arb, as it is known, underperformed the average hedge fund strategy by over 1,300 basis points. Another factor affecting performance is capital flows. After the Convert Arb index was down 7.7 percent for the first half of 2005, redemption notices came fast and furiously. The funds were forced to sell into a market in which there were no buyers, which drove returns even lower. The principal buyers of convertible bonds have been and remain hedge funds.

In earlier chapters we made considerable mention of the impact of liquidity in the investment markets. The forced selling into a highly illiquid market had a sad ending for several hedge funds and their investors. Three funds—Marin Capital Partners ($2.2 billion at its peak); Alta Partners ($1.2 billion at its peak); and Lakeshore International Fund ($669 million)— shut their doors.

Conversely, capital flows into a strategy can also foretell strong future performance. Along with capital flows, new fund formation is another key factor. The most robust example of these factors is the growth of the energy hedge fund strategy. In 2006 there were less than 500 funds that described themselves as having significant exposure to the energy sector. In early 2008, according to the Energy Hedge Fund Center (EHFC), there were more than 630 energy hedge funds. That included 362 energy specific funds and 272 energy related funds. It does not include the 210 commodity funds that have varying levels of energy exposure. The growth is continuing, since there is a spurt of fund creation dealing primarily with alternative energy solutions. This is clearly a much longer-tailed theme; however, I would urge caution, as fund strategies have life cycles no different from any other style or economic cycle.

BOTTOM-UP MANAGER ANALYSIS

The next step that needs to be done is the bottom-up manager analysis. The crux of the review and portfolio construction process is the fundamental analysis of the individual fund and its position in the portfolio. This process again is a mix of quantitative and qualitative measures that will be used to evaluate the possible contribution of each manager to the portfolio, primarily in terms of risk and return. In addition, ongoing developments in each manager's business that will influence future performance need to be assessed.

TEST OR MODEL THE PORTFOLIO

The final step as you begin the actual portfolio construction is to model or test how well the portfolio is diversified. Or to be perfectly clear, you want to have some assurance that your portfolio is not making the same trade a thousand times. One standard measure is correlation.

$$R = \frac{\sum_i \left[(x_i - \overline{x})(y_i - \overline{y}) \right]}{\sqrt{\sum_i \left[(x_i - \overline{x})^2 \right] \sum_i \left[(y_i - \overline{y})^2 \right]}}$$

1. Calculate the expressions $(x_i - \overline{x})$, $(y_i - \overline{y})$, their squares, and their product.
2. Determine the sums of squares $\sum (x_i - \overline{x})^2$ and $\sum (y_i - \overline{y})^2$, and the sum of products $\sum \left[(x_i - \overline{x})(y_i - \overline{y}) \right]$, then calculate value for R.
3. R^2 = the coefficient of correlation.

The coefficient of correlation essentially captures the extent to which the returns of x and y, in this case the returns of investment assets, move together. The resultant calculation provides a value of $+1$ to -1. The positive number as it approaches $+1.0$ demonstrates a high probability that the two return streams will move together. A high correlation between two investments can indicate a heightened risk in the funds. A correlation with a value of -1.0 leads to the conclusion that the return streams are more independent. It should be noted that the correlation between assets changes.

Table 8.2 compares the correlation of the MSCI EAFE Index to the S&P 500. For the 10 years ending December 31, 2001, the MSCI EAFE had a correlation of 0.56, or not highly correlated. Now let's skim over to the 10 years ending December 31, 2006. That correlation rose to 0.78. The MSCI EAFE and the S&P 500 have, as the world has become more global, seen the correlation of those markets increase. In fact, if you review the six 10-year periods, you will notice that the progression of the markets toward becoming more closely correlated has been steady over all the periods. This does not mean that you can invest in one market and not the other and reap similar diversification benefits. Quite the contrary; as quickly as the correlations rise, they also fall. If we look a little further down the table, we can see the opposite pattern in the Lehman Brothers 7-year Municipal Bond Index. For the 10 years ending December 31, 2001, the correlation is 0.26. By the fact of the 0.26 result, this index is already not highly correlated to

TABLE 8.2 Index Correlations

Correlation with S&P 500 Index	On 12/31/01 10 Years (1992–2001)	On 12/31/02 10 Years (1993–2002)	On 12/31/03 10 Years (1994–2003)	On 12/31/04 10 Years (1995–2004)	On 12/31/05 10 Years (1996–2005)	On 12/31/06 10 Years (1997–2006)
S&P 500 Index	1.00	1.00	1.00	1.00	1.00	1.00
S&P 400 Mid-Cap Index	0.79	0.86	0.86	0.87	0.85	0.84
S&P 600 Small-Cap Index	0.49	0.69	0.71	0.68	0.64	0.63
NASDAQ Composite (Price Return)	0.75	0.80	0.81	0.81	0.81	0.81
Russell 2000 Index	0.63	0.79	0.77	0.75	0.73	0.73
Wilshire 5000	0.99	0.99	0.99	0.99	0.99	0.99
MSCI World Free Gross	0.83	0.89	0.92	0.92	0.92	0.93
MSCI EAFE Net	0.56	0.65	0.75	0.74	0.76	0.78
MSCI Japan Net	0.24	0.25	0.34	0.39	0.38	0.45
MSCI Emerging Global Free Latin America Gross	0.07	0.25	0.38	0.34	0.46	0.49
MSCI Emerging Markets Free Gross	0.05	0.11	0.28	0.25	0.29	0.33
Lehman Brothers U.S. Aggregate (Taxable)	0.24	0.11	0.07	-0.04	-0.41	-0.39
Lehman Brothers 7-Year Municipal Bond Index	0.26	0.07	0.06	-0.05	-0.38	-0.37
10-Year U.S. Treasury Note	0.30	0.10	0.06	-0.03	-0.34	-0.31
International (J.P. Morgan Non-U.S. Bond)	0.48	0.25	0.34	0.32	0.20	0.21
Global (J.P. Morgan Global Government Bond)	0.48	0.06	0.14	0.09	-0.04	-0.03
Emerging Markets Bond Index (J.P. Morgan EMBI+)	0.26	0.21	0.31	0.25	0.18	0.06

(Continued)

TABLE 8.2 (*Continued*)

Correlation with S&P 500 Index	On 12/31/01 10 Years (1992–2001)	On 12/31/02 10 Years (1993–2002)	On 12/31/03 10 Years (1994–2003)	On 12/31/04 10 Years (1995–2004)	On 12/31/05 10 Years (1996–2005)	On 12/31/06 10 Years (1997–2006)
Goldman Sachs/Bloomberg U.S. Convertible Index	0.65	0.71	0.74	0.73	0.72	0.94
NAREIT (Real Estate Investment Trusts)	−0.17	−0.04	0.09	0.04	0.05	0.01
NCREIF Farmland Index (U.S. Farmland)	0.67	0.79	0.82	0.53	0.22	0.25
Cambridge Associates Private Equity Funds Index	0.80	0.86	0.89	0.87	0.83	0.81
Venture Economics All Private Equity Fund Index	0.41	0.48	0.45	0.43	0.43	0.43
HFRI Fund Weighted Composite Hedge Fund Index	0.41	0.58	0.69	0.68	0.65	0.63
HFRI Fund of Funds Index	0.29	0.38	0.48	0.45	0.45	0.43
MSCI Hedge Fund Composite Index	na	na	na	0.63	0.55	0.51
Commodity Research Bureau Total Return Index	0.05	−0.20	−0.14	−0.12	−0.21	−0.26
Barclay CTA Index (Commodity Trading Advisors)	0.54	0.22	0.25	0.19	0.05	−0.02
Handy & Harmon Spot Gold Price	−0.22	−0.52	−0.34	−0.37	−0.40	−0.30
Lehman Brothers TIPS Index/Bridgewater	−0.34	−0.48	−0.41	−0.52	−0.64	−0.63
Mei Moses Fine Art Index	0.24	0.36	0.42	0.38	0.18	0.21

Sources: Morgan Stanley Investment Management; Hedge Fund Research.

the S&P 500. If you now look at the 10-year period ending December 31, 2006, the correlation for the Lehman 7-year Municipal Bond Index has now dropped to −0.37, or hardly correlated at all.

Turning our attention to the hedge fund space, you will note that over the six periods the HFRI Fund Weighted Composite Hedge Fund Index saw the correlation rise from 0.41 to 0.63. This is not highly correlated, but also not a positive direction in searching for noncorrelating diversification. The good news is the 0.63 value has actually fallen over the last four 10-year periods (2002 *1/n* 2006). Part of the explanation for the rise in correlation is that most of the new funds in numbers and dollars are equity long/short funds, which by nature will have a higher correlation to the S&P 500. Also, as the long/short funds grow in assets under management, they begin to take on different risk/return profiles. Emerging managers have smaller asset bases and can move quickly between different styles and market caps. The larger managers, for liquidity purposes, need to move up the market cap scale and are likely to be closet indexers.

Another reason that the correlation of hedge funds has risen is a bit more worrisome. The major advantage over the long-only brethren of investments has been the hedge funds' ability to have some significant short positions or hedges (hence the name hedge funds). By shorting, the correlation to the traditional equity benchmarks falls, as does the fund market risk, which allows the hedge fund to protect capital. The reason this is worrisome is that huge sums of money are flowing to some of these large funds, which in turn has given rise to a new breed of hedge fund that is a mutual fund with fees on steroids. These large funds are becoming more index-like and are essentially providing an investor with a beta exposure with 1.5 percent management fees and 20 percent profit fees. As seen in Table 8.3, an analysis completed by Goldman Sachs research (13-f filings of 745 hedge funds) demonstrates that the net exposure to the long side of the portfolio has been high compared to the Russell 3000, even as the equity markets struggled in early 2008. There is only one sector that is net short: the financials. Also noticeable in this Table is that ETFs account for about 18 percent of the short positions, giving a slight indication that shorting is used only as a hedge and not as a true value added. Hedge funds currently own approximately 4.6 percent of the Russell 3000 index, up from 1 percent in 2001.

As a final note on correlations to the market benchmarks, you should observe that the correlation of the HFRI Fund of Funds Index has risen from 0.29 to 0.43, although it has fallen from its high of 0.48 for the 10-year period ending December 31, 2003. Although I have not seen any empirical evidence to support this, the rise in correlation of the various hedge fund indexes in the early 2000s may have more to do with the NASDAQ bubble than any other factor. After the bubble burst, the correlations, although

TABLE 8.3 Hedge Fund Sector Exposures (as of June 30, 2008)

	Overweights						Underweights				
	Materials	Energy	Telecom	Industrials	Technology	Utilities	Health Care	Consumer Discretionary	Consumer Staple	Financials	Totals
Long											
Stock Positions	$78.8	$129.6	$31.4	$106.3	$145.1	$32.9	$94.2	$109.7	$50.8	$92.6	$881.1
ETF Positions	0.6	3.1	0.4	1.3	3.0	0.4	1.4	1.1	1.2	2.7	15.1
Hedge Fund Long	$79.3	$132.6	$31.7	$107.6	$148.1	$33.3	$95.6	$110.9	$52.0	$95.3	$896.2
Short											
Stock Positions	$28.3	$59.8	$9.4	$55.8	$73.7	$15.9	$51.8	$85.3	$29.0	$102.7	$511.7
ETF Positions	3.7	20.3	2.1	7.7	15.8	3.1	9.3	9.1	6.8	15.9	93.9
Estimated Short	$32.1	$80.1	$11.5	$63.5	$89.5	$19.0	$61.1	$94.4	$35.8	$118.6	$605.6
Exposure											
Gross	$111.4	$212.8	$43.2	$171.0	$237.6	$52.3	$156.7	$205.3	$87.9	$213.8	$1,501.8
Net	47.3	52.5	20.2	44.1	58.5	14.4	34.5	16.4	16.2	(23.3)	290.7
%Net Long(Net/Long)	60%	40%	64%	41%	40%	43%	36%	15%	31%	−24%	32%
Net Sector Weighting(%)											
Hedge Fund Net Exposure	17%	19%	7%	16%	21%	5%	12%	6%	6%	−8%	100%
Russell3000	4.3	11.5	2.8	12.0	17.2	3.6	12.6	10.3	10.3	15.4	100%
Over/(Under)weight	1,566bp	718bp	445bp	369bp	368bp	148bp	−35bp	−447bp	−455bp	−2,366bp	

Source: Goldman Sachs Research.

returning to prior levels, have fallen somewhat as that market has yet to recover fully.

The next important correlation in the portfolio construction process is between the different hedge fund strategies themselves. This is important regardless of whether your goal is to have a fully diversified investment portfolio, or your own fund of hedge funds, or you are building a portfolio of equity long/short hedge funds. Examining the portfolio of managers and seeing how any new ones would fit the correlation between these different return streams is critical. Remember, objectives of the IPS were to increase returns, increase diversification, and protect capital. In building a diverse portfolio across all strategies you will find this a simpler task. As you can see in Table 8.4, the correlations are typically below 0.70 or not highly correlated. By virtue of the different strategies and the ability to short or hedge positions, the correlation between strategies is low.

If you are building a portfolio of equity long/short or even an emerging market fund, you must be careful that the managers selected have low correlations to each other. Understanding the underlying investment process and the universe the manager searches for investment ideas is key. A portfolio of eight large cap growth managers who use the Russell 1000 as its universe and First Call earnings growth projections will deliver, in all probability, highly correlated returns. Also, dependant on the managers' ability to short, they might also provide highly correlated returns to the Russell 1000. The overall aim of your portfolio construction process is to have managers who are alpha producers, but who are not highly correlated to either the markets or other managers in your portfolio.

PORTFOLIO OPTIMIZATION

As anyone who has taken an introductory course in finance can attest, portfolio optimization (which means Modern Portfolio Theory, or MPT) has an extensive list of literature. Only in recent times are we seeing Post-Modern Portfolio Theory, or PMPT, as the issues with MPT and how it relates to alternative investments are becoming more fully understood. Over the past 40-plus years, the academic assumption was that anything in the investment market is either mathematical or random noise. MPT is a strong mathematical tool, but its limits in hedge fund analysis are apparent. With PMPT, the goal is to meet a minimum return target by using alpha generating funds with low risk.

Typically a portfolio would use a mean-variance optimizer to allocate across all asset classes. With hedge funds using an unconstrained portfolio or only your best ideas is beginning to be the method of many sophisticated

TABLE 8.4 Strategy Correlations

	Agriculture	Convertible Arbitrage	Currency	Discretionary	Diversified	Emerging Markets	Event Driven	Financial	Fixed Income Arbitrage	Fund of Funds	Global Macro	Long/Short	Market Neutral	Systematic	Hedge Funds	CTAs	US Stocks	US Bonds
Agriculture	1.00	-0.10	0.28	0.37	0.27	-0.01	0.00	0.08	0.08	0.05	0.01	0.00	0.03	0.34	-0.02	0.06	0.02	0.11
Convertible Arb.		1.00	-0.07	0.00	0.00	0.42	0.54	-0.05	0.16	0.53	0.39	0.50	0.30	-0.03	0.57	0.02	0.34	0.02
Currency			1.00	0.87	0.40	-0.02	-0.11	0.23	-0.07	0.25	0.26	0.07	0.09	0.57	0.03	0.68	0.04	0.13
Discretionary				1.00	0.71	0.06	0.05	0.28	-0.02	0.32	0.11	0.11	0.05	0.50	0.11	0.67	0.06	0.09
Diversified					1.00	-0.07	-0.04	0.71	-0.05	0.23	-0.02	-0.02	0.04	0.89	-0.03	0.92	-0.02	0.04
Emerging Markets						1.00	0.70	-0.06	-0.05	0.75	0.35	0.67	0.13	-0.07	0.83	-0.04	0.57	0.01
Event Driven							1.00	-0.06	0.27	0.68	0.60	0.79	0.53	-0.08	0.88	-0.09	0.63	-0.08
Financial								1.00	-0.08	0.19	0.56	0.02	0.07	0.81	0.00	0.85	0.11	0.22
Fixed Income Arb.									1.00	0.18	0.32	0.09	0.09	-0.07	0.19	-0.06	-0.05	-0.14
Fund of Funds										1.00	0.26	0.78	0.40	0.24	0.84	0.25	0.45	0.06
Global Macro											1.00	0.71	0.30	0.34	0.68	0.38	0.36	0.32
Long/Short												1.00	0.40	0.00	0.93	0.00	0.67	0.05
Market Neutral													1.00	0.40	0.40	0.00	0.38	0.10
Systematic														1.00	0.35	0.20	-0.01	0.07
Hedge Funds															1.00	0.94	0.70	0.06
CTAs																1.00	-0.13	0.24
US Stocks																	1.00	0.24
US Bonds																		1.00

investors. In an MPT framework, the portfolios would be benchmark and/or style driven. This essentially produces a portfolio with significant dead weight. The overall goal is to produce alpha. Giving a manager the widest possible latitude to search for alpha and not be limited by a specific style box is one way of producing alpha. Unfortunately, this drives mathematicians wild. To use the optimizer, every manager needs to be in a box where historical returns for that style can then be tortured to bring specific results. Unfortunately, the markets are a "C" math student. The turning and twisting of the numbers only belie the fact that the historical numbers are the major source of output error of the MPT model.

Performance Outliers

In addition, focuses on probability of returns and fat-tailed returns is of little help. The stress testing of models is trying to quantify the damage of a 100-year event. The event is not truly observable since the amount of data is small, but its impact is much larger. Past outliers can in no way predict future outliers. One of the best analogies to this is weather forecasting. The local TV weatherman tells us Monday night that on Tuesday there will be a 10 percent chance of rain. As winds shift and temperatures change, we awake Tuesday to find that it is indeed raining. That 10 percent chance of rain is now a 100 percent certainty that it will rain. The forecast was of little use if you decided the probability was too low and skipped the umbrella. Similarly, when testing for portfolio outliers, we get a result that says we have a 2 percent chance of the market being down 10 percent. We wake up to a 9/11 terror attack and that probability is now 100 percent. Extreme events have no data. Positive fat-tailed events are typically on a long time scale, such as the NASDAQ rise in the 1990s or the rise in the price of oil in the 2000s. Negative fat-tailed events are typically on compressed time scales, such as the market crash in October 1987 or the demise of Bear Stearns. The negative fat-tailed risks are the risks that should be of the highest concern to hedge fund investors. Positive fat-tailed risk or upside is a perplexing concept. If you have upside movement or a large positive event, was it the risk? Success? We will discuss capital protection, or downside protection, more fully shortly.

I would like to add some final thoughts on optimization and portfolio diversification. Is there truly a need to run a portfolio optimizer when building your hedge fund portfolio? The return streams are normally distributed and there is the added complexity missing from the other, more traditional asset classes, in that hedge funds have the ability to leverage and short securities. Before we crank up the NASA satellites and the super computers to optimize a portfolio, we need to discuss some new research on naïve diversification.

The concept is simple and, in a nod to eco-friendly investing, the computers remain off. In 2001 Benartzi and Thaler found success by allocating equally among choices. The complicated math formula is: Allocation $= 1/n$ where n is equal to the number of possible investment choices. If you have four hedge funds, $1/4 = 25$ percent is allocated to each fund. This is not exactly elegant but quite simple in its execution.

Further study by Huberman and Jiang in 2006, examined applying naïve diversification to larger choices. The study tried to analyze how investors would allocate their funds if they were presented a much larger number of choices, say 10 or 12. The result was an adjusted $1/n$. Investors would choose three or four options and then allocate equally.

The most recent study on naïve diversification was published in 2008 in the *Review of Financial Studies* by Victor DeMiguel, Lorenzo Garlappi, and Raman Uppal. It was titled "Optimal Versus Naïve Diversification: How Inefficient is the $1/n$ Portfolio Strategy." The study revealed that out of 14 models evaluated, none is consistently better than the $1/n$ rule in terms of Sharpe Ratio. In other words, $1/n$ often outperformed the optimized models.

Downside Protection, or Preventing Relative Performance

In constructing portfolios, one additional factor needs to be examined and monitored quite closely in hedge funds, and that factor is downside protection. Downside protection from a portfolio level is the result of several decisions. First is the asset allocation decision, or the top-down strategy we discussed earlier in the chapter. It is quite necessary to be cognizant of any asset strategy that may be headed toward net outflows, since the fund's NAV will take a hit as the liquidity squeeze may overwhelm the fund. Investors may also find the Gate (a halt in redemption by the General Partner) slammed in their face. It is also important to know and understand the geographic exposure in the funds. The geographic risks are difficult to quantify in discernable terms other than percent exposure. The risks associated with geographic exposure tend to run along the lines of sovereign issues, currency issues, and certain issues surrounding a global conflict or crisis. For example, Italy has had 60 governments since World War II. Saudi Arabia has had one-family governance for 120 years. The real risk lies in Saudi Arabia, as the Middle East tends to be a power keg of issues, while Italy's government is more volatile but hardly revolutionary. The risk of a loss of capital can be mitigated at the top-down level with careful attention to the geographic exposure the funds have.

The bottom up approach offers more insight into how a manager will protect the fund's portfolio. Analysis and understanding of the past records of the funds will provide data about where the fund's performance was advanced or hurt due to exposures from their investment process. The use of leverage, net exposure, and ability to be profitable for the short side of the fund's portfolio in sub-par markets are the leading factors in providing downside protection.

Here in portfolio construction is where PMPT really earns its keep as an investing philosophy. First, instead of an artificially determined target of, say, risk-free rate plus 350 basis points, the IPS outlines the MAR or the drop dead number the client requires. From that we see the fallacy of relative investment performance. An old mentor of mine at W.H. Newbold's & Son, Inc. (no longer in existence), where we managed money for high net worth investors, told me "clients cannot spend relative money." PMPT emphasizes that clients do not view risk as a return below a benchmark, but think that risk is the loss of capital and spending power. Here the key to the risk reduction process is downside protection. Some people argue that it is impractical to expect all managers to provide 100 percent downside protection 100 percent of the time. I agree it would be foolish to expect that. It is equally foolish to consider it a portfolio management success to beat some market benchmark.

The importance of this is demonstrated in Tables 8.5 and 8.6. In Table 8.5, we see the amount of upside needed to regain losses. As the losses increase, the amount to reach par, so to speak, goes up at a much higher rate.

Table 8.6 illustrates how much upside is needed to match the S&P 500 return stream by avoiding downside. To clarify, in the 10-year period from 1996 to 2005, if an investor were to avoid all of the downside that the S&P 500 experienced, he would have to capture only 30 percent of the upside in order to capture the same return over that time period. A portfolio experiencing 50 percent of the S&P 500 downside would need only 64 percent of the upside. Less obvious from this exercise is that by preserving capital and lowering the downside capture, an investor has effectively lowered the overall risk of the portfolio. By using an unconstrained portfolio or your

TABLE 8.5 Recovering Investment Losses

Investment Loss (%)	Gains Needed to Recover (%)
10	11.1
20	25.0
30	42.9
40	66.7

Source: Morgan Stanley Investment Management.

TABLE 8.6　Downside Loss Lessens Upside Capture Requirements

Time	% Losses Incurred	Stock Market Return (%)	% Gains Needed
1 Year	0	3.0	23
(2005)	50	3.0	61
3 Years	0	12.4	61
(2003–2005)	50	12.4	80
10 Years	0	6.8	27
(1996–2005)	50	7.3	63
50 Years	0	6.8	28
(1956–2005)	50	6.8	63
Average		0	30
		50	64

Source: Crestmont Research.

best ideas, you maximize the alpha sources while removing the dead weight of beta sources and style boxes.

The final piece of the portfolio construction puzzle is the optimal number of managers needed to invest in a hedge fund portfolio. Theoretically, in equity portfolio management, the optimal number of stocks in a well-diversified portfolio is approximately 20. By increasing the number of stocks, the additional risk reduction is marginal (systemic risk cannot be entirely diversified away), and there is a rise in administrative work and costs.

Amin and Kat, using monthly return data on 455 hedge funds over the period June 1994 to May 2001, concluded that a portfolio of approximately 15 funds is optimal for standard deviation reduction, but can result in lower skewness and increased stock market correlation. In a later paper, Lhabitant and Vicin discovered that lowered skewness was the result of fixed income arbitrage and event-driven strategies. However, they also concluded that 15 to 20 was the optimal number of managers.

Any optimal portfolio will be a trade-off between the risks one is willing to assume and the return one can expect for taking that level of risk. This all leads to the next logical question: Is it prudent to consider a concentrated portfolio of hedge funds?

We have seen in the equity markets some highly successful concentrated funds. Can we successful implement the same type of strategy in the hedge fund area? The simple answer seems to be yes. As we have progressed from IPS to portfolio construction, we have examined various ways to reduce and mitigate risk in a hedge fund investment. During the due diligence process we quantitatively analyzed performance numbers to examine drawdowns, batting average, downside capture, and ability to effectively short or hedge the portfolio. All these measures help improve the probability of a positive outcome. During the top-down assessment, strategies were examined for a long-term positive fundamental environment and geographic diversification. Using PMPT, we have reduced the risk by eliminating the forecast of outcomes based on historical data and the reliance on benchmarks, which may lead to large output errors in expected and real returns. And finally, more may be gained by using a naïve diversification plan than by optimizing the portfolio.

The final point in dealing with portfolio construction is to be very aware of leverage. Leverage can enhance returns such as low volatility strategies like fixed income arbitrage. It also can cause havoc to returns if applied in large amounts or at the wrong levels. All leverage should be employed at the manager level. There are cases of FOFs that use leverage at the Master Fund level. This raises costs and makes the fund inherently more volatile. If borrowing costs are 6 percent annually, the fund must, on a monthly basis, return a minimum of 50 basis points just to break even. At the manager level, you must be careful that the fund stays within the guidelines established in the PPM. It should also be understood that typically PPMs are written in the broadest language in order to give managers maximum flexibility. Historically, a manager of a global macro fund may have used three to four times leverage in the fund. When managers come across some rough patches in the markets, they typically will leverage up in the hope of regaining lost ground. Margin calls on an over-leveraged fund can be deadly.

SUMMARY

While you build your portfolio, you must remember to be as consistent with your process as you would expect from your fund managers. As in picking an individual stock portfolio, problems begin when you make exceptions to your rules or make a dramatic break from your tried and true policies. This does not mean you cannot refine the policies over time. Know the difference between stubbornness and strength of conviction. Always review winners and losers. Learn what went right, what went wrong, and what took you by surprise. Remember, as I reminded you before, those who don't learn from history are apt to repeat it. This is as true in investments as in war.

CHAPTER 9

Navigating Buyers' Remorse

It's Always Darkest Before It Goes Completely Black

We have just spent several chapters walking through a due diligence process and then portfolio construction in order to arrive at a rational method for investing in hedge funds. After the reality has set in that you have allocated money to a hedge fund, it is not unusual that some doubts begin to slip into your mind. Did I make the right decision? Is there something I missed in reviewing this fund? Have I lost my mind entirely by investing in a hedge fund?

It is not unusual, if the fund doesn't have a lock-up period, to see investors redeem after a few months that were rocky or did not meet expectations. However, if you have performed a rigorous analysis of the fund and are still comfortable with the results of that analysis, redeeming is the wrong course of action. How, though, you may ask, can you get to a more comfortable level with your analysis?

One exercise I have found quite useful is to review past investments and, even more importantly, other funds that may have imploded. There are many things you can learn from hindsight. Reviewing past mistakes can help raise questions, provide guideposts, and give insight into what you should be on guard against in the new fund you are considering. In previous chapters we made mention of some high profile implosions such as Long Term Capital Management and Amaranth. Now we will list some other funds that have ceased to be, not from investment issues (broadly defined), but from operational and structural problems. In these cases you did not need a Cray supercomputer to foresee the problem, but merely an inquisitive mind.

We will also review second acts: those funds that have imploded and the responsible people then surfacing at another fund. Before we begin I would like to stress that, to date, fewer hedge funds have imploded than the number of corporations that disappear every year. In the "Reality TV" kind of pop culture we live in, it is easier and more profitable for news outlets, publications, and politicians to vilify the spawns of Satan known as hedge funds. Some of the bad press is certainly warranted, but I will leave those windmills for someone else to tilt at, and focus on how and why some funds have faded from existence and how an investor can protect himself.

It was difficult to decide where to place this chapter in the book—before due diligence or after the monitoring process? After much internal debate, I concluded that it was logical to insert the chapter here—after due diligence and portfolio construction and before monitoring. Once you have decided to make an investment, it is critical to closely monitor that position. In order to be vigilant in your monitoring process, it is helpful to review some investment tragedies that have come before your time and determine what clues or practices you can learn from these mistakes.

LONG TERM CAPITAL MANAGEMENT: POOR DIVERSIFICATION AND HIGH LEVERAGE ARE A DANGEROUS COMBINATION

Long Term Capital Management (LTCM) is the poster child for hedge fund failures. This hedge fund had at its roots a stellar cast of traders from Salomon Brothers led by bond trader John Meriwether. This star trading group, along with university professors and Nobel laureates Myron Scholes and Robert C. Merton, came together. Scholes and Merton developed sophisticated quantitative models for reversion to the mean on arbitrage trades that would be implemented by Salomon traders. For several years, it worked beyond most folks' wildest dreams, producing 40 percent returns per annum.

The key model was the Black-Scholes option model. It makes the key assumption that the volatility of a security is constant. Taking the lead from academics, many traders adopted faith in numeric certainties as it pertained to security pricing. Risk, as defined by these true believers, was volatility around the mean. Merton took this theory and applied it one step further. He assumed that volatility was so constant and smooth that prices move as a continuous series or, to non-academics, move without price jumps. As it was soon discovered, this was more an act of faith than a science. The 40 percent-plus returns only made LTCM more convinced these theories were correct and that all security movement could be reduced to a mathematical formula. The return stream gave them confidence, which people later described as arrogance, to begin applying these models into other areas besides fixed income arbitrage. Soon they were trading matched pairs and other equity securities. Underlying this were some operational issues that were either not seriously considered or just ignored, since performance was high.

One issue was how LTCM treated its prime brokers in the trades. LTCM would carve up trades between its prime brokers in order that any one of them would not fully understand the magnitude or impact of any trade. Additionally, the transaction was highly levered. Even in the trading of equities which are subject to Regulation T, LTCM worked around that 50 percent limit by using derivatives to obtain their specific equity exposure. LTCM, for example, would enter into a SAP contract with a bank. LTCM would pay some specified interest rate to the bank for the specific transaction; in return the bank would agree to pay LTCM whatever profit was made on the stock. This allowed enormous investments with no money down. The leverage of the fund was frightening. Since the fund was shrouded in secrecy even by hedge fund terms, the unsuspecting bankers had little idea of the extent to which the leverage was being used. In the summer of 1998, they were about to get a lesson.

LTCM through mid-August was not having a good year. There was little cause for alarm as every fund manager expects to have down periods. The fund had about $3.6 billion in capital, with roughly 40 percent of it being the monies of their own partners and employees. Going into mid-August, the fund was becoming more and more levered and, with an approximate capital base of around $4 billion, LTCM had positions in excess of $1.25 trillion. On August 17, Russia declared a debt moratorium. Western bondholders were left holding bonds that were not paying interest, and a devaluation of the Russian ruble was happening. By August 21 investors everywhere wanted out. The "flight to quality" was under way. A move to sell lower quality credits and buy less risky, lower yielding bonds was running through the global markets. The spreads between high yielding (lower credit) bonds and lower yielding (higher credit) were widening and LTCM was losing millions. Typical days in the U.S. swaps markets had seen movements of around one point.

One day in late August the U.S. swaps markets swung over 20 points. Moves similar to this one had occurred in 1987 and 1992. Unfortunately, such once-in-a-lifetime occurrences were not in LTCM's model. The markets worldwide were reaching a correlation of +1.0 on this day. LTCM had calculated with absolute mathematical certainty they could drop only $35 million in a single day, but on this day they dropped $553 million.

The rest of the unwinding of LTCM is a footnote to history as the major Wall Street firms and the Federal Reserve stepped in to promote an orderly liquidation. The total losses ended up being around $4.6 billion, with approximately 63 percent of those losses coming from swaps and equity volatility trades.

LESSONS FROM LONG TERM
CAPITAL MANAGEMENT

The Monday morning quarterbacking of the demise of LTCM began almost immediately, as many blamed the arrogance of the partners for the fast and furious falls. With the passage of time, we can take a more comprehensive view.

One of the clearest messages should be not to trust a blind reliance on any mathematical model. It is extremely important to understand what the key assumptions in the model are. The second lesson should be that models are just that—models. They do not have a drop-dead certainty. More certain is that "once-in-a-lifetime" events is a mathematical term, not one based in reality. These events happen with much more frequency than most would acknowledge. As we have said before, Mr. Market is a "C" student, but he does love to teach the smartest kid in the class a lesson or two.

Extreme leverage also played an enormous part in the rapid downfall. While the model pinpointed perceived value imbalances for the fund, the margin of profit was minuscule. The only way for a fund of that size to seize these opportunities was to employ large amounts of leverage. LTCM did, and apparently without any restraint. The large amounts of leverage also in the end created a liquidity squeeze for the fund. When the markets were conspiring against them, they could not unload positions without further driving down the value.

If we do a further analysis of the basic premise of reversion to the mean, we discover that LTCM in essence was making the same trade several thousand times. The combination of high leverage, blind faith in a model, and little true diversification led to the rapid and unforgiving meltdown of the fund. In the end, the tragedy that was LTCM was probably best described by one Wall Street strategist, Richard Bernstein of Merrill Lynch: "It seems LTCM was run by a bunch of guys who knew a lot about math and little about the markets."

BAYOU GROUP, LLC: DUE DILIGENCE IS A MUST

One of the lesser known but highly instructive hedge fund meltdowns was a Ponzi scheme perpetrated by the founder of Bayou Group, Samuel Israel. The fund after its launch in the mid-1990s had some performance issues.

LESSONS FROM BAYOU

Actually the lessons here are quite simple. One does not need extensive analysis but merely the ability to verify facts. A quick internet search would have revealed a couple of issues that should have made investors run and not walk away from this fund. In order to truly drive home the importance of dong the little things involving due diligence on any fund, investors should consider the following legal trauma that is ongoing in the Bayou saga. Investors who may not have noticed before investing, but eventually found something distasteful enough to redeem their funds, are not out of the woods.

A trustee liquidating Bayou has sued to attempt to reclaim more than $140 million from investors who got out early. This is not unusual—a disaster is usually followed up by a set of lawyers and a law suit. What makes this a little more biting is that the suit is claiming recapture of over $16 million in profit. The balance, $126 million, is the original money invested in Bayou. A judge in the U.S. Bankruptcy Court for the Southern District of New York ruled that the trustee could try to recoup the entire amount. The reasoning? As an alleged fraudulent conveyance, the money could possibly be returned to investors in order to perpetuate the fraud, thus denying a motion to dismiss by defendants of dozens of suits brought by the trustee. Even if successful, the trustee will still have only recovered about 50 cents on the dollar.

As an epilogue, Samuel Israel, Daniel Marino, and Matthew Marino (brother of Daniel) are all serving 20-year prison sentences for their roles in the fraud.

In 1998 Mr. Israel hired a new CFO and decided on a plan to recoup the fund's trading losses. Mr. Israel, a frenetic trader, planned to trade his way to large gains in order to offset the losses. The fund reported false NAVs and performance numbers in order to attract new investors. In order for the scheme to work, Bayou needed to replace its auditors; the firm Richmond-Fairfield was hired to oversee the fund's accounting. Soon it became harder and harder to maintain the breakneck pace needed for keeping the illusion alive. In 2005, Mr. Israel told investors he would be closing the fund; after raising $400 million, they had little capital (approximately $100 million) left. Several investors quickly sued to seek the return of their capital.

How could investors have protected themselves from this? Many folks believe that if a manager wishes to defraud someone, he will, and there is little that can be done. In some cases that have elaborate schemes, that may be true. Unfortunately for investors who did not bother to delve into or monitor the fund, they were soon parted from their money.

The new "independent" auditor hired, Richmond-Fairfield, which made the scheme work, is not exactly a household name in hedge fund circles. If investors had taken more than a cursory look at the newly hired firm, they would have discovered that the firm's principal was Daniel Marino, the newly hired CFO of the Bayou fund. Nearly all of the fund's trades were executed by Bayou Securities, owned by—yes, you guessed it—Mr. Israel. In 2003, Connecticut banking regulators fined the brokerage arm of Bayou $7,500 for having incomplete records. Also in 2003, an estranged partner in the business sued Bayou in federal court in Louisiana, alleging $7 million was missing from a trading account. The fund did pay approximately $50 million in commissions to the affiliated broker, or around 12.5 percent of the fund's capital. One final item was also discovered in Bayou's marketing materials. These materials distributed by the fund listed Mr. Israel as a former head trader for Omega Advisors (another hedge fund). This item is vigorously disputed by the firm's highly regarded founder and former Goldman Sachs partner, Leon Cooperman.

WOOD RIVER CAPITAL MANAGEMENT: A LACK OF EXPERIENCE AND AUDITING

Wood River is another hedge fund with some interesting twists that met its demise in 2005. The fund was launched in 2003 by John Whittier, who previously worked as a communications and media analyst at Donaldson, Lufkin and Jenrette (DLJ). Whittier had left DLJ in 1997 to form Wood River. He began the asset management firm with approximately $30 million in money from family and friends. In 1999, on the back of a roaring NASDAQ market, Wood River more than doubled in value. Despite the NASDAQ market slide of about 40 percent in 2000, Wood managed a paltry but surprising +2 percent return. The portfolio, however, declined in 2001 and 2002. Despite the lackluster returns, Whittier gathered enough assets to launch his hedge fund. Wood River touted solid returns in its marketing material, and in letters to the investors spoke of continued plans for expansion.

In 2005, things began to unravel a bit. In that year Wood River built up an enormous position in Endwave (ENWV). What was troublesome about this position is that in a lawsuit, the complainant claimed that they owned nearly half the outstanding shares of Endwave, and this accounted for more than 65 percent of the fund's $265 million in assets. As this position was being built, the stock price of Endwave from July 14 to September 15 fell from $53 to $31. By October it was trading down to $13. Investors in Wood River began to press for the return of their money and were unsuccessful.

LESSONS FROM WOOD RIVER

Similar to Bayou, the signs of issues were present in Wood River for those who did indeed do their homework. First, the fund's executives never presented any audited financials. In a brand new start-up this is not uncommon, since the audits are typically done at year end. However, Wood River, launched in 2003, did not provide any audited statements for 2003 or 2004. Red flags should have been flapping. This lack of reporting should naturally point investors to the audit firm. In its marketing materials under the organizational chart, Wood River listed American Express Tax and Business Services, Inc., a name quite similar to that of a large financial institution called American Express. Unfortunately for investors, this firm had no relationship at all to American Express. A quick check with American Express Tax and Business Services, Inc. would have revealed that they do not provide business audit services for hedge funds or anyone else.

On October 7 Wood River did finally file a form 13D with the SEC, stating it owned 40 percent or 4.3 million shares of Endwave. The filing contained no information as to price or date of acquisition.

In another quick check of the marketing material, it is discovered that Wood River advertised that its maximum sector exposure would be 15 to 20 percent and maximum position by size would be 5 to 8 percent at market value. Both of these stipulations were seriously violated by the Endwave holdings. Both the audit and the holdings were contrary to what investors were led to believe by Wood River marketing material.

For the true due diligence analyst, the warning signs go back a bit further. Whittier has a tax lien issued against him in April 2002 for $45,760. In July 2002 the state of Idaho issued a tax lien against him for $80,782 (released in February 2004 after payment). In August 2002, the owner of Wood River's San Francisco office sued Wood River for allegedly failing to pay three months' rent. Despite the early

(Continued)

LESSONS FROM WOOD RIVER (*Continued*)

warnings signs before the fund was launched, some very sophisticated investors placed money with Wood River. Once again, simple
research could have led to knowledge that would have prevented some
heart-wrenching loss of dollars. The use of highly quantitative number
crunching would not have uncovered the risk to investors; however, a
simple background check would have saved heartache.

In a legal footnote to the failure of Wood River, there is another
interesting lawsuit. A federal judge in Manhattan ruled that a lawsuit
brought under a Blue Sky law in Oregon against the firm's legal counsel
for allegedly aiding and abetting securities fraud by a client hedge fund
can move forward. New York law firm Seward & Kissell is being sued
under a state securities fraud statute or Blue Sky law. Under federal law,
aider and abettor claims against lawyers and accountants in securities
fraud cases are barred.

The investor claims that he invested $2.75 million in Wood River
based on the offering documents and marketing material. The material
led the investor to believe that a diversified investment strategy would
be followed. He also claims the law firm helped perpetuate that fraud,
as the law firm drafted some of those documents and its name was
included in the fund's prospectus. A New York Appellate Division
court had ruled in December 2007 that the law firm's work did not
constitute representations to investors and threw out the $200 million
suit filed there.

MOTHERROCK: THE LIQUIDITY SQUEEZE IN A SMALL MARKET WILL END BADLY WHEN VOLATILITY INCREASES

MotherRock was formed in December 2004 by Robert "Bo" Collins, former
head of the New York Mercantile Exchange (Nymex); John D'Agnostino,
former Nymex executive; Conrad Goerl, former Nymex trader; and Carol
Coale, former Prudential equity natural gas analyst. MotherRock was to use
this experienced global energy markets trading team to generate 18 to 22
percent annualized returns with a target VaR of approximately 5 percent
of NAV (with 95 percent confidence). The specific substrategies included
convenience yield curves arbitrage, which is the commodity equivalent to

interest yield curves. MotherRock also went long and short volatility positions through options or underlying derivative instruments. The portfolio would hold 300 total positions long and short. The fund grew quickly and was near $400 million near its peak in 2006. Energy prices were in the early stage of a long bull market, aided by Hurricanes Katrina and Rita. As the money came in quickly, MotherRock began to investigate other avenues to invest the cash flow and added a Chief Risk Officer to oversee its various risk management systems. They were also hiring PhDs to work with the equity research group to construct pair trades. MotherRock purchased a Nymex seat for about $1 million under the premise that they would see benefits since their trading costs would be cut in half. MotherRock also believed the value of the seat would not decline over the long term. All seemed to be going well.

By mid-2006, the volatility of the energy markets began to play havoc with MotherRock's portfolio. In June the portfolio experienced an estimated drawdown of approximately 19 percent. The VaR for June was a daily average of 1.69 percent with a single day high of 3.64 percent, all within its VaR guidelines. MotherRock attributed the losses to a number of factors, including losses on long volatility positions, losses from theta exposure, losses on long delta positions, Vega spread trades, and a large market to market drawdown on option structure with long maturities (December 2006). MotherRock reallocated capital to target allocations of 65/25/10 percent respectively in natural gas, crude oil, and equities. About two weeks later MotherRock revised the June loss to a drawdown of 24 percent. The difference was based on an initially incorrect clearing report. July turned out to be no more kind to MotherRock than June. On August 2, 2006, MotherRock informed investors that the fund sustained a significant loss in July and the fund would be winding down. All redemptions would be suspended. No performance estimate was provided, nor were monthly VaR levels or current margin levels.

On August 10, MotherRock sent a letter to investors outlining its plan to liquidate the fund. The plan was expected to take four to nine months. After the winddown period, its Limited Partner was expected to withdraw its interest. Investors would receive 90 percent of their interest within five days of the withdrawal date. The final 10 percent would be withheld pending the final audit. Over the next two weeks, MotherRock informed investors that they had received significant margin calls from its futures commission merchant, ABN Amro, and it was taking control of the assets. The Futures Commission merchant began to liquidate the portfolio. Investors were notified at this point that they might not receive any of their original investment. In less than three months, a fund that returned 20 percent net of fees in the prior year entirely melted away.

The entire portfolio was shopped around the Street in an effort to collect enough money to return some capital to investors. As is the case in distressed sales, the bottom kept falling since buyers had no need to step up and pay top dollar for damaged assets. The winner (?) of the fire sale was Amaranth.

LESSONS FROM MOTHERROCK

There are a couple of quick points to learn from the meltdown of MotherRock. The first is that even with a star-studded cast similar in stature to that of Long Term Capital Management, the outcomes are not assured nor will they necessarily be positive. Many folks put strong emphasis on pedigree. Examples like these show that pedigree by itself may not be an effective tool for screening funds.

Another lesson is the dependence on VaR as a measure of risk. Again with 95 percent certainty, MotherRock calculated a maximum loss of 5 percent of NAV. During the month of June when MotherRock reported a loss of 15, then 20, then finally 24 percent, they said that they did not violate their VaR guidelines. The average was 1.69 percent with a high of 3.64 percent, all well within mathematical reason.

Two other issues played a large part in the demise of the fund. The liquidity of the markets that MotherRock was investing in was thin. This lack of liquidity combined with margin calls will leave any fund with limited options if their book goes against their strategies. These two factors also played a major role in the final sale of the book to meet the margin calls. By the time the sale was being forced, there were few if any people that did not know the state of the fund's portfolio, driving down the price faster and farther than they would have liked.

The above factors are important for ongoing monitoring; however, there were some clues that maybe the risk investors were taking would be much higher than any VaR calculation would indicate. The first was despite its stellar team of Nymex traders, they were relatively inexperienced in trading equities. The second issue was the purchase of the Nymex seat as a fund asset. Despite the well-intentioned reasons, it is hard to justify the purchase. It is the hedge fund version of buying a Gulfstream jet for an IPO company. The initial good performance they experienced in 2005 tends to overshadow some of the little things that in isolation may not mean much but in aggregate can cause some catastrophic results. With many funds when things are good they are very good, but when they turn bad it can be deadly.

AMARANTH: LIQUIDITY AND CONCENTRATED PORTFOLIOS CAN DRAG A FUND DOWN AS THE TREND OF ANY TRADE EVENTUALLY REVERSES

While the drama played out rather quietly with MotherRock, another one was slowly building. This one was set in motion even before Amaranth bought the assets from the liquidated MotherRock fund. In September 2000, Nicholas Maounis left Paloma Partners LLC and founded Amaranth with $600 million in assets. It was a multi-strategy fund trading securities of merging companies, distressed debt, convertible bonds, and stock. As the hedge fund world grew, so did Amaranth, growing to $7.5 billion by the end of 2005. Amaranth was producing returns of 15 percent since inception, handily outdistancing the peer group.

In 2002, Amaranth wanted to add energy trading to its stable. Meanwhile, at our neighbors to the north, Brian Hunter was making a name for himself as a natural gas trader for TransCanada Corp. and then later Deutsche Bank. He earned a master in mathematics before entering the trading world in 1998. Mr. Hunter left Deutsche in April 2004 and shortly thereafter joined Amaranth in what would be a short-lived and volatile experience.

In early 2005, market conditions were not favorable to a couple of Amaranth's key strategies, primarily convertibles and credit spreads. According to Hedge Fund Research Inc., convertible bonds were down over 6 percent by May. Amaranth was hit further when Ford and GM were downgraded to junk status by Standard & Poor's. The energy space continued to do well. With that as a backdrop, Brain Hunter was offered a $1 million bonus to join Steven Cohen's SAC Capital Advisors LLC. Maounis, seeing most strategies under pressure, did not want to lose his burgeoning energy trader. Maounis countered that proposal by making Hunter co-head of the energy trading desk and giving him more trading authority. By the end of 2005 Hunter was the highest paid trader at Amaranth. His new deal earned Hunter 15 percent of any profits he made (10 percent average for others). Hunter earned $75 million in 2005, largely on a Katrina bet for natural gas prices. After the successful year Hunter moved his family and eight traders back to Calgary to open an office. Despite some poor results from other strategies, Amaranth's multistrategy fund returned 15 percent.

Going into 2006 the strategy Hunter employed did not vary from the previous two years. He was betting the difference between natural gas prices in the winter (March delivery contracts) and summer months (April delivery contracts) would widen. The trades were extended out to 2012 as Maounis allocated $1 billion in capital out of the roughly $7 billion fund. His bet was correct. In April the fund returned 13 percent, putting Amaranth up nearly

30 percent for the year while peer multistrategy funds were up an average of 5.3 percent.

This huge outperformance began to make some investors nervous and they started to question the concentrated strategy. Investors were told that the trades were not highly risky because it was an arbitrage of the pricing disparities and not a directional bet on gas. In May some of those worst fears began to surface. The spreads narrowed 0.37 from $3.64, causing Hunter to lose $1 billion. The logical thing would have been to cut natural gas positions that held large profits; however, the Street knew the positions and the need to raise cash and they were not in much of a charitable mood to pay current prices. This forced Amaranth to raise cash by liquidating the books of other stock and convertible bond traders. Taking a step back, this only complicated the allocation picture. By the end of June, Hunter was trading approximately 56 percent of the fund's assets and was responsible for 78 percent of the performance. From June through August, the energy and commodities positions earned the fund $1.35 billion, with a majority of those gains coming in August.

The month of September would not be as kind to Amaranth. As the weather cooled so did demand for natural gas. On September 14, natural gas prices plummeted 10 percent and Amaranth lost $560 million, or nearly 42 percent of the enormous profit they made during the summer months. The bet on natural gas spreads between the March 2007 and April 2007 contracts fell 69 percent to 0.63 cents.

Mr. Market came knocking with margin calls. The fund liquidated positions in equities, convertibles, and European loans. This did not stop the flood of margin calls. Within one week Hunter's bet on natural gas lost approximately $4.6 billion. By the end of September Amaranth had lost 70 percent or $6.6 billion of its assets. JP Morgan, one of the fund's prime brokers, and Citadel took over the book of Amaranth's natural gas positions on September 20. Although this did not immediately shut down Amaranth, the end was clearly at hand.

LESSONS FROM AMARANTH

In what has been one of the fastest demises of a hedge fund, the decline with the aid of 20/20 hindsight offers some clear lessons. What may be the most surprising is how this occurred so soon on the tail of the MotherRock debacle. The fall of Amaranth will be discussed for years to come. The list of culprits bantered about for blame is lack of regulation

(Continued)

(always a favorite), greed, and lack of risk controls, arrogance, human frailty, and ignorant bliss. We will discuss the last one first.

Ignorant bliss is not meant to deride any of the individual or fund investors in Amaranth. It is a human condition in which when the fund is providing enormous returns, we turn a blind eye to some of the most glaring issues that can turn your smile into a frown. The tell-tale signs were not just the outperformance of the fund of normal benchmarks, it was exceeding any benchmark measure and by a wide margin. To put this in quantitative terms, the returns of the fund were positive fat-tailed returns. In mathematical parlance the probability of these being routine are quite small, the one-hundred-year event. Red flags should have been raised just on the extreme event and the possibility it would continue. The natural question that should have been raised is, "would there be a countervailing fat-tailed negative event?" The answer in the end was yes. Sometimes a cynical view of such strong performance should be taken. One should question strong outperformance as intensely as underperformance. The probability of it continually reoccurring is small, especially given that the manager, in this case, was making essentially the same trade for two years. The law of averages caught up. The reversal was quick and unforgiving. For comparison, LTCM's downdraft in August 1988 was eight standard deviations. The loss for Amaranth on September 15 was nine standard deviations.

The call for more regulation of hedge funds was heard immediately after this failure, as is the case when most investments go bad for people who have willingly and knowingly invested in something that does not work out as planned. In the case of Amaranth, there was no fraud or underhanded dealings but merely highly volatile investments that went awry. No amount of government regulation will prevent this type of blow-up. The loss of $6 billion in a matter of weeks far exceeds the loss of value in hedge funds, due to fraud, of approximately $1 billion.

Investors again learned the lessons that risk is not asymmetric. Amaranth made outsized bets relative to its portfolio in energy and they were essential to the market in natural gas trading. The fund's positions were enormous compared to the open positions in the futures markets. The lesson of strained liquidity and the commodity markets' poor two-sided flow were the same lessons that MotherRock learned. There was no natural counterparty to offload positions when it was essential to do so. Similarly, the types of and size of trades that Amaranth was

(Continued)

LESSONS FROM AMARANTH (*Continued*)

engaging in were not the best kept secret on the Street. Once again the few natural buyers stepped aside in order to buy positions at a lower price. In a liquidity squeeze in these markets the manager is up the proverbial creek without a paddle and the boat is taking on water.

By performing simple performance attribution analysis against the benchmark and returns-based analysis, investors would have seen a red flag as the performance and lack of diversification would be completely apparent. If you are diligent about how your portfolio is constructed, you would have deduced that your risk levels rose and the initial thesis for investing in a multistrategy fund had evaporated. The high level of exposure to energy would have led you to conclude that you invested in an energy fund instead.

There is one further point to ongoing due diligence that investors must do. A quick check on Brian Hunter would have uncovered that when he left Deutsche Bank in 2004 he filed suit for the payment of his bonus. Hunter contends he made $40 million for the bank in 2003 and $100 million in the past three years. The bank had responded that the bonus was at the discretion of the bank managers. Was it greed on the part of the bank? In December of 2003 Hunter and his trading partners were up around $76 million for the year. In the first week of December the desk lost a bit over $51 million or 67 percent of the profits. In his suit against Deutsche Bank, Mr. Hunter attributed the loss to "unprecedented and unforeseeable run-up in gas prices," a line and market action that was soon to be repeated.

RECENT EVENTS: OSPRAIE FUND

One fund that has seen a recent demise is the Ospraie Fund, a U.S. based commodity hedge fund. This fund is the flagship fund at $2.8 billion (formerly) of Ospraie Management, which also runs three other hedge funds totaling over $4 billion in assets. As the energy, mining, and natural resource markets sold off sharply in August 2008, the Ospraie fund dropped 26.72 percent and is now down 38.79 percent year-to-date. The greater than 30 percent drawdown triggered a provision allowing investors to redeem out of the fund irrespective of lock-up provisions. This resulted in a decision to shut down the fund and return money to the investors. However, the redemptions will be staggered. Ospraie planned to distribute 40 percent of the fund's asset by September 30, 2008, and an additional 40 percent by year-end. The remaining assets are illiquid in nature, according to the fund, and will be distributed as liquidity is available. They have estimated it could take three years to liquidate certain portions of the portfolio. Before this fund-ending drawdown, Ospraie delivered about 15 percent per annum returns to investors. This new twist will take that number down to around the 8 percent level.

Ospraie had done well compared to most Commodity Trading Advisors (CTAs) since its founding in 1999. The fund grew to a large size and needed to invest in more illiquid markets to obtain the same octane returns for investors. CTAs are famous for being trend followers and making large directional bets. When the trend is right, profits are sky high. The markets they trade in also tend to be quite volatile, and being on the wrong side of a commodity trade was quite hazardous to investors. It is interesting to note the 30 percent drawdown provision that many surely thought was a get-out-of-jail-free card. Concerns should have been raised to investors that in July they were nearly halfway to the trigger point of 30 percent. It can be expected to witness high volatility in these types of funds; however, it seems quite apparent that directional bets ruled the portfolio and the investor had little in the way of hedged protection in the event of what happened. This is another example of outsized upside leading to outsized downside.

YOUR FINAL EXAM

From the above outlined hedge fund catastrophes, here are the five top causes of hedge fund collapses, in no particular order.

1. **Fraud is one cause we have seen in several instances.** It should be noted that this type of collapse is usually found in mid- to small-sized hedge funds. They tend to be harder to root out, but with consistent and persistent due diligence there are warming signs that should give you pause. If the resulting follow-up does not give you a sense of comfort, don't invest or redeem. There are over 10,000 hedge funds; find another.

2. **Once-in-a-lifetime market events that catastrophically affect the underlying investment theme or trading of the fund.** Whether it was widening of credit spreads for LTCM or collapse of natural gas spreads for Amaranth or other disruption to an arbitrage strategy, the suddenness and magnitude of the negatively fat-tailed event are never foreseen, and rarely is there a contingency plan to deal with such events in place.

3. **Leverage is a dual edge sword for hedge funds.** It can enhance returns in areas which the underlying strategy cannot support. The downside is that leverage can quickly change a trading strategy. The margin terms

can in some instances be changed and not to the fund's advantage. When there is turmoil in the market, the broker or bank can quickly reassess their risk exposure and demand a higher margin haircut. During this turmoil the portfolio may fall in value, forcing margin calls to produce higher levels of collateral from a portfolio that can't support them.

4. **Investor redemptions also contribute to the number of hedge fund blow-ups.** During improbable market events or concerns over leverage, investors begin to panic and the number of redemptions jumps. Hedge funds typically have little cash and thus are forced to liquidate positions. This can put the fund in a death spiral as margin calls may be occurring simultaneously.

5. **Forced liquidation of the fund's portfolio is the likely next step when margin calls and investor redemptions kick into high gear.** These liquidations can occur to meet the margin requirements that are necessary. Typically it is the part of the portfolio that has a lower risk profile and better liquidity. Unfortunately, when the portfolio is under stress these assets are also typically the best performing parts of the portfolio. The other assets are the ones under stress and they have poor liquidity terms. If the hedge fund gets to the stage where they are selling portions or the entire portfolio to another entity, it usually is the last shovel full of dirt being thrown on the body. The fund has little leverage in negotiating terms or price, and the sale is usually one of last resort.

APPLYING YOUR EDUCATION

Now you understand why the decision to put this chapter before the one on portfolio monitoring and review makes sense. Apply the following steps.

1. Review your strategy and the market prospects.
2. Verify factual details of the hedge fund.
3. Understand the market and investment process.
4. Quantify liquidity parameters.
5. Operation infrastructure in small firms is paramount.
6. Question all data.
7. Be as cynical about good as well as poor investment returns.

As you have progressed through the due diligence process you have obtained a fairly good snapshot of the fund. What you have discovered in this chapter is that the snapshot can change quickly and with some adverse consequences. As has been stressed throughout the book, reliance on quantitative measures is only half the job. The quantitative analysis does not provide you with answers but merely questions that need to be researched. Taking the time to verify even what seems to be the most routine data like the fund's auditor or principal's background can defend you from headline risk. Investors should understand that strategies and managers have capacity limits. A strategic exit plan needs to be in place before an investment is made. Good performance can be as frightening as bad performance. An investor needs to know the source of return and how likely that performance is to be repeated and at what level. It is also important to know the histories of the fund managers and not just their pedigree. Pedigree is what is discussed at cocktail parties, while what they accomplished is the stuff that makes good fund managers.

Coming from a well-respected hedge fund franchise is only a start. There are limits to the value of pedigree. Think in terms of how you might pick a doctor. Would you want to be treated by one of the top five graduates of Harvard or Johns Hopkins medical school or one that finishes near the bottom? Of course those schools might tell you that they have the Lake Woebegone effect on students, where everyone is above average. But are you willing to take that chance? Also discussed were some of the legal actions coming as a result of the hedge fund implosions. I possess no particular legal expertise, but I have offered some of these cases as a way of outlining options available to investors and what pitfalls may lie ahead if you find yourself in the midst of these meltdowns.

THE IMPORTANCE OF SECOND ACTS

On Wall Street, as in politics, there are many second acts. In the high pressure high stake world of investments, there are many sound investment professionals that have lost large amounts of money. George Soros, Paul Tudor Jones, and Warren Buffett, just to name of few, have had their share of stumbles. One of the overriding differences is that while their bets, if you allow me to use that term, may have been large, the risk parameters and controls were more than adequate to withstand a catastrophic downturn, liquidity squeeze, or unforeseen event.

Others have not performed as admirably as investors may have hoped, but they still manage to return to the front lines as people provide capital in the hope that the tragedy will not be repeated.

Robert "Bo" Collins, the founder of MotherRock, has set up a new venture to raise about $200 million. The firm 1.618 Group LLC was set up in early 2007. Collins received $100 million from one person who is not identified. 1.618 is a mathematical reference to Fibonacci analysis. 1.618 is known as Phi or the golden ratio. Technical traders use Fibonacci analysis to determine when the price of a commodity might change direction. Only time will reveal if anything was learned form the MotherRock implosion.

Brian Hunter, the former Amaranth energy trader, is back advising Peak Ridge Commodity Volatility fund run by Peak Ridge Capital Group, a Boston-based private equity fund. Mr. Hunter is still dealing with legal fall-out in the aftermath of Amaranth. The Federal Energy Regulatory Commission is proceeding with an action against him charging that he manipulated natural gas prices.

Everyone should seek and allow forgiveness. Investors in hedge funds should do so without the risk of exposing capital to the possibility of the fund being closed after the second act.

CHAPTER 10

Monitoring Your Flock

I Walk in the Valley of Darkness, I Fear No Evil

Diligentia maximum etiam mediocris ingeni subsidium.
(Diligence is a very great help even to a mediocre intelligence.)
—Seneca

Investors have spent several months combing through paperwork and data to find a comfort level in choosing a particular hedge fund or group of hedge funds. Many are relieved that the arduous process is over. Unfortunately for the true investor, one phase is over and a new one begins: monitoring of the chosen funds. In the prior months, there was little at stake besides time. Now with capital invested, our process and conclusions are being tested.

The due diligence process takes on a slightly different tone for several reasons. Most obvious for you and the hedge fund is that you are now an interested party. You are rooting for the manager to succeed, and the manager wants the investment to be successful in the hope you will invest more money or possibly tell your friends. After all, "country club marketing" is still one of the most successful distribution channels in the investment business. An investor should approach the ongoing duty of care in a similarly systematic way as he approached the original work. The views may be a bit different; however, the end result, a feeling of comfort with the fund and the manager, is still the end result.

The factors to be reviewed will be similar but the data reviewed will be looked at in view of the changing market and economic environments and the fund's reaction to those events. The major areas of post-investment monitoring are:

- Performance.
- Portfolio exposures.
- Performance trends.
- Peer group analysis.
- Strategy review.
- Fund size and performance impact.
- Management and personnel reviews.
- Third party vendors.
- Regulatory and legal risk.
- Business continuity risk.

This chapter will deal with each of the above topics and will make suggestions as to how to refine your post-investment monitoring.

EVERYONE'S FAVORITE METRIC: PERFORMANCE

Probably the easiest place to start and one nearly everyone turns to first is to review ongoing performance of the fund, which seems simple enough. Let us first review some of the items we learned in the due diligence process. First, are we comfortable with the classification and public market benchmark that the fund is identified with according to the database reports and the fund's own reports? For the purposes of this monitoring example, we are going to assume that the fund is classified as an equity long/short fund with the Russell 2000 as its benchmark. We have maintained a list of four other long/short hedge funds with similar investment strategies as well. So let's begin!

In Table 10.1 we see the typical monthly performance report that the fund sends to investors and interested prospects. The table demonstrates the fund's performance on a monthly basis and compares year-to-date (YTD) with the appropriate benchmark, in this case the Russell 2000. Since we have just invested in this fund, we do not need to spend much time on this table other than to review how we did this month and how the fund stands up against the benchmark YTD. The fund is up for the month (+0.32 percent), however the index was up sharply (+3.61 percent). The fund still is far outstripping the benchmark by 1,285 basis points, +10.23 percent versus −2.62 percent for the YTD in what has been a volatile market. It is always good to have positive performance in your first month of investment for a couple of reasons. First, the obvious reason is that it is from an investment standpoint a good end. Second, it provides the investor with a level of confidence

TABLE 10.1 HF Partners' Historical Performance (%)

	Jan	Feb	Mar	Apr	May	Jun	Jul	Aug	Sep	Oct	Nov	Dec	YTD	Russ 2000
2005	2.80	1.77	1.65	2.24	−1.38	3.50	−0.36	1.80	1.57	2.08	−1.81	−0.39	14.16	4.55
2006	1.83	−0.53	0.25	0.07	−0.34	−2.44	1.48	4.12	−0.15	−2.19	2.62	2.33	7.06	18.37
2007	0.81	1.46	1.13	1.72	4.64	−0.41	−2.28	0.33	0.55	4.91	−2.39	0.13	10.83	−1.57
2008	−3.82	1.43	3.41	1.30	2.77	5.33	−0.67	0.32					10.23	−2.62

(maybe false) that he made the correct decision. This may seem like a sense-less point; however, consider the case if the benchmark was up +3.61 percent while the fund was down even marginally at −0.32 percent. You immediately question your decision and the fund management, and you begin laying the groundwork toward redeeming out of the fund. Everyone enters as a long-term investor until a disappointment is at hand.

That does not mean that your cynicism should evaporate. It puts various questions in your mind, for both now and later returns analysis of returns: Does this manager underperform in strong markets? Has the manager made a large short bet? Are the manager's short selections not on par with his long selections? The monthly returns shown in Table 10.1 have already given us some indication about at least one of those questions. This manager does seem to underperform in strong markets. It also shows that this manager sharply outperforms in down markets, not only on a relative basis but, more importantly, on an absolute basis. One of the points stressed in earlier chapters is the downside protection advantage that hedge funds have over traditional managers.

PORTFOLIO EXPOSURES

What do we need to review next? Most managers do not provide full transparency but many provide exposure levels to investors. Table 10.2 is the position summary of our manager that corresponds to the performance reported in Table 10.1. In Table 10.2 the manager has provided some interesting information as to how he has positioned the portfolio over the previous three-plus years.

The easiest observation is that over the time period the fund has essentially run a portfolio with 23 longs and 25 shorts with an average net exposure of 13. What has changed over time is that the portfolio has become less neutral. In 2005 and 2006 the average net exposure was 4 to 5 percent with little movement until late 2006. As we move through 2006 and 2007, we see the average net exposure hit double digits and the monthly average change significantly in some instances.

Remember, quantitative numbers give us questions, not answers! Has the manager changed his approach? Let's look again at the numbers revealed in Table 10.2. First let's note the consistencies of the manager across time. The average percent long exposure and the number of long positions were consistent within a reasonable range for the data. But what about the average percent short exposure and consequently the average percent gross exposure? They both have changed significantly. The average percent short exposure has fallen from the high 90 percent to the low 70 to 80 percent

TABLE 10.2 Position Summary

	Average Long % Exposure	Average Short % Exposure	Average Gross % Exposure	Average Net % Exposure	Number of Longs	Number of Shorts
Jan-05	101	99	199	2	26	23
Feb-05	100	99	199	1	27	18
Mar-05	99	95	194	4	25	19
Apr-05	98	94	191	4	28	19
May-05	98	96	195	2	26	18
Jun-05	99	96	196	3	23	23
Jul-05	100	96	196	4	22	24
Aug-05	99	95	194	4	23	21
Sep-05	96	93	189	4	25	24
Oct-05	99	92	191	7	27	27
Nov-05	102	94	197	8	22	26
Dec-05	101	95	196	6	23	19
Jan-06	100	96	196	4	24	23
Feb-06	99	97	196	2	22	25
Mar-06	99	98	197	1	22	28
Apr-06	97	96	193	2	19	27
May-06	97	91	187	6	19	29
Jun-06	95	90	184	5	20	29
Jul-06	97	95	192	2	22	33
Aug-06	101	95	195	6	24	34
Sep-06	95	86	181	9	22	23
Oct-06	92	87	179	6	24	16
Nov-06	94	84	178	10	22	22
Dec-06	94	79	173	15	21	20
Jan-07	96	79	175	17	22	18
Feb-07	94	79	173	15	22	14
Mar-07	91	75	166	16	22	17
Apr-07	96	78	174	17	24	20
May-07	96	76	172	19	23	25
Jun-07	93	75	168	18	23	23
Jul-07	95	72	167	22	21	24
Aug-07	91	73	164	18	20	29
Sep-07	90	80	170	11	20	34
Oct-07	98	77	174	21	25	34
Nov-07	102	72	173	30	24	34
Dec-07	104	74	178	31	24	37
Jan-08	105	76	182	29	22	33
Feb-08	99	81	180	18	22	35

(Continued)

TABLE 10.2 (*Continued*)

	Average Long % Exposure	Average Short % Exposure	Average Gross % Exposure	Average Net % Exposure	Number of Longs	Number of Shorts
Mar-08	96	86	182	11	23	39
Apr-08	98	88	187	10	22	40
May-08	97	87	185	10	21	38
Jun-08	92	81	172	11	22	43
Jul-08	90	80	170	10	21	39
Aug-08	93	83	176	10	22	38
AVG.	97	84	181	13	23	25

range in 2007 and 2008. At the same time the average percent gross exposure had dropped as well. As quick cross-check to the column with number of short positions shows a significant increase as well.

Quickly a number of questions arise. Did the manager change his investment process? Has there been value-added with this change? Some of this should come up in the original due diligence process and is a key point in the ongoing monitoring. One of the realities of hedge fund managers is that many are closet long only managers and will short only a few stocks, usually as a sector call or various ETFs that will hedge some of the fund's long positions. For some investors this is a red flag and an almost automatic rejection. In some cases, such as a manager running a concentrated portfolio or a strategy where there is not a solid way to hedge risk, PIPES comes to mind. Shorting in this manner is certainly acceptable. This allows the manager to pursue absolute returns in all market environments without the additional risk of stock selection.

A separate reason for this progression is that the manager may have little or no shorting experience. As the fund is starting up and the object is to put up some solid numbers early on for marketing reasons, the focus is on long positions and shorting can only add downside risk to the portfolio. As the manager gets comfortable in the operation and assets grow, the fund can and may throw more resources at building a short book in the portfolio. The hoped for result of this progression is to generate positive returns in both sides of the portfolio and produce alpha regardless of the market level. In Table 10.1, one of the observations is that the manager performed all right in strong markets but did very well in weak markets. That may be the direct result of this shift to a more active short book. The point to take away from Table 10.2 is to gauge several levels of the portfolio holdings. One is that leverage is not heavily used here. Another is that the management of this fund has moved from being a passive "hedger" to one where value is being added from the short side of the portfolio. Be a keen observer of trends. Sometimes you can pick up some important information on the content of the portfolio without having full and complete transparency.

Now we need to answer the question: Is the manager really adding value for the short side of the portfolio, as we inferred from the above observations? One additional piece of information that managers will send to you as an investor is a breakout of its performance attribution between the longs and shorts of the portfolio. Our fund manager here does provide that very information for us. In Table 10.3 the fund breaks out the long performance contribution by month and the short contributions by month as well as the comparison of the total fund performance versus the Russell 2000 index.

PERFORMANCE TRENDS

As keen trend spotters, what can we ascertain from this fund information? The quick and dirty observations are that the average long returns are +1.54 percent, the short returns are −0.32 percent. The average Russell 2000 return was +0.47 percent while the fund's average return was +0.94 percent. The fund's long positions exceed the Russell returns, on average, by over 100 basis points. The short selection returns were negative but only underperformed the Russell by less than 80 basis points. From the table we can also calculate a batting average for each. The long positions were positive in 30 periods or 68 percent of the time. The short positions were less successful, being positive during 20 periods or 45 percent of the time. Combined, the portfolio was positive 68 percent of the time. Can we conclude that the short book added value? Not entirely. We can, however, observe that the performance levels of the shorts were not in direct proportion to the index, which can lead us to the conclusion that the shorting was at least partially effective for this manager.

One final test that we can run from Table 10.3 is how our manager correlates to the index. Thanks to the magic of computers, we can readily see that this manager has a correlation of 0.082. More plainly, this manager has a low correlation to the Russell 2000 index, which tells us that the manager we have just hired provides us with some protection that we will not be heavily subjected to market downdrafts. Again, you are providing downside protection for your invested funds.

This is now the ground work for the ongoing monitoring of your hedge fund investment. In the upcoming months you will continue to compare

TABLE 10.3 Portfolio Attribution

	Long Attribution (%)	Short Attribution (%)	Russell 2000 %	Fund Return %
Jan-05	0.17	3.40	−4.17	2.80
Feb-05	4.42	−2.14	1.69	1.77
Mar-05	0.66	1.46	−2.86	1.65
Apr-05	−2.60	5.45	−5.73	2.24
May-05	4.84	−6.57	6.55	−1.38
Jun-05	7.68	−3.38	3.86	3.50
Jul-05	3.92	−4.27	6.34	−0.36
Aug-05	0.43	1.83	−1.85	1.80
Sep-05	0.80	1.13	0.31	1.57
Oct-05	−0.49	3.10	−3.10	2.08
Nov-05	1.93	−4.21	4.85	−1.81
Dec-05	−0.85	0.32	−0.46	−0.39
Jan-06	9.05	−6.81	8.97	1.83
Feb-06	−0.79	0.22	−0.28	−0.53
Mar-06	4.65	−4.24	4.85	0.25
Apr-06	−0.14	0.38	−0.02	0.07
May-06	−4.58	4.23	−5.62	−0.34
Jun-06	−2.20	−0.37	0.64	−2.44
Jul-06	−0.86	2.43	−3.25	1.48
Aug-06	6.55	−1.30	2.96	4.12
Sep-06	1.95	−2.05	0.83	−0.15
Oct-06	1.59	−4.21	5.76	−2.19
Nov-06	4.77	−1.44	2.63	2.62
Dec-06	3.49	−0.54	0.33	2.33
Jan-07	2.94	−1.86	1.67	0.81
Feb-07	1.84	0.04	−0.79	1.46
Mar-07	2.08	−0.62	1.07	1.13
Apr-07	4.57	−2.38	1.80	1.72
May-07	8.45	−2.61	4.10	4.64
Jun-07	−1.02	0.55	−1.46	−0.41
Jul-07	−6.85	4.18	−6.84	−2.28
Aug-07	1.03	−0.62	2.27	0.33
Sep-07	2.24	−1.55	1.72	0.55
Oct-07	7.34	−1.23	2.87	4.91
Nov-07	−7.51	4.72	−7.18	−2.39
Dec-07	−0.43	0.75	−0.06	0.13
Jan-08	−8.19	4.49	−6.82	−3.82
Feb-08	−0.98	2.55	−3.71	1.43

(Continued)

TABLE 10.3 (*Continued*)

	Long Attribution (%)	Short Attribution (%)	Russell 2000 %	Fund Return %
Mar-08	2.82	0.97	0.42	3.41
Apr-08	6.00	−4.28	4.19	1.30
May-08	6.68	−3.19	4.59	2.77
Jun-08	−0.89	7.51	−7.70	5.33
Jul-08	0.24	−1.02	3.70	−0.67
Aug-08	3.15	−2.70	3.61	0.32
Average	*1.54*	*−0.32*	*0.47*	*0.94*
		Correl.	*0.082*	

this baseline and look for *sustained* changes in the trends that you have discovered in your investment manager. I stress sustained changes in trends. A one-month change in trend is something to view, but only if there are other clues that may be noticeable in the fund and its operations. A change for a second straight month probably warrants a call to the fund to try to understand if there is a more permanent trend that is beginning to develop and whether it changes the original thesis of your investment. Going back to our example in this chapter; there was a sustained change in the trend of exposure and the number of shorts. A call to the fund in mid-2006 would have informed you that the fund had indeed added a change in its short book from just hedging to producing alpha with individual stock shorts.

PEER GROUP ANALYSIS

Now that you have reviewed everyone's favorite marker, performance, you can turn your attention to other data that you will need to monitor on an ongoing basis. In the review of performance, some of this monitoring has been done. The comparison of the fund's performance and correlation to the benchmark has been noted. In Table 10.4, it is time to examine how your fund has performed versus your peer group.

A glance at the peer review does not show anything extraordinary, although Peer #2 has shown much more volatility than the other members of this group. Even though it is not germane to this analysis, it is always a good idea to obtain a better understanding of any fund. In another time it would be useful to dig deeper as to why this fund was included in this peer group. The next step would be to compare the fund result to the general

TABLE 10.4 Peer Group Comparison

	Our Fund	Peer #1	Peer #2	Peer #3	Peer #4
Jan	−3.82	−4.07	−3.26	−0.98	−4.44
Feb	1.43	1.89	1.41	1.01	1.56
Mar	3.41	3.99	6.32	1.29	1.54
Apr	1.30	1.22	0.88	1.59	1.17
May	2.77	2.23	3.68	2.32	2.84
Jun	5.33	4.99	6.74	5.42	4.55
Jul	−0.67	−0.92	−2.31	−0.88	−0.87
Aug	0.32	−0.06	−0.32	0.91	0.03

hedge fund equity long/short monthly results, if you have the computational power to segment small cap equity long/short funds. This is really not very constructive and you may ask why bother? You should be cognizant of the markets and how the asset class in general is reacting to current and past market conditions. By itself this is not a breakthrough analysis but it is another data point as you monitor this fund, other funds, the hedge fund world, and the markets. Asking what am I missing or what can go wrong will help you analyze data and give you clues to future signs that you can catch.

STRATEGY REVIEWS

From a monitoring standpoint, you can now step back and review the hedge fund world from a strategy standpoint. Early in the due diligence process, the investment committee, or whoever is leading the process, decided that from a portfolio standpoint or future alpha generating sector, they should find a fund in the small cap hedge fund space. On a monthly, or no less than a quarterly, basis it is prudent to review whether those assumptions are still intact. In addition to looking at the hedge fund universe, it can be a useful exercise to review return streams from the mutual fund world. Mutual funds tend to have larger asset bases in most strategies than hedge funds. The comparison can give one additional clue that the hedge fund is providing alpha. The larger size of a small cap mutual fund will in most instances be a drag on performance.

In Chapter 2, we reviewed research that showed smaller managers outperformed the larger ones. This outcome is applicable to long only ones as well. If your fund and group are consistently underperforming the mutual fund data, you might need to consider your investment strategy at several levels.

TABLE 10.5 Hedge Fund Strategy Asset Flows—6 Months

Strategy	$Flows (million)	% Change
European Long/Short	450.89	−7.7
Global Long/Short	3,619.24	9.9
U.S. Long/Short	1,129.14	16.0
Japan Long/Short	−359.55	−48.7

Period ending August 2008.

FUND SIZE AND PERFORMANCE IMPACT

The natural next level of monitoring should be asset flows in and out of the strategy and your invested fund. From a strategy standpoint, a one month shot again is a heads up but looking at the six month flow is more valuable. In Table 10.5 the flows in several categories in dollar terms and percentages is reviewed.

The table reveals that money for the past six months is still favorably impacting the U.S and global equity long/short markets. There have been considerable outflows in Japan and it would appear that trend may be picking up steam in the European long/short markets as well. In Figure 10.1 we next track the impact of net asset growth and the return stream of the fund. It can be determined from the chart that performance remains

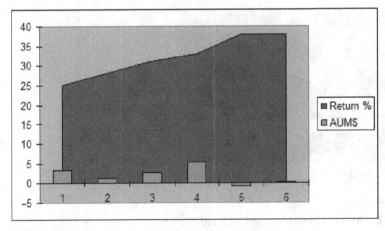

FIGURE 10.1 Invested Fund—Returns vs. $AUM

consistent even as the assets under management are growing. More precisely, the ability to generate alpha has not yet been compromised for this manager.

In Figure 10.2 we see a different set of conditions and results for another fund. This chart is measuring the year end AUM for a fund and compares it to the annual return of another small cap fund. After the fund had a strong start we see a sharp increase in net inflow of dollars to the fund. Those dollars are met with rather disappointing results. Again, as we have seen in Chapter 2, funds experiencing sharp inflows of money or funds that have grown substantially larger than is ideal for a given strategy will see performance suffering. With these two charts as a backdrop, it should be an ongoing point of monitoring to see the fund flows and AUM of a manager. You need to compare the monthly AUM with the original targets for the fund that you received during your due diligence process. If the manager changes that target, a red flag should be raised. If the fund is still within a comfortable range of its original target but has seen a large increase in AUM accompanied by a mediocre performance results in the process, another red flag should be raised.

Under this circumstance, the rapidity that a manager can put money to work comes into question. In an effort to put the new funds to work, the manager may do one of two things, neither an ideal outcome. First and worst, the manager may stray from the initial core competency of the portfolio team. For example, the manager's valuation metrics for new purchases may be strained to put the new money to work. Whether the manager stretches

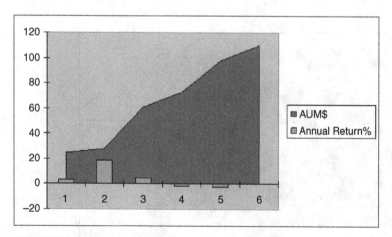

FIGURE 10.2 AUM$ Growth vs. Annual Fund Returns

the financial metric of the new stock or capitalization size you are now in a riskier fund than your original proposition. Secondly, the manager may use a place holder in the portfolio.

A sector ETF or an index ETF may be used to provide additional long exposure. This will at best provide beat exposure and some relative performance for a portion of the portfolio. These red flags are to be heeded. As the fund becomes larger than expected or grows faster than funds can be put to work, investors must consider redemption options. Otherwise one can expect mediocre performance to visit shortly.

MANAGEMENT AND PERSONNEL REVIEWS

Any changes to the management of the firm or additions (or subtractions), especially to the investment team, should be reported immediately by a fund manager. As a normal course of business, in any conversation with the fund manager you should inquire about any changes that have occurred or may be contemplated.

First, let us consider the investment team. In the due diligence process you obtained detailed information about the investment team and quite possibly a roadmap as to the growth plans for the investment team. Typically, in start-up funds they will add a new analyst or trader at the level of AUM obtained. Question the fund if there are any changes to the plan, either positively or negatively. On the positive side, if the fund has sped up its hiring plan it may be a positive sign that new assets are expected or that the fund wants to help performance by lessening the duties of one person or by adding additional skills from someone else. Of course, the new person will need to be vetted at some point by you and your due diligence team. In the meantime, a channel check through your hedge fund contacts will provide some initial answers and possible comfort.

Of further importance would be the change or addition of any person on the business, back, middle, or front office side of the fund. You are quite aware that in small start-up funds the biggest risk leading to fund failure is that the business infrastructure is insufficient. What is even more significant is the qualifications of the fund's personnel. As we discovered in Chapter 9, the addition of a CFO or accountant is not necessarily a sleep-well-at-night hire. Here the due diligence of these folks is an immediate requirement when you are notified or discover that additional personnel is on board. Remember that just the hiring is not the answer, and you must be comfortable that the hire has been made for the right reasons and not part of a much larger nefarious plot.

At this point, you may be thinking that performing this function makes one a deep pessimist. Quite possibly that is true. The other side is that if you are pessimistic, you will rarely be disappointed.

THIRD-PARTY VENDORS

You have now gone through the progress of the firm. From performance to asset growth to personnel changes, you have set up a monitoring process for evaluating whether the fund you have invested monies in remains the fund you thought it would be in your portfolio.

The next part of the monitoring process should include all outside vendors that service the fund. The following are the typical third-party vendors of most hedge funds: prime broker, auditor, legal counsel, administrator, and third-party marketer.

The prime broker is key to discovering if the information about the fund is consistent. At least quarterly, a prime broker check will give confirmation as to whether the asset under management is consistent with the level the fund is claiming. You may also ask the fund to provide a list of assets. Here you can get a peek into the types of investments the manager has made, how aligned the manager is to its investment process, and are they adhering to security and sector maximums as marketed. It should be noted that some fund managers may balk at providing the current month statements. And that, to be fair, is reasonable. The concept of intellectual capital is something that is real to many fund managers. It is also reasonable that you need some sort of access to a manager's holdings to verify assets and holdings. If the manager refuses, and some may, it then becomes a decision as to whether you can live with no level of transparency and whether the manager's integrity is above reproach. You may come to the conclusion that the answer is yes.

The investor also needs to be concerned about the health and wellbeing of the prime broker(s). The prime broker may add a certain amount of default or counterparty risk depending on the amount of leverage, use of derivatives, and other bundled services of the broker. The financing arrangements and the legal structure of the brokers can add operational complexities, in particular in data aggregation and additional documentation. In recent months, Bear Stearns and Lehman Brothers have disappeared, creating problems for investors and hedge funds alike.

The investor needs to understand how the prime broker holds collateral and which assets may be hypothecated. Cash levels in the hedge fund and where they are held need to be monitored as well. The hedge fund needs to know that the prime broker has excess SIPC (Securities Investor Protection Act of 1970) and what are the terms. Additionally, the hedge fund portion of the assets/P&L may not be covered by SIPC.

From the investor's standpoint, the health of the prime broker is a concern in the event that the prime broker files for bankruptcy. In bankruptcy, SIPC would distribute securities to customers, but in the event of a shortfall it will cover only $500,000 in securities and $100,000 in cash. Any excess might fall to the general creditor line. During the bankruptcy proceeding the SIPC trustee may sell accounts to another broker dealer, which could take two to four weeks or, if there are no takers for the business or there was fraud involved, the unwind process could take more than three months.

Regardless of the ultimate disposition of the broker, it will impact performance on the investor's returns and may delay the return of funds in the event a redemption was planned.

The fund administrators and auditors are also sources for information. Lack of an independent administrator or auditor should raise some red flags. We saw in Chapter 9 the end result from the lack of a legitimate auditor. It will not be unusual for an auditor only to confirm that they indeed have been hired by the fund for audit services. If the auditor is a reputable firm, that will give some degree of comfort. A small unknown auditor will be worth time and effort spent to determine their level of competence and integrity. Checks with the state and local accounting boards or the AICPA may be required to confirm the legitimacy of an auditor.

The administrator will be providing you with your NAV. Pricing policies and other issues related to performance and fees can be ascertained. Just like medical students, some graduate at the top of their class and others reside near the bottom. It is essential to gain comfort with the administrator. Requests for information are given more serious consideration as recent court rulings have put administrators and auditors on the wrong end of lawsuits as funds have imploded.

You should also be aware that at some point there is a high probability that you be blindsided by some aspect of the fund of which you were completely unaware. Regardless of how much assorted detail, such as percent of portfolio in top ten holdings or weightings of the sectors in the long and short book, you have no definitive verification that the numbers you are analyzing are indeed true. You can derive certain inferences from this information, but true accuracy is not one of them. One of the biggest fears of folks who perform due diligence is headline risk. Will you wake up one day and read about your fund in a negative fashion in the *Wall Street Journal*?

REGULATORY AND LEGAL RISK

As you gather information form the fund on an ongoing basis, you get a clearer picture as to the level of regulatory and legal risk to which you may be exposed. Not all funds are registered with the SEC. If they are, that is not a Good Housekeeping Seal of Approval. It is merely a function that the fund has gone through the process, often for little else than a marketing gain. That is not to demean the effort of some funds that do register and feel strongly that to insure a "culture of compliance" is not just a punch line but a business decision. There are folks that notice the adviser is a registered investment adviser and believe they somehow have an angel on their shoulder. The SEC has been overwhelmed by the growth of the hedge fund business and is even more overwhelmed in the lack of understanding of how hedge funds work and operate. They have moved up the learning curve but still have a long way to go. In recent years the SEC has moved to a risk rating system to schedule how frequently managers need to be reviewed and audited by the SEC. The SEC has moved most hedge funds to a three-year or less time frame, while more traditional advisers are on a three to five year schedule.

Other legal risks that many fund investors ignore are the civil or tax cases or charges against some advisers. Tax liens, IRS charges, and DUIs are among the areas that should raise a flag to investors. Random and regular background searches on your manager may yield some useful information. If there is a dissatisfied investor or ex-employee that has filed suit against the manager, there are a couple of reasons to worry. First and foremost is that the charges may be true. Secondly, if there seems to be a growing list of these, it raises a strong concern that there is a deeper underlying problem with the firm. Finally, all of the legal action is draining to the fund's resources and a distraction from its real business at hand—finding alpha.

BUSINESS CONTINUITY RISK

The above issues funnel into one primary issue that is at the root of the hedge fund world: business continuity. Any one of the above issues can deliver a fatal blow to the small nascent hedge fund. The firm needs sufficient infrastructure to withstand short term disruptions to its operations, distractions to the managers, and ample resources to withstand any temporary slowdown to its business plan.

In the due diligence process, the manager disclosed its business continuity plan to assure investors that catastrophic events beyond everyone's control do not leave investors in a lurch as to the disposition of their funds. As the fund and firm grow, you should also see improvements to the continuity plan. Third-party vendors that specialize in delivering back-up service, plus computer and data protection. will be seen as essential as the fund moves from a start-up to its more mature stage. When some firms become of sufficient size they develop there own off-site infrastructure and back-up systems, which they feel gives them more control in what is typically an uncontrollable system.

A FINAL WORD ON MONITORING

As you expand your flock of funds, you will most likely get the feeling that you walk in the shadow of darkness, especially as the strategies are new and become more complex. It is important to remember several key items. If you are not comfortable with a manager or strategy—*redeem*! No amount of return can compensate for the constant fear that there is something wrong and you may be the last to figure it out. There are thousands and thousands of funds. Find one to your liking.

Next, as President Reagan was fond of saying, "trust but verify." There are some aspects of the business for which you must get direct confirmation from a reliable independent third party.

Finally, as your third grade school teacher told you, the only dumb question is the one you didn't ask. Be persistent in your approach and determined to have all aspects of the fund's operations completely understood. You will make mistakes. Everyone does. If you think you have not made a mistake, I will offer two thoughts. One is wait, yours is coming, or you are not really trying. The key is to learn from your mistakes and apply what you learn to any future situation. Being a hedge fund historian is sometimes more useful than being a hedge fund mathematician.

Sample Investment
Policy Statement

Investment Policy Statement

The purpose of Funds is to support the mission by providing a reliable source of funds for current and future use. The Funds assets have an indefinite time horizon that runs concurrently with the existence of the family in perpetuity. As such, the investment portfolio assumes a time horizon that may extend beyond a normal market cycle and therefore may assume an appropriate level of risk as measured by the standard deviation and downside deviation of annual returns. It is expected that professional management and portfolio diversification will smooth volatility and assure a Minimum Acceptable Return (MAR). Investment of the Funds is the responsibility of the Investment Committee (Committee). The Committee recommends investment objectives and policies, recommends asset allocation, selects investment Managers, and monitors the Funds investment program. The Committee will be advised by the Family Office (FO), who will analyze investment policies and management strategies, make recommendations to the Committee, and supervise operations and investment activities. This Investment Policy should not change frequently. In particular, short-term changes in the financial markets should not require adjustments to this Investment Policy.

I. STATEMENT OF INVESTMENT OBJECTIVES

The Funds will seek to maximize long-term total returns consistent with prudent levels of risk. Investment returns are expected to preserve or enhance the real value of the Funds to provide a MAR that will support the family activities. Funds are expected to generate a MAR, net of fees, of XX percent over a rolling 3-year period. Funds MAR governs the rate at which funds are released to the family for their current spending. The MAR will be reviewed annually by the Investment Committee for recommendation and approval.

II. ASSET ALLOCATION AND REBALANCING

To achieve its investment objectives, the Fund will be allocated among a number of asset classes. These asset classes may include domestic equity, domestic fixed income, international developed equity, international emerging markets equity, and international fixed income, alternative investments (absolute return) and directional hedge funds, private equity, venture capital, real assets, and cash. The purpose of allocating the investment portfolio asset classes is to ensure the proper level of diversification within the Fund.

The Committee will review and recommend asset class allocation targets and minimum/maximum ranges no less frequently than annually. The Asset Allocation Policy Table attached to this document defines the present policy target asset allocation percentages of the families' portfolio. The Committee may appoint Investment Managers (Managers) or select pooled investments with an objective to be fully invested at all times. If at any time a Manager elects to be invested at less than 90 percent, the Committee shall be notified. Managers are expected to diversify holdings consistent with prudent levels of risk.

Asset allocations shall be made among various asset classes including the following, subject to the limitations stated in the Asset Allocation Policy Table.

A. Domestic Equity Portfolio

The domestic equity portfolio will be invested on the basis of total return, including dividend yield and capital appreciation.

The return, risk, and cost dynamics of each sub-class/style (i.e., large cap, small cap, growth, value, etc.) will be evaluated to determine whether active or passive management is appropriate under the circumstances existing at the time.

Within the guidelines and restrictions, Managers have discretion over the timing and selection of equity securities and are expected not to time the market.

B. International Equity Portfolio

The Funds international equity portfolio will be invested in stocks of international issuers on the basis of total return, including dividend yield and capital appreciation. No more than 10 percent of the international equity portfolio may be invested in emerging markets (i.e., countries in the Morgan Stanley Capital International Emerging Markets Free Index and other non-EAFE markets.) Currency hedging as a defensive strategy is permitted in global or international equity portfolios.

C. Alternative Investments

Alternative Investments involve investing in non-traditional asset classes and in traditional asset classes structured in a non-traditional manner. Managers are expected to use their specific investments skills to generate long-term equity-like returns that are not highly correlated to traditional asset classes. Absolute Return (marketable) and Directional hedge fund investment strategies, such as, long versus short, tactical asset allocation, distressed securities, and arbitrage strategies, among others may be used to enhance investment returns and overall portfolio diversification. Investment commitments to alternative asset Managers will be made to attempt to achieve an average investment in subclasses of alternative investments at or below the individual target levels established for each subclass. The Funds non-marketable alternative investment portfolio will be invested in venture capital, leveraged buyouts, distressed debt, timber, energy, and other investments recommended by the committee in order to produce the combined or individual effects of reducing overall portfolio risk or to generate expected returns that exceed those available from domestic and international equities. Non-marketable alternative investments in aggregate will be valued at cost for purposes of determining whether they are within the permitted allocation target level. Investments in alternative assets will be made primarily in Funds, a limited partner relying upon the expertise of experienced general partners. The alternative investment portfolio will be invested across a broad spectrum of underlying investments up to the target level for each asset subclass that should realize expected returns over a period of ten years. Net commitments (total commitments minus distributions) to a single manager may not represent more than 15 percent of the asset allocation target for alternative investments.

Managers for alternative investments shall provide, in writing, the policies and procedures used in periodic portfolio valuation. These policies and procedures along with portfolio composition are to be reviewed with the

Family at least annually. At a minimum, the Manager will address the following:

- Nature of underlying investments, including factors such as complexity, liquidity, volatility and frequency of trading.
- Methodology and assumptions used in valuation.
- Role of advisory committee in valuations.
- Current membership and experience of advisory committee members.
- Checks and balances in place to ensure a fair evaluation process.
- Specific guidelines for marketable alternative investments are listed in Appendix I.

D. Fixed Income Portfolio

Fixed income Investments may be managed to pursue opportunities presented by changes in interest rates, credit ratings, and maturity premiums, with the objective of meeting or exceeding the results of the fixed income market as represented by the annualized returns of specific indices over an annualized moving three- and five-year time period. The fixed income portfolio may include municipal bonds and U.S., non-U.S., or emerging market fixed income instruments.

E. Real Asset Portfolio

A portion of the portfolio will be invested by Managers who are expected to use their specific investment skills to generate returns that have lower correlations to the U.S. stock market. Real Estate and commodity investments may be made in a broad spectrum of investments including publicly traded Real Estate Investment Trusts (REITs), open- or closed-end funds, limited partnerships, Exchange-traded funds (ETF).

F. Asset Allocation Rebalancing

Marketable asset classes that exceed tolerance ranges will be rebalanced to target levels quarterly. Excess allocations intended for non-marketable asset categories will be carried, prior to their investment in non-marketable assets, in one or more other asset classes after consultation with the Investment Consultant and approval from the Chair of the Investment Committee.

The Russell 3000 will be used as a proxy for the domestic equities market. Domestic equity portfolios and strategies selected for the portfolio will be chosen with the goal of forming a domestic equity portfolio that is similar in capitalization relative to the Russell 3000 index.

Tolerance ranges for portfolio rebalancing will be established by multiplying target ranges times the expected volatility (standard deviation) updated annually by the FO for each portfolio target allocation, rounded up to the closest whole percentage point. (Example: An asset class with an expected volatility of 17 percent and a portfolio target allocation of 10 percent would result in 17 percent times 10 percent equals 1.7 percent rounded up to 2 percent. The asset class will be rebalanced quarterly when the tolerance exceeds plus or minus 2 percent; i.e., when the actual portfolio allocation to that asset class is over 12 percent or below 8 percent, the asset class is rebalanced to 10 percent.)

III. GUIDELINES FOR THE SELECTION OF FIXED-INCOME SECURITIES

A. Diversification

Except for the U.S. government, its Federal Agencies or instrumentalities, no more than 5 percent of the fixed-income portfolio at cost, or 10 percent at market value, shall be invested in any one guarantor, issuer, or pool of assets. In addition, Managers are expected to exercise prudence in diversifying the Fund's investment by sector and industry.

B. Investment Quality

U.S. FIXED INCOME—All fixed income obligations must be rated investment grade BBB/Baa or better by either Standard & Poor's or Moody's Investors Service, except that bonds not receiving a rating may be purchased under the following circumstances:
- The issue is guaranteed by the U.S. government, its Federal Agencies or instrumentalities.
- Other comparable debt of the issuer is rated investment grade by Standard & Poor's or Moody's Investors Service.

Securities downgraded in credit quality rating subsequent to purchase, resulting in the violation of the policy guidelines, may be held at the Manager's discretion. This is subject to immediate notification to the FO of such a change in rating.

NON-U.S. FIXED INCOME—For funds invested with a Manager in a separately held account, the non-U.S. assets held by such Manager must be investment grade fixed income securities (or securities deemed of comparable quality by the Manager) of issuers located outside the United States. All fixed income obligations must be rated

investment grade BBB/Baa or better. The average quality rating of
the non-U.S. fixed income portfolio must be A or better.

GLOBAL FIXED INCOME—The Global fixed income asset class will
be comprised of investment grade fixed income securities and may
be comprised of domestic or global issues. All bonds must be rated
BBB or better.

MUNICIPAL FIXED INCOME—Strategies for this asset category will
be comprised of U.S. fixed income instruments of state and local
authorities with the legal capacity to float municipal securities. All
municipal bonds held will be investment grade or have an indenture
mechanism to guarantee principal such as backed by another higher
rated entity, escrowed to maturity, or insured.

C. Duration

In general, the average duration of managed fixed income assets (excluding
global high yield fixed income) will be maintained within the range of the
average duration of the designated bond index plus or minus one and one-
half years.

IV. GUIDELINES FOR SELECTION OF EQUITY INVESTMENTS

Diversification for Each Manager (Long Only)

No more than 5 percent at cost, or 10 percent at market value, shall be
invested in any single issuer. In addition, Managers are expected to exercise
prudence in diversifying the Fund's investments by sector and industry with
weightings no more than two times the Manager's comparable benchmark.

V. STANDARDS OF PERFORMANCE

A. Performance Relative to Risk

The stated goal for the total portfolio is to generate a Minimum Acceptable
Return of XX percent over rolling 3-year periods.

Broad portfolio diversification is expected to provide an aggregate risk
(volatility) for the total portfolio that is lower than that of a market index
weighted to match the asset mix of the portfolio.

The disciplined approach to investment is intended to be consistent over
time and among asset classes. Incremental changes to asset class allocation
will be proposed or new classes added when such actions are anticipated to
improve returns and/or reduce risk.

B. Peer Group

Performance of the Managers in the portfolio will also be compared to a peer universe with similar investment styles. It is expected that the total portfolio will perform above the median performance in the comparable fund universe provided by the FO.

Managers are expected to equal or exceed the return of the agreed benchmark and generally perform in the top 40th percentile (40 percent) or better of their respective peer group over a market cycle (3–5 years), as measured by a broad performance database that evaluates Managers as to style, risk, and return.

C. Indices

1. Performance of the Fund (net of fees) and its component asset classes will be measured against benchmark returns of comparable portfolios as follows:

   Total Fund Aggregated weighted return equal to the actual asset class composite market value as a percentage of total portfolio market value multiplied times the selected benchmarks for the asset class composites.

   U.S. Equity

   Large Cap: Russell 1000 Index

   Mid Cap: Russell Mid Cap Index

   Small Cap: Russell 2000 Index

   International Equity

   Non-U.S. Developed: MSCI EAFE Index

   Emerging Markets: MSCI Emerging Market Index

   Absolute Return Composite 91 Days T-Bill + 450 Basis Points

   Non-Marketable Composite Total Non-Marketable actual return

   Real Assets

   CPI-Urban Index

   NAREIT Index

   Goldman Sachs Commodity Index

   Fixed Income Composite

   Global Fixed Income: Citigroup Global Bond Index

   Municipal Bonds: Lehman Intermediate Muni Bond Index

2. **MARKETABLE ALTERNATIVE INVESTMENTS**—Performance will be compared to 91-day U.S. T-Bills plus 450 basis points. Period to

period performance for marketable alternative assets will also be compared to the HFRI Hedge Fund or Fund-of-Funds Index benchmark to
assess relative asset class movement and volatility.

3. **NON-MARKETABLE ALTERNATIVE INVESTMENTS**—The primary objective is to obtain equivalent or higher U.S. equity returns
over multi-year periods, with reduced volatility and lower risk (standard deviation) for the equity portfolio. Actual non-marketable alternative investment returns will be used as the benchmark. Non-marketable
alternative investment performance will also be compared to the Russell 3000 plus 300 basis points per annum to assess relative asset class
movement and volatility.

4. **REAL ESTATE**—Investments will be compared to the NAREIT index.

5. **U.S. FIXED INCOME**—Fixed income performance will be compared
to the total return of the Lehman Aggregate Bond Index.

6. **INTERNATIONAL FIXED INCOME**—Performance will be compared
to the total return of the Citigroup WGBI Non-U.S. Unhedged Index.

7. **TREASURY INFLATION PROTECTED SECURITIES (TIPS)**—Performance will be compared to the Merrill Lynch U.S. Treasury Inflation
Index.

8. **GLOBAL FIXED INCOME**

   A. **GLOBAL FIXED INCOME**—Performance will be compared to
   the Citigroup Global Bond Index.

   B. **INTERNATIONAL EMERGING MARKETS DEBT**—Performance will be compared to the J.P. Morgan Emerging Markets
   Bond Index.

   The benchmark will be a weighed average of A + B. based on the
   overall allocation in the Global High Yield Category.

9. **CASH INVESTMENTS**—Performance will be compared to the Lipper
Institutional Money Market Funds Index.

D. Trading and Execution Guidelines

Manager(s) shall have the discretion to execute securities transactions with
brokerage firms of their choosing, based upon the quality of execution ren-
dered, the value of research information provided, the financial health and
integrity of the brokerage firm, and the overall efficiency in transacting
securities trades. In the case of separate accounts, the Committee retains
the right to direct brokerage commissions subject to best execution. When
the Manager(s) directs commissions on behalf of the Fund, the direction
will be contingent upon the institution being competitive in both price and

execution for the specific transaction. FO will be consulted and utilized for new or transferred portfolios when cost-efficient.

E. Investment Monitoring

At least annually, the Committee will conduct performance evaluations at the total Fund, asset class, and individual Manager Levels. At the total Fund level, the Committee will analyze results relative to the MAR, the real rate of return and the benchmark indices for the total Fund. Further, investment results will be reviewed relative to the effects of policy decisions and the impact of deviations from policy allocations that may require portfolio rebalancing.

On the asset class and individual Manager levels, results will be evaluated relative to benchmarks (net of fees) assigned to Managers and selected pooled investments. These benchmarks are a vital element in the evaluation of individual and aggregate Manager Performance within each asset class.

G. Selection of Investment Consulting Services

The Committee may utilize the services of FO for specific due diligence, screening/evaluation of Managers, performance monitoring, asset allocation, and other services that the Committee may deem necessary that may exceed the scope of this IPS.

H. Custodial Services/Risk

All assets held by any custodian on behalf of the Family shall be registered in "street names" or "nominee names." The Family will provide FO with the appropriate authority to receive on-line and electronic transmissions of portfolio holdings and monitoring in order to provide all needed reporting.

Custodians may only lend securities within the terms and conditions of specific written agreements executed by an authorized member of the Family.

VI. SELECTION OF MANAGERS

The Committee may select and appoint Managers or commit investments to limited partnerships for a specific investment style or strategy provided that the overall objectives of the Fund are satisfied.

Managers (traditional asset classes) are expected to have a sound business infrastructure, have a minimum of $50 million in assets under firm management, an investment record of 3 years,* and strong relative performance against style-based benchmarks, and must provide a quarterly statement of assets and quarterly investment performance evaluation statements.

Alternative investment managers must have demonstrated experience of 3 years and 6 months documented performance, $25 million in assets under firm management, and provide monthly or quarterly statements from a non-affiliated administrative entity and annual audited statements from a recognizable accounting firm. Leverage in single strategy funds will be limited to no more than 3:1. Fund of Hedge fund managers will not be allowable.

VII. RESPONSIBILITIES OF MANAGERS

A. Adherence to Statement of Investment Objectives and Policy Guidelines

1. All Managers are expected to observe the specific limitations, guidelines, and philosophies stated herein or in any amendments hereto, or other written instructions from the Family. Where commingled funds are utilized in the Fund (including, but not limited to partnerships, commingled trusts, and mutual funds), the Committee recognizes the Manager's duty to manage the investments in the commingled vehicle consistent with the commingled funds prospectus or other operative document.
2. The Manager's acceptance of the responsibility of managing a portion of the Fund will constitute a ratification of this statement, affirming its belief that it is realistically capable of achieving the Fund's investment objectives within the guidelines and limitations stated herein.

B. Communication and Reporting

The FO shall communicate on a regular basis with the Committee on all significant matters pertaining to this Investment Policy and the management of the portfolio.

FO must provide quarterly valuation reports and quarterly and annual investments performance reports.

Committee and the FO will meet at least quarterly to review this Investment Policy and the continued feasibility of achieving the stated investment objectives and goals.

---

* Historic performance may include the Manager's experience at a former investment firm.

Specific areas of review shall include:

1. Asset allocation and portfolio performance.
2. Evaluation of each fund/Manager's results.
3. Fund/Manager's adherence to the investment policy guidelines.
4. Material changes in the Manager's organization, ownership, investment philosophy, and/or personnel.

C. Discretionary Authority

Each Manager will be responsible for making all investment decisions including proxy voting for all assets placed under its management and will be held accountable for achieving the investment objectives stated herein. Such "discretion" includes decisions to buy, hold, and sell securities (including cash and equivalents) in amounts and proportions that are reflective of the Manager's current investment strategy and are compatible with the Fund's investment guidelines.

Marketable Alternative Portfolio Investment Guidelines   The purpose of portfolio guidelines is to clearly define performance objectives, state the investment approach, and to control risk. Portfolio guidelines should be subject to ongoing review. A change in the allocation to the strategy or the Investment Committee's risk tolerance can be among the reasons for a guideline review.

Performance Objective:

> The strategic objective of the Marketable Alternative ("Hedge Fund" or "HF") portfolio is to earn an annualized return that exceeds the annualized rate of return of the three-month U.S. Treasury bill by 5.0 percent. The HF portfolio should also provide diversification benefits to the overall portfolio by offering returns that have low correlation to the performance of other asset classes.

Portfolio Guidelines:

> 1. Permissible investments include funds that invest primarily in a combination of:
>   a. *Long/Short strategies* (including U.S., dedicated Non-U.S., short bias, and global equities).
>   b. *Relative Value strategies* (including equity market neutral, convertible bond arbitrage, and fixed income).
>   c. *Event Driven strategies* (including distressed securities, special situations, capital structure arbitrage, relative value credit, and risk arbitrage strategies.
>   d. *Directional strategies* (including global asset allocation, CTA and global macro).

2. Target rebalance range and maximum allocation for the strategies are:

	Target Range	Max
Long/Short Equity	20–40%	50%
Event Driven	20–40%	50%
Relative Value	20–40%	50%
Directional	5–20%	25%

3. Direct single-strategy, multi-strategy and fund-of-funds investments are permitted. Leverage will be limited to no more than 3:1.
4. No investment with any single manager can represent more than 15 percent of the HF portfolio.
5. No investment with any single fund may exceed 20 percent of that fund's total assets under management.
6. Total HF portfolio forecast downside risk shall be maintained at a level of no more than 7.5 percent of total invested HF capital based on realized and pro forma risk measured quarterly.
7. No more than 15 percent of the total HF portfolio risk budget may be derived from any single manager.
8. Currency hedging as a defensive strategy is permitted in global and international portfolios.
9. Derivative securities may be used within asset portfolios provided that investments in such instruments do not cause the portfolio to be exposed to an asset class not expressly approved in this policy. Derivatives may not be used in non-alternative asset portfolios to add additional risk or leverage, but may be used to control risk or establish exposures to asset classes.
10. Except for Relaxed Short Constraint (130/30 or similar funds), Absolute Return Strategies, and other hedge fund strategy investments, the Managers will not employ short selling without prior written approval by the Family.

Sample ADV Part II with ADV Schedule F

This SEC form must be delivered to clients within 48 hours after meeting. It contains basic information on business, investment style, and associated people. (See Figures B.1 and B.2.)

FORM ADV

Uniform Application for Investment Adviser Registration

Part II - Page 1

Name of Investment Adviser:

Address:	(Number and Street)	(City)	(State)	(Zip Code)	Area Code:	Telephone number:
					( )	

This part of Form ADV gives information about the investment adviser and its business for the use of clients.
The information has not been approved or verified by any governmental authority.

Table of Contents

Item Number	Item	Page
1	Advisory Services and Fees	2
2	Types of Clients	2
3	Types of Investments	3
4	Methods of Analysis, Sources of Information and Investment Strategies	3
5	Education and Business Standards	4
6	Education and Business Background	4
7	Other Business Activities	4
8	Other Financial Industry Activities or Affiliations	4
9	Participation or Interest in Client Transactions	5
10	Conditions for Managing Accounts	5
11	Review of Accounts	5
12	Investment or Brokerage Discretion	6
13	Additional Compensation	6
14	Balance Sheet	6
	Continuation Sheet	Schedule F
	Balance Sheet, if required	Schedule G

(Schedules A, B, C, D, and E are included with Part I of this Form, for the use of regulatory bodies, and are not distributed to clients.)

Potential persons who are to respond to the collection of information contained in this form
are not required to respond unless the form displays a currently valid OMB control number.

SEC 1707 (01-08)
File 3 of 4

FIGURE B.1   Sample ADV Part II Form

FORM ADV Part II - Page 2	Applicant:	SEC File Number: 801-	Date:

1. A. **Advisory Services and Fees.** (check the applicable boxes)   For each type of service provided, state the approximate % of total advisory billings from that service. (See instruction below.)

Applicant:

- ☐ (1) Provides investment supervisory services .... _____ %
- ☐ (2) Manages investment advisory accounts not involving investment supervisory services .... _____ %
- ☐ (3) Furnishes investment advice through consultations not included in either service described above .... _____ %
- ☐ (4) Issues periodicals about securities by subscription .... _____ %
- ☐ (5) Issues special reports about securities not included in any service described above .... _____ %
- ☐ (6) Issues, not as part of any service described above, any charts, graphs, formulas, or other devices which clients may use to evaluate securities .... _____ %
- ☐ (7) On more than an occasional basis, furnishes advice to clients on matters not involving securities ...... _____ %
- ☐ (8) Provides a timing service .... _____ %
- ☐ (9) Furnishes advice about securities in any manner not described above .... _____ %

(Percentages should be based on applicant's last fiscal year. If applicant has not completed its first fiscal year, provide estimates of advisory billings for that year and state that the percentages are estimates.)

　　　Yes　　No

B. Does applicant call any of the services it checked above financial planning or some similar term? .... ☐　　☐

C. Applicant offers investment advisory services for: (check all that apply)

- ☐ (1) A percentage of assets under management　　　☐ (4) Subscription fees
- ☐ (2) Hourly charges　　　☐ (5) Commissions
- ☐ (3) Fixed fees (not including subscription fees)　　　☐ (6) Other

D. For each checked box in A above, describe on Schedule F:

- • the services provided, including the name of any publication or report issued by the adviser on a subscription basis or for a fee
- • applicant's basic fee schedule, how fees are charged and whether its fees are negotiable
- • when compensation is payable, and if compensation is payable before service is provided, how a client may get a refund or may terminate an investment advisory contract before its expiration date

2. **Types of clients** - Applicant generally provides investment advice to: (check those that apply)

- ☐ A. Individuals　　　☐ E. Trusts, estates, or charitable organizations
- ☐ B. Banks or thrift institutions　　　☐ F. Corporations or business entities other than those listed above
- ☐ C. Investment companies　　　☐ G. Other (describe on Schedule F)
- ☐ D. Pension and profit sharing plans

Answer all items. Complete amended pages in full, circle amended items and file with execution page (page 1).

FIGURE B.1 *(Continued)*

FORM ADV Part II - Page 3	Applicant:	SEC File Number: 801-	Date:

3. Types of Investments. Applicant offers advice on the following: (check those that apply)

☐ A. Equity securities

☐ (1) exchange-listed securities
☐ (2) securities traded over-the-counter
☐ (3) foreign issuers

☐ B. Warrants

☐ C. Corporate debt securities (other than commercial paper)

☐ D. Commercial paper

☐ E. Certificates of deposit

☐ F. Municipal securities

G. Investment company securities:
☐ (1) variable life insurance
☐ (2) variable annuities
☐ (3) mutual fund shares

☐ H. United States government securities

I. Options contracts on:
☐ (1) securities
☐ (2) commodities

J. Futures contracts on:
☐ (1) tangibles
☐ (2) intangibles

K. Interests in partnerships investing in:
☐ (1) real estate
☐ (2) oil and gas interests
☐ (3) other (explain on Schedule F)

☐ L. Other (explain on Schedule F)

4. Methods of Analysis, Sources of Information, and Investment Strategies.

A. Applicant's security analysis methods include: (check those that apply)

(1) ☐ Charting
(2) ☐ Fundamental
(3) ☐ Technical

(4) ☐ Cyclical
(5) ☐ Other (explain on Schedule F)

B. The main sources of information applicant uses include: (check those that apply)

(1) ☐ Financial newspapers and magazines
(2) ☐ Inspections of corporate activities
(3) ☐ Research materials prepared by others
(4) ☐ Corporate rating services

(5) ☐ Timing services
(6) ☐ Annual reports, prospectuses, filings with the Securities and Exchange Commission
(7) ☐ Company press releases
(8) ☐ Other (explain on Schedule F)

C. The investment strategies used to implement any investment advice given to clients include: (check those that apply)

(1) ☐ Long term purchases (securities held at least a year)
(2) ☐ Short term purchases (securities sold within a year)
(3) ☐ Trading (securities sold within 30 days)
(4) ☐ Short sales

(5) ☐ Margin transactions
(6) ☐ Option writing, including covered options, uncovered options or spreading strategies
(7) ☐ Other (explain on Schedule F)

Answer all items. Complete amended pages in full, circle amended items and file with execution page (page 1).

FIGURE B.1 (*Continued*)

FORM ADV Part II - Page 4	Applicant:	SEC File Number: 801-	Date:

5. Education and Business Standards.

Are there any general standards of education or business experience that applicant requires of those involved in determining or giving investment advice to clients? .... Yes ☐ No ☐
(If yes, describe these standards on Schedule F.)

6. Education and Business Background.

For:

• each member of the investment committee or group that determines general investment advice to be given to clients, or

• if the applicant has no investment committee or group, each individual who determines general investment advice given to clients (if more than five, respond only for their supervisors)

• each principal executive officer of applicant or each person with similar status or performing similar functions.

On Schedule F, give the:
• name   • formal education after high school
• year of birth   • business background for the preceding five years

7. Other Business Activities. (check those that apply)

☐ A. Applicant is actively engaged in a business other than giving investment advice.

☐ B. Applicant sells products or services other than investment advice to clients.

☐ C. The principal business of applicant or its principal executive officers involves something other than providing investment advice.
(For each checked box describe the other activities, including the time spent on them, on Schedule F.)

8. Other Financial Industry Activities or Affiliations. (check those that apply)

☐ A. Applicant is registered (or has an application pending) as a securities broker-dealer.

☐ B. Applicant is registered (or has an application pending) as a futures commission merchant, commodity pool operator or commodity trading adviser.

C. Applicant has arrangements that are material to its advisory business or its clients with a related person who is a:

☐ (1) broker-dealer   ☐ (7) accounting firm

☐ (2) investment company   ☐ (8) law firm

☐ (3) other investment adviser   ☐ (9) insurance company or agency

☐ (4) financial planning firm   ☐ (10) pension consultant

☐ (5) commodity pool operator, commodity trading adviser or futures commission merchant   ☐ (11) real estate broker or dealer

☐ (6) banking or thrift institution   ☐ (12) entity that creates or packages limited partnerships

(For each checked box in C, on Schedule F identify the related person and describe the relationship and the arrangements.)

D. Is applicant or a related person a general partner in any partnership in which clients are solicited to invest?. . Yes ☐ No ☐
(If yes, describe on Schedule F the partnerships and what they invest in.)

Answer all items. Complete amended pages in full, circle amended items and file with execution page (page 1).

FIGURE B.1 *(Continued)*

FORM ADV Part II - Page 5	Applicant:	SEC File Number: 801-	Date:

9. Participation or Interest in Client Transactions.

Applicant or a related person: (check those that apply)

☐ A. As principal, buys securities for itself from or sells securities it owns to any client.

☐ B. As broker or agent effects securities transactions for compensation for any client.

☐ C. As broker or agent for any person other than a client effects transactions in which client securities are sold to or bought from a brokerage customer.

☐ D. Recommends to clients that they buy or sell securities or investment products in which the applicant or a related person has some financial interest.

☐ E. Buys or sells for itself securities that it also recommends to clients.

(For each box checked, describe on Schedule F when the applicant or a related person engages in these transactions and what restrictions, internal procedures, or disclosures are used for conflicts of interest in those transactions.)

Describe, on Schedule F, your code of ethics, and state that you will provide a copy of your code of ethics to any client or prospective client upon request.

10. Conditions for Managing Accounts. Does the applicant provide investment supervisory services, manage investment advisory accounts or hold itself out as providing financial planning or some similarly termed services *and* impose a minimum dollar value of assets or other conditions for starting or maintaining an account?

Yes ☐   No ☐

(If yes, describe on Schedule F)

11. Review of Accounts. If applicant provides investment supervisory services, manages investment advisory accounts, or holds itself out as providing financial planning or some similarly termed services:

A. Describe below the reviews and reviewers of the accounts. **For reviews,** include their frequency, different levels, and triggering factors. **For reviewers,** include the number of reviewers, their titles and functions, instructions they receive from applicant on performing reviews, and number of accounts assigned each.

B. Describe below the nature and frequency of regular reports to clients on their accounts.

Answer all items. Complete amended pages in full, circle amended items and file with execution page (page 1).

FIGURE B.1 *(Continued)*

FORM ADV Part II - Page 6	Applicant:	SEC File Number: 801-	Date:

12. Investment or Brokerage Discretion.

   A.   Does applicant or any related person have authority to determine, without obtaining specific client consent, the:

                                                          Yes   No

       (1)   securities to be bought or sold? .... ☐   ☐

                                                          Yes   No

       (2)   amount of the securities to be bought or sold? .... ☐   ☐

                                                          Yes   No

       (3)   broker or dealer to be used? .... ☐   ☐

                                                          Yes   No

       (4)   commission rates paid? .... ☐   ☐

                                                          Yes   No

   B.   Does applicant or a related person suggest brokers to clients? .... ☐   ☐

       For each yes answer to A describe on Schedule F any limitations on the authority. For each yes to A(3), A(4) or B, describe on Schedule F the factors considered in selecting brokers and determining the reasonableness of their commissions. If the value of products, research and services given to the applicant or a related person is a factor, describe:

          •   the products, research and services

          •   whether clients may pay commissions higher than those obtainable from other brokers in return for those products and services

          •   whether research is used to service all of applicant's accounts or just those accounts paying for it; and

          •   any procedures the applicant used during the last fiscal year to direct client transactions to a particular broker in return for product and research services received.

13.   Additional Compensation.

   Does the applicant or a related person have any arrangements, oral or in writing, where it:

                                                          Yes   No

   A.   is paid cash by or receives some economic benefit (including commissions, equipment or non-research services) from a non-client in connection with giving advice to clients? .... ☐   ☐

                                                          Yes   No

   B.   directly or indirectly compensates any person for client referrals?. .... ☐   ☐

                          (For each yes, describe the arrangements on Schedule F.)

14.   Balance Sheet. Applicant must provide a balance sheet for the most recent fiscal year on Schedule G if applicant:

          •   has custody of client funds or securities (unless applicant is registered or registering only with the Securities and Exchange Commission); or

          •   requires prepayment of more than $500 in fees per client and 6 or more months in advance

                                                          Yes   No

       Has applicant provided a Schedule G balance sheet? .... ☐   ☐

Answer all items. Complete amended pages in full, circle amended items and file with execution page (page 1).

FIGURE B.1   *(Continued)*

Schedule F of Form ADV Continuation Sheet for Form ADV Part II	Applicant:	SEC File Number: 801-	Date:

(Do not use this Schedule as a continuation sheet for Form ADV Part I or any other schedules.)

1. Full name of applicant exactly as stated in Item 1A of Part I of Form ADV:	IRS Empl. Ident. No.:
Item of Form (identify)	Answer

Complete amended pages in full, circle amended items and file with execution page (page 1).

FIGURE B.1 (*Continued*)

Schedule G of Form ADV Balance Sheet	Applicant:		SEC File Number: 801-	Date:

(Answers in Response to Form ADV Part II Item 14.)

1. Full name of applicant exactly as stated in Item 1A of Part I of Form ADV:	IRS Empl. Ident. No.:

Instructions

1. The balance sheet must be:

   A. Prepared in accordance with generally accepted accounting principles

   B. Audited by an independent public accountant

   C. Accompanied by a note stating the principles used to prepare it, the basis of included securities, and any other explanations required for clarity.

2. Securities included at cost should show their market or fair value parenthetically.

3. Qualifications and any accompanying independent accountant's report must conform to Article 2 of Regulation S-X (17 CFR 210.2-01 et. seq.).

4. Sole proprietor investment advisers:

   A. Must show investment advisory business assets and liabilities separate from other business and personal assets and liabilities

   B. May aggregate other business and personal asset and liabilities unless there is an asset deficiency in the total financial position.

Complete amended pages in full, circle amended items and file with execution page (page 1).

FIGURE B.1 (*Continued*)

Schedule H of Form ADV Page 1	Applicant:	SEC File Number: 801-	Date:

(for sponsors of wrap fee programs)

Name of wrap fee program or programs described in attached brochure:

1. **Applicability of Schedule.** This Schedule must be completed by applicants that are compensated under a wrap fee program for sponsoring, organizing, or administering the program, or for selecting, or providing advice to clients regarding the selection of, other investment advisers in the program ("sponsors"). A wrap fee program is any program under which a specified fee or fees not based directly upon transactions in a client's account is charged for investment advisory services (which may include portfolio management or advice concerning the selection of other investment advisers) and execution of client transactions.

2. **Use of Schedule.** This Schedule sets forth the information the sponsor must include in the wrap fee brochure it is required to deliver or offer to deliver to clients and prospective clients of its wrap fee programs under Rule 204-3 under the federal Advisers Act and similar rules of jurisdictions. The wrap fee brochure prepared in response to this Schedule must be filed with the Commission as part of Form ADV by completing the identifying information on this Schedule and attaching the brochure. Brochures should be prepared separately, not on copies of this Schedule. Any wrap fee brochure filed with the Commission as part of an amendment to Form ADV shall contain in the upper right corner of the cover page the sponsors' registration number (801-).

3. **General Contents of Brochure.** Unlike Parts I and II of this form, this Schedule is not organized in "check-the-box" format. These instructions, including the requests for information in Item 7 below, should not be repeated in the brochure. Rather, this Schedule describes minimum disclosures that must be made in the brochure to satisfy the sponsor's duty to disclose all material facts about the sponsor and its wrap fee programs. **Nothing in this Schedule relieves the sponsor from any obligation under any provision of the federal Advisers Act or rules thereunder, or other federal or state law to disclose information to its advisory clients or prospective advisory clients not specifically required by this Schedule.**

4. **Multiple Sponsors.** If two or more persons fall within the definition of "sponsor" in Item 1 above for a single wrap fee program, only one such sponsor need complete the Schedule. The sponsors may choose among themselves the sponsor that will complete the Schedule.

5. **Omission of Inapplicable Information.** Any information not specifically required by this Schedule that is included in the brochure should be applicable to clients and prospective clients of the sponsor's wrap fee programs. If the sponsor is required to complete this Schedule with respect to more than one wrap fee program, the sponsor may omit from the brochure furnished to clients and prospective clients of any wrap fee program or programs information required by this Schedule that is not applicable to clients or prospective clients of that wrap fee program or programs. If a sponsor of more than one wrap fee program prepares separate wrap fee brochures for clients of different programs, each brochure must be filed with the Commission and the jurisdictions attached to a separate copy of this Schedule. Each such brochure must state that the sponsor sponsors other wrap fee programs and state how brochures for those programs may be obtained.

6. **Updating.** Sponsors are required to file an amendment to the brochure promptly after any information in the brochure becomes materially inaccurate. Amendments may be made by use of a "sticker", i.e., a supplement affixed to the brochure that indicates what information is being added or updated and states the new or revised information, as long as the resulting brochure is readable. Stickers should be dated and should be incorporated into the text of the brochure when the brochure itself is revised.

7. **Contents of Brochure.** Include in the brochure prepared in response to this Schedule:

   (a) on the cover page, the sponsor's name, address, telephone number, and the following legend in bold type or some other prominent fashion:

   This brochure provides clients with information about [name of sponsor] and the [name of program or programs] that should be considered before becoming a client of the [name of program or programs]. This information has not been approved or verified by any governmental authority.

   (b) a table of contents reflecting the subject headings in the sponsor's brochure.

   (c) the amount of the wrap fee charged for each program or, if fees vary according to a schedule established by the sponsor, a table setting forth the fee schedule, whether such fees are negotiable, the portion of the total fee (or the range of such amounts) paid to persons providing advice to clients regarding the purchase or sale of specific securities under the program ("portfolio managers"), and the services provided under each program (including the types of portfolio management services);

FIGURE B.1 (Continued)

Schedule H of Form ADV Page 2	Applicant:	SEC File Number: 801-	Date:

(d) a statement that the program may cost the client more or less than purchasing such services separately and a statement of the factors that bear upon the relative cost of the program (*e.g.*, the cost of the services if provided separately and the trading activity in the client's account);

(e) if applicable, a statement that the person recommending the program to the client receives compensation as a result of the client's participation in the program, that the amount of this compensation may be more than what the person would receive if the client participated in other programs of the sponsor or paid separately for investment advice, brokerage, and other services, and that the person may therefore have a financial incentive to recommend the wrap fee program over other programs or services;

(f) a description of the nature of any fees that the client may pay in addition to the wrap fee and the circumstances under which these fees may be paid (including, if applicable, mutual fund expenses and mark-ups, mark-downs, or spreads paid to market makers from whom securities were obtained by the wrap fee broker);

(g) how the program's portfolio managers are selected and reviewed, the basis upon which portfolio managers are recommended or chosen for particular clients, and the circumstances under which the sponsor will replace or recommend the replacement of the portfolio manager;

(h) (1) if applicable, a statement to the effect that portfolio manager performance information is not reviewed by the sponsor or a third party and/or that performance information is not calculated on a uniform and consistent basis,

   (2) if performance information is reviewed to determine its accuracy, the name of the party who reviews the information and a brief description of the nature of the review,

   (3) a reference to any standards (*i.e.*, industry standards or standards usely solely by the sponsor) under which performance information may be calculated;

(i) a description of the information about the client that is communicated by the sponsor to the client's portfolio manager, and how often or under what circumstances the sponsor provides updated information about the client to the portfolio manager;

(j) any restrictions on the ability of clients to contact and consult with portfolio managers;

(k) in narrative text, the information required by Items 7 and 8 of Part II of this form and, as applicable to clients of the wrap fee program, the information required by Items 2, 5, 6, 9A and C, 10, 11, 13 and 14 of Part II;

(l) if any practice or relationship disclosed in response to Item 7, 8, 9A, 9C and 13 of Part II presents a conflict between the interests of the sponsor and those of its clients, explain the nature of any such conflict of interest; and

(m) if the sponsor or its divisions or employees covered under the same investment adviser registration as the sponsor act as portfolio managers for a wrap fee program described in the brochure, a brief, general description of the investments and investment strategies utilized by those portfolio managers.

8. *Organization and Cross References.* Except for the cover page requirements in Item 7(a) above, information contained in the brochure need not follow the order of the items listed in Item 7. However, the brochure should not be organized in such a manner that important information called by the form is obscured.

Set forth below the page(s) of the brochure on which the various disclosures required by Item 7 are provided.

		Page(s)			*Page(s)*			*Page(s)*
Item	7(a)	cover	Item	7(f)		Item	7(j)	
	#7(b)			#7(g)			#7(k)	
	#7(c)			#7(h)			#7(l)	
	#7(d)			#7(i)			#7(m)	
	#7(e)							

FIGURE B.1 (*Continued*)

Schedule F of	Applicant:	SEC File Number: Date:
Form ADV	PCM	**801-XXXX 5/6/2003**
Continuation Sheet for Form ADV II		

SAMPLE

1. Full name of applicant exactly as stated in Item 1A of Part I of Form ADV
    PCM.

Page 2 Item 1D

Investment Advisory services provided to clients are based on the need and objectives of the client. These may be established through an initial meeting with PCM or through written investment objectives submitted by the client. The relevant facts relating to management of the client's account are examined and appropriate strategies are developed to obtain the client's desired goals. Thereafter, the client receives a written quarterly evaluation of the account accompanied by an analysis of performance. PCM is also available for periodic meetings at the request of the client. In the event that PCM is contracted as a sub-adviser, client contact may be restricted. PCM provides this service to individuals, pension and profit sharing plans, trusts, estates, charitable organizations, and corporations. PCM will provide evaluations on the liquidation and distribution of trusts and estates. PCM will manage accounts on a discretionary basis. Account supervision is guided by the stated objectives of the client (i.e., maximum capital appreciation, growth, income, or growth and income). Asset allocation parameters are assigned to each account

FEES—PERCENTAGE OF ASSETS UNDER MANAGEMENT

The client is charged an annual fee for services, which is billed quarterly and payable in arrears. Each quarterly fee is 25% of the appropriate annual fee applied to the market value of the account, including cash equivalents, on the last day of the quarter. Registrant's standard fee schedule is as follows:

Equity and Balanced Accounts

ASSETS	ANNUAL FEE
Up to $10,000,000	0.75%
Over $10,000,000	0.50%

Fixed Income Accounts

ASSETS	ANNUAL FEE
Up to $20,000,000	0.50%
Over $20,000,000	0.25%

Pooled Investment Vehicles

PCM charges a 1% management fee and a 20% performance fee based in profits in excess of a hurdle rate in the pooled investment vehicles.

FIGURE B.2   Sample ADV Schedule F
Form ADV is not a solicitation of investment service. Advisor mentioned is a ficticious name.

Page 2 Item 1D (Continued)

While it is general policy of PCM to charge fees to clients in accordance with the fee schedule in effect at the time of the charge, fees are subject to negotiation and modification due to special circumstances, such as constraints imposed by substantial capital gains, the client is an eleemosynary organization, and/or the account is that of a related person of the Registrant. Either party may terminate the advisory relationship at any time by giving the other written notice of termination. Fees paid in advance will be prorated to the termination date, and any unearned portion thereof will be returned to the client.

Page 3 Item 3L

PCM actively manages the equity and fixed portion of the portfolios. Investments in these segments are designed to provide above-average total returns, including yield, where applicable, and capital appreciation. In the equity segment, convertible bonds and exchange-traded funds (ETFs) may be used. In the fixed income portion, taxable and tax-exempt securities are used where most appropriate given a client's federal tax status.

When appropriate to the needs of the client, PCM may recommend the use of wash sales, short sales, or margin transactions. These strategies involve certain additional risk, and they will be recommended when consistent with the client's stated tolerance for risk.

PCM is the general partner of a pooled investment vehicle that invests in publicly traded securities and other investment vehicles. When appropriate PCM may use ETFs, options, futures, and short sales in the management of the pooled investment vehicles.

Page 3 Item 4A(5)

The PCM approach to stock selection starts with a universe of approximately 3,000 companies, which are subjected to a proprietary quantitative screening process. Potential purchase candidates are based on several factors, including attractive fundamental valuation, earnings momentum, and relative price strength. Further fundamental and economic analysis is done on those companies that meet the quantitative guidelines.

Page 4 Item 5

Registrant requires those responsible for giving investment advice to have:

1. a college degree, and

2. minimum of two years experience in the investment field

Page 4 Item 6

FIGURE B.2 *(Continued)*

Mr. Portfolio Manager (Born 1956) Chief Investment Officer

The Portfolio Manager started PCM in 2002. PM is President and Chief Investment Officer and Senior Portfolio Manager for international and domestic portfolios. PM has 20 years' experience in professional asset management. Prior to founding PCM, PM was Director of Equity Research and Portfolio Manager for a mutual fund and separate accounts at Home Trust Company (2000–2002). These responsibilities included supervision of nine portfolio managers, traders, and research analysts. His other experience includes serving as Chief Investment.Officer of Bank Advisers (1999–2000), Senior Portfolio Manager at Value Asset Management (1993–1999), and Managing Partner at ML Capital Management (1990–1993). PM is an active member of the Association for Investment Management and Research (AIMR) and the Financial Analysts of Philadelphia, Inc. He received his BA and MBA from State University (1978) and has successfully completed the NASD Series 7, 63, and 65 examinations.

Page 5 Item 9D & 9E

PCM or individuals associated with PCM may purchase or sell securities identical to recommendations to clients for their personal accounts. In addition, any related person(s) may have an interest or position in securities that also may be recommended to a client.

It is the expressed policy of PCM that no person employed by PCM may purchase or sell any security prior to a transaction being implemented for an advisory account, therefore preventing such employees from benefiting from transactions placed on behalf of advisory clients. As these situations represent a conflict of interest, PCM has established the following restrictions in order to ensure its fiduciary responsibilities:

1. An employee of PCM shall not buy or sell securities with a preferred interest to a client.
2. PCM prohibits investment personnel from acquiring securities in an initial public offering.
3. PCM prohibits investment personnel from purchasing privately offered securities.
4. PCM prohibits investment personnel from buying or selling securities used by client accounts for at least seven days before and after trading for client accounts.
5. PCM requires all investment personnel to disclose all personal securities holdings upon commencement of employment and thereafter on a quarterly basis.
6. PCM requires that all employees must act in accordance with all applicable Federal and State regulations governing registered investment advisory practices.
7. Any individual not in observance of the above personal trading policies may be subject to termination.

Page 5 Item 10

PCM has a minimum fee of $2,500 that relates to a minimum account size of $500,000. Management has the right to waive the minimum fee.

Page 5 Item 11A & 11B

Investment policy and strategy is determined by the Chief Investment Officer. Equities and fixed income are reviewed at least weekly to assess current holdings, implement portfolio strategies, and take action on buy/sell candidates.

On a monthly or quarterly basis, as mandated by the account, the Chief Investment Officer reviews individual accounts for cash, performance, and compliance with client investment objectives. Concurrently, with the preparation of these reports, the Chief Investment Officer reviews account holdings, buys and sells, commissions, turnover, and special client instructions.

FIGURE B.2   (*Continued*)

Investment advisory accounts receive a quarterly evaluation that lists securities owned, market value, and yield. Valuations are accompanied by a performance analysis. Registrant meets with clients periodically and encourages regular telephone or electronic mail contact to review investment objectives and strategies.

Page 6 Item 12A & 12B

PCM has investment or brokerage discretion for its clients. Limitations on the degree of such authority vary and are determined by the individual client. PCM selects broker-dealers based upon their execution capabilities. In the event that a client directs PCM to use a particular broker-dealer, the Registrant may not be able to negotiate and obtain the best commission rates, obtain volume discounts, or receive the best execution.

Investment decisions are generally applied to all accounts utilizing a particular strategy taking into consideration client restrictions, instructions, individual needs, and cash balances. Due to these issues, however, there may be a disparities in securities purchased, prices, or commissions among clients in a particular strategy.

FIGURE B.2 (*Continued*)

Form ADV is not a solicitation of investment service. Advisor mentioned is a ficticious name.

Hedge Fund Manager Due Diligence Questionnaire

Please read the following instructions before completing this questionnaire:

1. All questions must be completed.
2. Type or select answers to each question. The tab key will take you to the next field.
3. If any questions are not applicable or the answer is not available, please answer as N/A.
4. If any answer is larger than the space available, please include it in an attachment that references the page and section number. Answer only the question asked. Any additional information required will be requested.

In addition to a hard copy, please submit an electronic version of this questionnaire on a CD/DVD in Microsoft Word format. Please be sure to include an electronic copy of your firm's latest Form ADV in Parts I & II.

I. BACKGROUND

A. Firm Name & Address
B. Contacts
C. Ownership & Affiliates
   Your firm is organized as a:
   List ALL owners of your firm:

Explain owners' relationship to firm:

List ALL related companies:

Explain related companies' relationship to firm:

D. Other offices

List the locations where the firm has other offices.

E. History

List names, positions held, and dates of all professional-level personnel hires in the past five years.

List names, positions held, and dates of all professional-level personnel departures in the past five years.

Provide information pertaining to any organizational changes that have occurred during the past 10 years that a prudent investment professional would consider significant.

F. Important Dates

Date assets were first managed:

Date current investment process initiated:

Date present firm was operative:

Exact date of SEC filing, if applicable:

G. Personnel

1. Number of employees

   Portfolio managers

   Analysts (NOT included above)

   Client service/marketing (NOT included above)

   Administrators (NOT included above)

   Other professionals (NOT included above)

   Other full-time employees (NOT included above)

   Total Employees

2. Provide an organizational flow chart.

3. Indicate the strategy and/or geographics of expertise for portfolio managers and analyst specialists. If your Portfolio Manager/Analyst is a generalist only, please mark the "Generalist" box.

	Strategy Expertise	Geographic Expertise	Generalist
Portfolio Managers			
Analysts			

H. Indicate the name of your insurance carrier and the dollar amount of your coverage:

> Errors & Omissions: Coverage: $
> Fiduciary Liability: Coverage: $

II. INVESTMENT PROCESS, STRATEGY, AND PHILOSOPHY

A. Provide the names and titles of all members of the investment policy or strategy committee.
B. What individual discretion does each portfolio manager have in structuring portfolios? (See below)
C. What is the frequency of regularly scheduled investment policy or strategy meetings?
D. Describe the process by which an investment idea is originated and implemented. Include a flow chart.
E. Describe your strategy and philosophy toward investment and manager selection.
F. Describe how the strategy has changed since the fund's inception.
G. Describe your target returns and estimates of volatility. Explain how you arrived at each figure.
H. Describe your competitive edge.
 I. How does your strategy affect the capacities of your managers? Detail how much money each underlying hedge fund can manage based upon your strategy.
 J. Will new money be accepted from current investors after capacity is reached? If so, what is the "soft-close" figure? Is there a hard-close figure?
K. State all potential conflicts of interest that might arise between the fund of funds and the underlying hedge fund managers. Do any of the underlying hedge funds pay the fund of funds for any services? If so, which funds and which services? Is there any fee sharing arrangement between the fund and the underlying funds?

III. BUSINESS PLANS

A. Describe future plans and activities for your firm.
B. Describe the details of any new investment services you plan to introduce.

C. Describe any plans to cap or limit your growth in terms of total assets. Total dollars? Do you have a maximum asset size based on your capacity restraints?

IV. MANAGER SELECTION AND RESEARCH

A. What criteria do you use to select underlying managers? How are managers and strategies excluded from consideration? What are the common characteristics of the managers in your portfolio?
B. Describe in detail how you source your managers. Do you use personal contacts, databases, prime brokers, or other information?
C. Describe how your research team is structured. Describe the individual responsibilities and contributions/specialties of each team member.

V. MANAGER MONITORING AND RISK MANAGEMENT

A. Describe the risks inherent in your portfolio—what can go wrong? Address each of the following: volatility risk, credit risk, liquidity risk, geopolitical risk, leverage risk, and fraud risk.
B. How much leverage do you typically use and how is it monitored? Is there an independent check on this leverage? Does the fund of funds manager ever use leverage at the fund of funds level? If so, what are the parameters, and is there a maximum amount that can be used?
C. How much derivative exposure is allowed and how is it monitored?
D. Describe the transparency you have with regard to underlying managers and their investments. Is there any third-party check?
E. What is your diversification policy with regard to number of managers, sector, industry, and geographic distribution?
F. What are the criteria for manager termination? Provide an example of in which managers were hired and fired, including the reasons why.
G. What is the average turnover of the portfolio?
H. Do you provide performance attribution information and reports? If so, describe how this works.
I. What types of risk management tools are used, and are they internal, external, or both?

VI. PERFORMANCE AND FEES

A. Do you report performance on a net or gross basis, or both? Will the fund of funds provide performance data on the underlying managers to the consultant, and if so, is this data net and/or gross of fees?

B. Do you publish estimates of the fund's performance? If so, how often?
C. When, how, and how often do you report performance? Have you failed to meet this schedule any time in the past year?
D. Do you charge a performance fee? Is there a hurdle rate? A high water mark? Describe.
E. Do you charge an up-front placement fee? Describe.
F. What are your fees and how do they compare with comparable fund of funds investments?
G. What are the total fees that I will be paying, including those of the underlying managers?

VII. COMPLIANCE AND CLIENT REPORTING

A. With which regulatory authorities are you registered?
B. Has the SEC, CFTC, or any other regulator ever audited your firm? Specify.
C. What is the timing of K-1s, 1099s, or other tax reporting for U.S. investors?
D. Describe any past or pending regulatory action or litigation. Please attach formal filings.

VIII. PERSONNEL

A. Describe your remuneration and incentive policy. How do you retain good employees?
B. What has been your personnel turnover?
C. Have any principals of the firm been subject to regulatory action? Do any have a criminal or civil record? Provide details.
D. What background checks do you perform on the underlying managers?

IX. OPERATIONS AND ADMINISTRATION

A. When can investments be redeemed or tendered? Describe the redemption process.
B. Do you have a lock-up period? Describe.
C. How often are the underlying funds valued? Do you check if they employ fair valuation methodology?
D. Do you have a disaster recovery program and other emergency procedures? Describe.

X. TAXES

A. Do any of the underlying managers use strategies to reduce the tax impact of the investment style? Describe.
B. What percent of your gains historically have been long-term? Has it varied year by year? Why?
C. Do you offer estimated after-tax returns for taxable clients? Describe.
D. What provisions has the fund of funds made for avoiding UBTI (Unrelated Business Taxable Income) for its tax-exempt clients?

XI. PERFORMANCE (SEE APPENDIX 6)

Year End	Product Gross & Net	Benchmark
January 2001		
February 2001		
March 2001		
April 2001		
May 2001		
June 2001		
July 2001		
August 2001		
September 2001		
October 2001		
November 2001		
December 2001		
Annual Return 2001		
January 2002		
February 2002		
March 2002		
April 2002		
May 2002		
June 2002		
July 2002		
August 2002		
September 2002		
October 2002		
November 2002		
December 2002		
Annual Return 2002		
January 2003		

Year End	Product Gross & Net	Benchmark
February 2003		
March 2003		
April 2003		
May 2003		
June 2003		
July 2003		
August 2003		
September 2003		
October 2003		
November 2003		
December 2003		
Annual Return 2003		
January 2004		
February 2004		
March 2004		
April 2004		
May 2004		
June 2004		
July 2004		
August 2004		
September 2004		
October 2004		
November 2004		
December 2004		
Annual Return 2004		
January 2005		
February 2005		
March 2005		
April 2005		
May 2005		
June 2005		
July 2005		
August 2005		
September 2005		
October 2005		
November 2005		
December 2005		
Annual Return 2005		
January 2006		
February 2006		
March 2006		

Year End	Product Gross & Net	Benchmark
April 2006		
May 2006		
June 2006		
July 2006		
August 2006		
September 2006		
October 2006		
November 2006		
December 2006		
Annual Return 2006		
January 2007		
February 2007		
March 2007		
April 2007		
May 2007		
June 2007		
July 2007		
August 2007		
September 2007		

Year End	Product	Benchmark
Annualized 3-year (most recent quarter-end) 7/2004-6/2007		
Annualized 5-year (most recent quarter-end) 9/2002-8/2007		

Year End	Product	Benchmark
Annualized 3-year (most recent quarter-end) 7/2004–6/2007		
Annualized 5-year (most recent quarter-end) 9/2002–8/2007		

ATTACHMENTS

- Appendix 1. Organizational flow chart
- Appendix 2. Biographies of personnel

- Appendix 3. Fee schedule
- ADV—Part I & II
- Appendix 4. Marketing brochure
- Appendix 5. Reference list
- Appendix 6. Monthly performance record
- Appendix 7. Research process

U.S. Equity Long/Short Managers

Proposal Questionnaire

As prescribed in Section V of the Request for Proposal, all respondents are required to submit responses and documentation as requested on this questionnaire. The information requested must be provided in the prescribed format; all questions must be repeated in their entirety before the answers are given. Responses that deviate materially from the prescribed format may lead to the rejection of the Proposal.

A. ORGANIZATION

1. Product Name:_____
2. Describe the firm's ownership structure (Sub-chapter S, LLP, public, etc.) and provide an organizational chart.
3. Provide historical background of your firm.
4. Indicate your firm's fiduciary classification:

   Bank   Insurance Co   Registered Investment   Advisor   Hedge Fund   Other

5. Provide the current ADV or explain the nature of the exemption.
6. Explain any legal judgments associated with the firm or your parent company within the last five years. Specify whether the firm is involved in any pending litigation or investigations (SEC, CFA Institute, etc.).
7. What level of errors and omissions insurance does the firm carry? List the insurance carriers supplying the coverage and show the amount carried by each.
8. What level of fiduciary liability insurance does the firm carry? List the insurance carriers supplying the coverage and show the amount carried by each.

9. Do your employees sign a written code of conduct? If so, how is it enforced?

10. Describe any restructuring or organizational changes that have occurred within the firm over the past three years. Discuss any planned organizational changes that could be implemented in the near future.

11. What is the approximate percent of total firm revenue generated by this product?

12. Will you accept a performance-based fee?

B. INVESTMENT PROFESSIONALS (PRODUCT SPECIFIC)

13. Please list the portfolio managers, research analysts, traders, and client service officers directly involved with the product. Include a brief biography of each.

14. For the investment professionals listed in question 13, please provide the following information using the format below:

% Ownership of Firm	% of Time on Long/Short Product	Years of Experience Managing Long/Short Products	Years with Firm	Years of Overall Investment Experience	Degree/ Designation

15. Identify the investment professionals that would be responsible for this portfolio and explain their roles and responsibilities in the investment decision-making process.

16. The minimum qualifications for this product require that the key portfolio managers and traders for the product have at least three years of experience shorting stocks. Please identify the portfolio managers and traders that have this experience and provide details of that experience.

17. Disclose the number of investment professionals affiliated with the subject product that have joined or left the firm within the last three years. Include their title and responsibilities and, for the investment professionals who left the firm, the reason for leaving and the person who is the replacement.

18. Explain to what extent investment professionals are rewarded for performance versus revenue in the firm or product.

19. Please state what percentage of top management and key product professionals' net worth is in the firm and the product/strategy. Is any percentage of current compensation deferred into the firm's products?
20. Have you devised a succession plan for management of the product? If so, what is it?

C. INVESTMENT PHILOSOPHY AND PROCESS

21. Describe the investment philosophy, strategy, and investment style (i.e., top-down, bottom-up, fundamental, quantitative, technical, contrarian), including the importance of each component. Besides common stocks, what other securities will be used in this strategy? Include all other investment instruments. What is the appropriate benchmark for this product? Why?
22. Describe the decision-making and portfolio construction processes. Please explain the process in ranking stocks. Please contrast and identify tactical or strategic allocation decisions to specific sectors/industries and factors. Disclose sub-advisors and how their expertise is incorporated into the process.
23. Describe how your firm determined the appropriate amount of shorting for this strategy. Is this position going to be held constant or float according to market conditions? How often do you plan to rebalance back to the target short position?
24. Describe your sell discipline. What factors dictate your sell discipline and how do they rank in importance?
25. What quantitative models do you use in your process? What factors are used in the model? Are the factors weighted equally or do some factors have more weight than others? Are the factor weights static or dynamic?
26. Who owns the model? Who developed and maintains the model(s)? How do you measure its effectiveness?
27. Describe how research (internal, external, and sell-side) is utilized and incorporated into the portfolio. Please indicate sources of external information including sub-advisor relationships.
28. Please describe your risk control systems. Include in your answer the constraints put on various exposures (sector, market capitalization, individual securities, tracking error). What other ways does this strategy attempt to control risk?
29. Explain why this product should add value over the benchmark. Does this product plan to add value on the short side? Is the value added

coming from stock selection or another source (include both the long side and the short side in your answer)?

30. What has been the targeted annual portfolio turnover for the subject product? How does the turnover for this product differ from the long-only product? Explain why.

31. What is the typical number of securities for the subject product? How does it differ from the long-only product? Explain why.

32. Explain the use of cash in the investment process.

33. What is your expected active return (alpha)? What is the expected tracking error of this product to its benchmark? Is there a targeted information ratio? How do these statistics compare to the long-only product? Explain why they differ.

34. Regarding the investment process: (1) explain its shortcomings or limitations; (2) describe the market environments in which our product will have difficulty outperforming; (3) what would cause you to reevaluate the process; (4) explain any enhancements you have made, and/or are being worked on but not yet implemented, to the investment process in the last five years.

35. Does your product perform differently in periods of high market volatility versus periods of low volatility? If so, please explain how and why.

D. TRADING PROCESS AND SYSTEMS

36. Please describe how trading is conducted for the subject product and how it differs from the trading for your long-only products. Include your trader's experience in shorting stocks.

37. Are stop losses used as a risk control on the short trades? Why or why not?

38. Describe your firm's automated systems for trading and their integration with the back office and the portfolio management team. Does your current portfolio management, trading and accounting systems have the ability to handle shorts?

39. This strategy requires that the short positions in the portfolio not exceed 35 percent of the portfolio. Does your trading system have the ability to put a hard cap on the amount of shorting? Include details on other compliance tools available to monitor client guidelines.

40. For this product, provide a summary of trade execution performance over the last year. Describe how performance is measured and indicate if this is evaluated internally or externally. If externally, what service or services are used? Include details on how this information is integrated into the overall trading strategy. If the subject product does not have

one year of live history, please provide any history available along with a one year report of the manager's long-only product.

41. This strategy requires that the manager have extensive experience working with Prime Brokers. Please describe your experience working with Prime Brokers and provide a copy of a prime brokerage transaction report with the client name removed.

42. How does the firm establish relationships with prime brokers?

43. Provide a recent example of a difficult short trade and how it was handled. Discuss the trading strategy and its implementation including sources of inventory and liquidity. Discuss your experience with a short squeeze and how it was handled.

44. Transaction costs can have a big impact on the performance of a portfolio. Trading stocks short can add additional transaction costs. Explain in detail how your traders try minimizing the additional costs of trading shorts.

45. Provide a recent example of a trade error. Discuss how it occurred, how it was identified, how it was resolved, and what changes have been made to prevent such an error from occurring again.

46. Appendix A at the end of this questionnaire contains a list of reports and requirements that we will likely need for this product. Although some of the reports may be provided by Prime Brokers or other third parties, it is the manager's responsibility that all the information requested in Appendix A be provided to us. Is there anything in Appendix A that would present a problem or difficulty for your firm?

47. Provide the percent of this product's trades which generate soft dollars (both research and third-party soft dollars). List the recipients of the all soft dollars and the products/services received for these soft dollars (both research and third-party).

E. PERFORMANCE

IMPORTANT. This portion of the questionnaire is broken up into three sections. Please read the instructions to each section carefully before completing.

Section 1. Long/Short Performance Results

Complete this section only if your firm currently has a long/short product with live history. The product must have a limit of up to 35 percent short positions. The minimum qualifications for this product are one year of live performance history and $100 million in assets. If your product does not

meet the minimum qualifications, you may still complete this section but you
must also complete the sections for the long-only product and the simulated
portfolio. Please provide returns that are gross of fees.

48. Provide the product's monthly performance returns through December
    31, 2006. Please provide up to five years of data, if it is available. Please
    include benchmark returns for the same period. Also provide 12 months
    of month-end holdings through December 31, 2006 (or time period
    that is available). The file should contain the security name, cusip, and
    number of shares (on a diskette or CD in Microsoft Excel format).
49. Are the returns provided compliant with the CFA Institute PPS/GIPS
    standards? If not, why not? Specify if the performance is a carve-out of
    another product. Specify the product and give the methodology of the
    carve-out. Does it meet CFAI standards for carve-outs?
50. Provide the annualized returns of the proposed product, the appropriate
    benchmark (please specify) along with lowest and highest performing
    portfolios within the same strategy using the format below through
    December 31, 2006.

Annualized Returns	Last Year	Last 2 Years	Last 3 Years	Last 5 Years
Product				
Highest Portfolio				
Lowest Portfolio				
Benchmark				
Value Added				

51. Provide the returns of the proposed product, the appropriate benchmark
    (please specify) along with the lowest and highest performing portfolios
    in the strategy ending December 31, 2006, using the format below.

Calendar Year Returns	2006	2005	2004	2003	2002	2001
Composite						
Highest Portfolio						
Lowest Portfolio						
Benchmark						
Value Added						

52. Please provide 3- and 5-year (if available) Sortino Ratios for this product as of December 31, 2006.
53. Provide a sector performance attribution report using GICs sectors of the proposed product for the trailing 12 months (or time period available if less than 12 months) ending December 31, 2006, using the format below. Please specify the benchmark used for this comparison.

	Representative Portfolio			Benchmark			2 Factor Attribution		
	Portfolio Average Weight	Total Return	Contribution to Return	Benchmark Average Weight	Total Return	Contribution to Return	Allocation Effect	Stock Selection	Total
Sector Long									
Consumer Disc									
Consumer Staples									
Energy									
Financials									
Health Care									
Industrials									
Technology									
Materials									
Telecommunication									
Utilities									
Sector Short									
Consumer Disc									
Consumer Staples									
Energy									
Financials									
Health Care									
Industrials									
Technology									
Materials									
Telecommunication									
Utilities									
Total									

54. Provide market capitalization performance attribution report of the proposed product for the trailing 12 months (or time period available if less than 12 months) ending December 31, 2006, using the format below. Please specify the benchmark used for this comparison.

	Representative Portfolio			Benchmark			2 Factor Attribution		
	Portfolio Average Weight	Total Return	Contribution to Return	Benchmark Average Weight	Total Return	Contribution to Return	Allocation Effect	Stock Selection	Total
Capitalization Breakdown Long									
Over $50 billion									
$25–$50 billion									
$10–$25 billion									
$5–$10 billion									
$1–$5 billion									
$0–$1 billion									
Capitalization Breakdown Short									
Over $50 billion									
$25–$50 billion									
$10–$25 billion									
$5–$10 billion									
$1–$5 billion									
$0–$1 billion									
Total									

55. Provide the characteristics of a representative portfolio of the long/short product and the appropriate benchmark using the format provided below. Please specify the benchmark used for this comparison.

Measure	Representative Portfolio			Benchmark		
	12/31/06	12/31/05	12/31/04	5/31/06	12/31/05	12/31/04
Price/ Earnings						
Price/Book						
Price/Cash Flows						
Dividend Yield						
Earnings Growth						
Weighted Avg Mkt Cap						
Beta						

Section 2. Long-Only Enhanced Index Performance Results

This section is for performance results for the long-only product that has the same alpha engine as the proposed long/short product. The minimum qualifications, if submitting long-only performance, are three years of live performance history and $500 million in assets. Please provide returns that are gross of fees.

56. Provide the product's monthly performance returns through December 31, 2006. Please provide up to 10 years of data if it is available. Please include benchmark returns for the same period. Also provide 12 months of month-end holdings through December 31, 2006. The file should contain the security name, cusip, and number of shares (on a diskette or CD in Microsoft Excel format).

57. Are the returns provided compliant with the CFA Institute PPS/GIPS standards? If not, why not? Specify if the performance is a carve-out of another product. Specify the product and give the methodology of the carve-out. Does it meet CFAI standards for carve-outs?

58. Provide the annualized returns of the long-only product, the appropriate benchmark (please specify) along with lowest and highest performing portfolios within the same strategy using the format below through December 31, 2006.

Annualized Returns	Last Year	Last 2 Years	Last 3 Years	Last 5 Years	Last 7 Years	Last 10 Years
Product						
Highest Portfolio						
Lowest Portfolio						
Benchmark						
Value added						

59. Provide the returns of the long-only product, the appropriate benchmark (please specify) along with the lowest and highest performing portfolios in the strategy ending December 31, 2006, using the format below.

Calendar Year Returns	YTD 2006	2005	2004	2003	2002	2001	2000	1999	1998	1997	1996
Composite											
Highest Portfolio											
Lowest Portfolio											
Benchmark											
Value Added											

60. Please provide 3-, 5- and 10- (if available) year information ratios for this product as of December 31, 2006.

61. Provide a sector performance attribution report using GICs sectors of the long-only product for the trailing 12 months ending December 31, 2006, using the format below. Please specify the benchmark used for this comparison.

	Representative Portfolio			Benchmark			2 Factor Attribution		
	Portfolio Average Weight	Total Return	Contribution to Return	Benchmark Average Weight	Total Return	Contribution to Return	Allocation Effect	Stock Selection	Total
Sector Long									
Consumer Disc									
Consumer Staples									
Energy									
Financials									
Health Care									
Industrials									
Technology									
Materials									
Telecom-munication									
Utilities									
Total									

62. Provide market capitalization performance attribution report of the long-only product for the trailing 12 months (or time period available if less than 12 months) ending December 31, 2006 using the format below. Please specify the benchmark used for this comparison.

	Representative Portfolio			Benchmark			2 Factor Attribution		
	Portfolio Average Weight	Total Return	Contribution to Return	Benchmark Average Weight	Total Return	Contribution to Return	Allocation Effect	Stock Selection	Total
Capitalization Breakdown Long									
Over $50 billion									
$25–$50 billion									
$10–$25 billion									
$5–$10 billion									
$1–$5 billion									
$0–$1 billion									
Total									

63. Provide the characteristics of a representative portfolio of the long-only product and the appropriate benchmark using the format provided below. Please specify the benchmark used for this comparison.

Measure	Representative Portfolio			Benchmark		
	12/31/06	12/31/05	12/31/04	5/31/06	12/31/05	12/31/04
Price/ Earnings						
Price/Book						
Price/Cash Flows						
Dividend Yield						
Earnings Growth						
Weighted Avg Mkt Cap						
Beta						

Section 3. Simulated Long/Short Performance Results

If you complete Section 2 (long-only results) instead of Section 1, please complete this section as well. The subject product must have a limit of no more than 35 percent in short positions. The minimum qualification for simulated returns is 10 years of performance history. Please provide returns that are gross of fees.

64. Provide the product's monthly performance returns through December 31, 2006. Please provide at least 10 years of data. Please include benchmark returns for the same period. Also provide 12 months of

month-end holdings through May 31, 2006. The file should contain the security name, cusip, and number of shares (on a diskette or CD in Microsoft Excel format).

65. Provide the annualized returns of the simulated portfolio, the appropriate benchmark (please specify) using the format below through December 31, 2006.

Annualized Return	Last Year	Last 2 Years	Last 3 Years	Last 5 Years	Last 7 Years	Last 10 Years
Simulated Product						
Benchmark						
Value Added						

66. Provide the returns of the simulated portfolio and the appropriate benchmark (please specify) for the period ending December 31, 2006, using the format below.

Calendar Year Returns	YTD 2006	2005	2004	2003	2002	2001	2000	1999	1998	1997
Simulated Product										
Benchmark										
Value Added										

67. Please provide 3-, 5-, and 10-year Sortino Ratios as of December 31, 2006.

68. Provide a sector performance attribution report using the GICs sectors of the simulated portfolio for the trailing 12 months ending December 31, 2006, using the format below. Please specify the benchmark used for this comparison.

	Representative Portfolio			Benchmark			2 Factor Attribution		
	Portfolio Average Weight	Total Return	Contribution to Return	Benchmark Average Weight	Total Return	Contribution to Return	Allocation Effect	Stock Selection	Total
Sector Long									
Consumer Disc									
Consumer Staples									
Energy									
Financials									
Health Care									
Industrials									
Technology									
Materials									
Telecommunication									
Utilities									
Sector Short									
Consumer Disc									
Consumer Staples									
Energy									
Financials									
Health Care									
Industrials									
Technology									
Materials									
Telecommunication									
Utilities									
Total									

69. Provide market capitalization performance attribution report of the simulated portfolio for the trailing 12 months ending December 31, 2006, using the format below. Please specify the benchmark used for this comparison.

	Representative Portfolio			Benchmark			2 Factor Attribution		
	Portfolio Average Weight	Total Return	Contribution to Return	Benchmark Average Weight	Total Return	Contribution to Return	Allocation Effect	Stock Selection	Total
Capitalization Breakdown Long									
Over $50 billion									
$25–$50 billion									
$10–$25 billion									
$5–$10 billion									
$1–$5 billion									
$0–$1 billion									
Over $50 billion									
Capitalization Breakdown Short									
$25–$50 billion									
$10–$25 billion									
$5–$10 billion									
$1–$5 billion									
$0–$1 billion									
Total									

70. Provide the characteristics for the simulated portfolio and the appropriate benchmark using the format provided below. Please specify the benchmark used for this comparison.

Measure	Representative Portfolio			Benchmark		
	12/31/06	12/31/05	12/31/04	5/31/06	12/31/05	12/31/04
Price/ Earnings						
Price/Book						
Beta						
Dividend Yield						
Earnings Growth						
Weighted Average Market Cap						
Beta						

71. What was the frequency of rebalancing?
72. Did you include transaction costs in your simulation? What were the assumed costs and how realistic are they?
73. Did you factor any cash, and cash flows, in the simulation?
74. Did you factor in the availability of shorts in the simulation?
75. Did you take into account the short rebate in the simulation?
76. Did the simulation have any controls on leverage or was it allowed to float?
77. Did you take a haircut on the simulated returns? If so, how much?
78. When comparing the returns of the long-only product to the long/short product, were the returns for both simulated, or is the long-only returns actual? If both are simulated, are the assumptions the same for both?

F. COMPOSITE/PRODUCT INFORMATION

IMPORTANT. This portion of the questionnaire is broken up into two sections. Please read the instructions to each section carefully before completing.

Section 1. Long/Short Performance Results

Complete this section only if your firm currently has a long/short product with live history. The product must have a limit of up to 35 percent short positions. The minimum qualifications for this product are one year of live performance history and $25 million in assets.

79. Is the product included in a composite? If so, how many composites are associated with this product? How do they differ? How many accounts from the following type(s) of portfolios are included?

Fully Discretionary Separate Account Portfolios Only	
Restricted Portfolios	
Commingled Vehicles	
Other (Please Specify)	

80. As of December 31, 2006 and the prior two calendar year-end periods, specify the percentage of product assets included in the composite's performance. If the percentage is low, please comment.

	% of Composite
December 31, 2006	
December 31, 2005	
December 31, 2004	

81. Provide the following most recent calendar year-end investment product information for the firm's separate (Sep.) and commingled (Comm.) accounts (U.S.-based investors only). If you have significant Non-U.S. clients, please list in a separate similar table, the number of accounts and the amount of assets.

Year	# of Commingled Accounts	$ in Commingled Accounts	# of Separate Accounts	$ in Separate Accounts	Total $ in Product	# of U.S. Tax-Exempt Accounts	$ in U.S. Tax-Exempt Accounts
5/31/06							
12/31/05							
12/31/04							
12/31/03							

82. What are the asset sizes of the three largest separate accounts in the product and who is the client for each? If the client name is confidential, describe the client (i.e. the type of client, total asset size, etc.).

83. What is the asset capacity in dollars of the subject product? How is it derived?

84. What is the benchmark used for the majority of the product's assets? Please specify other benchmarks that can be used for this product. What is the length of the performance history for each different benchmark? Describe any change in the portfolio construction process if a different benchmark is used.

Section 2. Long-Only Enhanced Index Performance Results

This section is for the long-only product with live history that has the same alpha engine as the long/short product being proposed. The minimum qualifications for this product are three years of live performance history and $500 million in assets.

85. Is the product included in a composite? If so, how many composites are associated with this product? How do they differ? How many accounts from the following type(s) of portfolios are included?

Fully Discretionary Separate Account Portfolios Only	
Restricted Portfolios	
Commingled Vehicles	
Other (Please Specify)	

86. As of December 31, 2006 and the prior two calendar year-end periods, specify the percentage of product assets included in the composite's performance. If the percentage is low, please comment.

	% of Composite
December 31, 2006	
December 31, 2005	
December 31, 2004	

87. Provide the following most recent calendar year-end investment product information for the firm's separate (Sep.) and commingled (Comm.) accounts (U.S.-based investors only). If you have significant Non-U.S. clients, please list in a separate similar table, the number of accounts and the amount of assets.

Year	# of Commingled Accounts	$ in Commingled Accounts	# of Separate Accounts	$ in Separate Accounts	Total $ in Product	# of U.S. Tax-Exempt Accounts	$ in U.S. Tax-Exempt Accounts
12/31/06							
12/31/05							
12/31/04							
12/31/03							

88. What are the asset sizes of the three largest separate accounts in the product and who is the client for each?
89. What is the asset capacity in dollars of the subject product? How is it derived?
90. What is the benchmark used for the majority of the product's assets? Please specify other benchmarks that can be used for this product. What is the length of the performance history for each different benchmark? Describe any change in the portfolio construction process if a different benchmark is used.

REFERENCES

91. Please provide three references for the long/short subject product (name, title, firm, telephone number, and length of time the firm has been a client). If you do not currently have a long/short product with live clients, please provide three references for your long-only product. U.S. tax-exempt institutional account references are preferred.

92. Please provide three contacts (name and telephone number) that have terminated the subject product within the last three years, along with the corresponding asset values at the time of termination. If your long/short product does not have three years of live performance history, please provide three contacts that have terminated the related long-only product within the last three years. Please include the corresponding asset values at the time of termination. U.S. tax-exempt institutional account contacts are preferred.

Bibliography

Adrian, Tobias. "Measuring Risk in the Hedge Fund Sector." *Federal Reserve Bank of New York Research* (March/April 2007).

Agarwal, Vikas, and Narayan Y. Naik. "Risks and Portfolio Decisions Involving Hedge Funds." *Review of Financial Studies* (2004): 63–98.

Anderson, Jenny. "Navigating the Hedge Fund Maze in a Leveraged World." *New York Times* (April 6, 2007).

Avery, Helen. "The Funds of Hedge Funds That Are Too Hot to Handle." *Euromoney* (November 2006): 87–91.

Beckers, Stan. "Hedge Fund Asset Allocation, Risk Management, Manager Selection and More." *CFA Institute Webcasts* (February 22, 2007).

Brighton House Associates. "Quarterly Research Report—Q2 2008." Marlborough, MA, 2008.

Brinson, Gary P., Brian D. Singer, and Gilbert L. Beebower. "Determinants of Portfolio Performance II: An Update." *Financial Analysts Journal* (May/June 1991): 40–48.

Brinson, Gary P., L. Randolph Hood, and Gilbert L. Beebower. "Determinants of Portfolio Performance." *Financial Analysts Journal* (July/August 1986): 39–44.

Chaudhry, Ashraf, and Helen L. Johnson. "The Efficacy of the Sortino Ratio and Other Benchmarked Perormance Measures Under Skewed Return Distributions." *Australian Journal of Management* (March 2008): 485–500.

Christory, Corentin, Stephane Daul, and Jean-Rene Giraud. "Quantification of Hedge Fund Risk." *Edhec-Risk Asset Management Research* (January 2007).

Coroneos, Elise. "Storm in a Side Pocket." www.hfmweek.com (February 1–7, 2007).

Darst, David M. *Mastering the Art of Asset Allocation*. New York: McGraw Hill, 2007.

Esterling. Ed. "Perpsectives on Hedge Fund Investing." *Crestmont Research* (February 2005).

Grinold, Richard C., and Ronald N. Kahn. *Active Portfolio Management*. Chicago: Irwin Publishing, 1995.

Hsieh, David A. "The Search for Alpha-Sources of Future Hedge Fund Returns." *CFA Institute Conference Proceedings Quarterly* (2006).

Hurley, Mark P., and Yvonne N. Kanner. "Analysis of the Effect of Size on Small Cap Mutual Fund Performance." *Northern Trust* (March 2006).

Investment Advisor Search. [Online] Available at www.sec.gov.

Investor Risk Committee. "Valuation Concepts for Investment Companies and Financial Institutions and Their Stakeholders." *International Association of Financial Engineers* (June 8, 2004).

Jacobius, Arleen. " Acting on Faith." *Pensions & Investments* (February 5, 2007).

Jones, Meredith, and Milt Baehr. "Investment Statistics: A Primer." *Strategic Financial Solutions* (2005).

Kirschner, Sam, Eldon C. Mayer, and Lee Kessler. *The Investor's Guide to Hedge Funds*. Hoboken, NJ: John Wiley & Sons, 2006.

Krum, Ted. "Potential Benefits of Investing With Emerging Managers." *Northern Trust's Insights on...* (March 2006).

Krum, Ted. "The Performance Advantage of Small Portfolio Management Firms." *Journal of Investing* (Spring 1995).

Le Sourd, Veronique. "Hedge Fund Performance in 2007." *Edhec-Risk Asset Management Research* (February 2008).

Lo, Andrew W. "The Dynamics of the Hedge Fund Industry." *Research Foundation of CFA Institute* (2005).

Lowenstein, Roger. *When Genius Failed: The Rise and Fall of Long Term Capital Management*. New York: Random House, 2000.

Malkiel, Burton G., and Atanu Saha. "Hedge Funds: Risk and Return." *Financial Analysts Journal* (November/December 2005): 80–88.

Mangiero, Susan M. *Risk Management for Pensions, Endowments, and Foundations*. Hoboken, NJ: John Wiley & Sons, 2005.

Mangini, Douglas. "Building Portfolios with Beta Aware Investing." *Morgan Stanley Investment Management* (July 2008).

Maxey, Daisy. "Fraud, Market Conduct Among Regulators Hedge-Fund Concerns." *Dow Jones Newswires* (March 6, 2007).

Nowak, Gregory J. "Pension Protection Act of 2006." *Pepper Hamilton LLP—Investment Management Update* (August 2006).

Panzier, Ron. "Observation on Hedge Fund Due Diligence: Risk Management Procedures." *Emerging Manager Focus* (2007).

Pension Protection Act of 2006. [Online] Available at www.fi360.com.

Performance Measurements. [Online] Available at www.math.uwaterloo.ca.

Rahl, Leslie, and Lisa Polsky. "A New Approach to Risk-Adjusted Asset Allocation for Hedge Fund Investing." *Capital Market Risk Advisors* (2004).

Rom, Brian M., and Kathleen W. Ferguson. "Post-Modern Portfolio Theory Comes of Age." *The Journal of Investing* (Fall 1994).

Saphir, Ann. "Mansueto's Hedge Fund Headaches; Morningstar Chief Investment Pools Aren't Forthcoming." *Crain's Chicago Business* (March 5, 2007).

Schoyer, William S. "The Changing Nature of Hedge Funds." *CFA Institute Webcasts* (April 27, 2006).

Sivathambu, Shamillia. "Solving the Hedge Fund Asset Allocation Puzzle." www.hfmweek.com. (May 24-30 2007): 17–18.

Soerensen, Jan Tang. "Hedge Fund Portfolio Construction." Master of Arts in Law and Diplomacy Thesis, Tufts University (April 2006).

Statistics Used in Manager/Advisor Analysis. [Online] www.cta-online.com.

Swensen, David F. *Pioneering Portfolio Management*. New York: Free Press, 2000.

Swensen, David F. *Unconventional Success*. New York: Free Press, 2005.

Swisher, Pete. "Post Modern Portfolio Theory." www.fpanet.org/journal (2005).

Till, Hilary, "EDHEC Comments on the Amaranth Case: Early :Lessons from the Debacle." *EDHEC Risk and Asset Management Research* (2006).

Till, Hilary. "Measuring Risk-Adjusted Retirns in Alternative Investments." *Edhec-Risk Asset Management Research* (July 2006).

Welch, Scott D., "Consulting to the Ultra Affluent." *CFA Institute Conference Proceedings Quarterly* (March 2008).

Wilmott, Paul. *Paul Wilmott Introduces Quantitative Finance*. New York: John Wiley & Sons, 2001.

Index

A

ADV sample form, 203–217
AIMR-Performance Presentation Standards,
      66–67
Albourne, 24
Alpha, 49
Alta Partners, 141
Altvest, 40
Amaranth, 3, 87, 165–168
Amin, Gaurav S., 73, 152
Arbitrage, 5–6, 141
Assets
   growth, 105
   rebalancing allocation, 194–195
Assets Under Management (AUM), 2, 29, 43,
      65
   allocation, 11–25
      profiles, 14
   versus annual fund returns, 184
Association for Investment Management and
      Research, 67
AUM. *See* Assets Under Management
Average return, 49

B

Barclays Global HedgeSource, 30
Bayou Group, 7, 81, 158–160
Berkshire Hathaway, 81
Black-Scholes option model, 156–157
Bloomberg.com, 54
Braeside Capital, 6
Brokers, 43–45
   audit and prime, 106
Buffett, Warren, 11, 81, 171
Bullfrog, 4
Business plans, 221–222

C

California Public Employees Retirement
      Systems (CalPERS), 29
CalPERS (California Public Employees
      Retirement Systems), 29

Capital Asset Pricing Model (CAPM), 16
CAPM. *See* Capital Asset Pricing Model
CBOE. *See* Chicago Board of Option Exchange
CCI Healthcare, 6, 104
Cerebus, 111
Chicago Board of Option Exchange (CBOE), 95
CNBC, 54
Coale, Carol, 162
Cohen, Steven, 165
Collins, Robert "Bo," 162, 171
Colton, C.C., 115
Commodity Trading Advisors (CTAs), 169
Complexity risk, 98–99
Concentration risk, 89
Contrarian Capital, 6
Counterparty risk, 94
Credit risk, 95–96, 97
   mortgage delinquency, 96
Cresmont Holdings LLC, 74
Crestmont Research, 30
CSFB/Tremont Global Macro Index, 68
CTAs. *See* Commodity Trading Advisors

D

D'Agnostino, John, 162
Databases, 53
DDQ. *See* Due Diligence Questionnaire
Derivatives risk, 100–101
Deutsche Bank, 165, 168
DLJ. *See* Donaldson, Lufkin and Jenrette
Dollar Weighted Return (DWR), 61–62
Donaldson, Lufkin and Jenrette (DLJ), 160
Dow-Jones Industrial Average, 73
Down capture, 52
Downside deviation, 49–50
Drawdown, 52
   analysis, 77
Due diligence, 37, 173. *See also* Due Diligence
      Questionnaire
   alternative investments process, 116
   background checks, 130–131
   checklist, 17

Due diligence (*Continued*)
  consistency, 122–123
  investment team, 123–124
  for a manager, 42
  manager summary, 131, 132–134
  master feeder structure, 117–118
  model ranking, 131, 134, 136
  on-site visit, 111–112, 120–126
  operational, 127–129
  of the organization, 119–120
    infrastructure, 124
  preparation of final evaluation, 126–129
  process, 115–138
  ranking model, 135–136
Due Diligence Questionnaire (DDQ), 56–60,
    103–110, 117. *See also* Due diligence
  sample, 219–227
Duration Capital, 6
DWR. *See* Dollar Weighted Return

E
Easterling, Ed, 74
EdHec, 7
Education, 170–171
EHFC. *See* Energy Hedge Fund Center
Endowments, 4–5, 29
EndWave (ENWV), 106, 161
Energy Hedge Fund Center (EHFC), 141
Enron, 81
ENWV. *See* EndWave
Equity investments, 196
ERISA law, 20–21
ETFs. *See* Exchange Traded Funds
Eton Park, 3–4
Event-driven strategies, 6
Exchange Traded Funds (ETFs), 125, 178

F
Fannie Mae, 95
Federal Reserve, 95, 157
Fibonacci analysis, 171–172
Fiduciary
  responsibilities, 11–25
  tips for, 22–24
Financial Analysts Journal, 12, 73
Financial Times, 54
Fixed income securities, 195–196
Fixed income strategies, 6
FOFs. *See* Funds of funds
FOHF. *See* Fund of hedge funds
Fox Financial, 54
Fraud, 169

Freddie Mac, 95
Fund of hedge funds (FOHF), 18–19
Funds of funds (FOFs), 1–2

G
GAIM, 45
Gain to loss ratio, 52
GARP (Growth At a Reasonable Price), 71
General Partnership (GP), 48
GIPS. *See* Global Investment Performance
    Standards
Global Investment Performance Standards
    (GIPS), 66
Global markets, 9
Goerl, Conrad, 162
Goldman Sachs, 3
Goldstein, Phillip, 4
Google, 54
GP. *See* General Partnership
Guidant Capital, 6

H
Halcyon, 6
HedgeFund.net, 30, 45
Hedge Fund of Funds (HFOF), 28
Hedge Fund Research (HFRI), 30, 165
  Equity Index, 68, 69–70
  Fund Weighted Composite Index, 68,
    145–147
Hedge funds. *See also* Due Diligence
    Questionnaire
  annual returns versus return per unit risk, 33
  art versus science of, 8–9
  asset growth, 105
  AUM growth versus annual fund returns,
    184
  business structure, 117
  compliance, 58, 223
  conferences and industry events, 45–46
  Congressional intervention, 4
  databases, 48–53
  description of, 5–7
  frequency distribution of monthly returns, 65
  fundamental data, 122
  fund brochures and documents, 110–111
  goals of the firm, 124
  growth of, 2–3
  history of, 1
  holdings, 125
  incubators and platforms, 47–48
  indexes. *See* Indexes
  infrastructure, 124

large versus small, 27–40
  aligned interests, 38–39
  attrition rates, 36
  diminishing returns, 39–40
  invested interests, 37–38
  outperformance of small funds, 37
  performance of new small funds, 34–36
  returns, 28
  small fund advantage, 29–33
  trend line analysis, 40
leverage and, 17–19
monitoring, 189
monthly return attribution and exposure
    levels, 72
net fund return analyis, 126
on-site visit, 111–112
operations and administration, 223
organization, 119
past performance, 9
peer analysis, 71–72
performance, 58, 103–113, 224–226
  analysis, 61–79
personnel, 223
portfolio construction, 139–153
publications, 46–47
regulation, 167
research, 29–33
risk management, 57–58, 106–108. *See also*
    Risks
  regulatory and legal risk, 188
risk matrix, 84
risks. *See* Risks
sector exposures, 146
size and impact, 183–185
sources of returns, 124–126
strategies, 7–8, 19–20, 34–36
  asset flows, 183
  bottom-up manager analysis, 141
  correlations, 148–149
  historical annual returns, 69–70
  reviews, 182–183
  top-down analysis, 140–141
structure, 16–20
types of, 5–6
web sites, 48–53
HFOF. *See* Hedge Fund of Funds
HFRI. *See* Hedge Fund Research
HFR Industry, 3
Highbridge, 6
High watermark risk, 87–89
Hsieh, Dr. David A., 30
Hunter, Brian, 165, 168, 172

I
IBM, 27
Indexes
  annual net returns, 140
  correlations, 143–144
  CSFB/Tremont Global Macro Index, 68
  hedge fund annual net returns, 140
  HFRI Equity Index, 68, 69–70
  HFRI Fund Weighted Composite Index, 68
  large hedge fund, 32
  Lehman Aggregate, 76
  medium hedge fund, 31
  MSCI EAFE, 142
  NASDAQ, 68
  risk/return comparison, 15
  Russell, 74, 78, 179
  small hedge fund, 31
Infovest21, 45
Institutional Investor, 45
Internal Revenue Service (IRS), 117
Internet, 54
Investment consulting services, 198
Investment Policy Statement (IPS), 9–10.
    See also Managers
asset allocation and rebalancing, 192–195
  alternative investments, 193–194
  domestic equity portfolio, 192
  fixed income portfolio, 194
  international equity portfolio, 193
  real asset portfolio, 194
guidelines
  for selection of equity investments, 196
  for selection of fixed-income securities,
    195–196
    diversification, 195
    duration, 196
    investment quality, 195–196
  for trading and execution, 198–199
manager's articulation of the investment
    process, 121–122
purposes of, 11–2
responsibilities of managers, 200–202
  adherence to statement of investment
    objectives and policy guidelines, 200
  communication and reporting, 200–201
  discretionary authority, 201–202
sample, 191–202
selection of managers, 199–200
standards of performance, 196–199
  custodial services/risk, 199
  indices, 197–198
  investment monitoring, 199

Investment Policy Statement (IPS) (*Continued*)
  peer group, 197
  performance relative to risk, 196
  selection of investment consulting services, 199
  statement of investment objectives, 191–192
Investments, 193–194. *See also* U.S. Equity
  long/short managers proposal questionnaire
  advisors, 21
  alternate, 13–16
  alternative process, 116
  manager, 21
  monitoring, 199
  philosophy and process, 231
  recovering losses, 151–152
  search and selection process, 24–25
  socially responsible, 20
  stewards of, 21
Investors, 126
  redemptions, 170
IPS. *See* Investment Policy Statement
IRS. *See* Internal Revenue Service
Israel, Samuel, 158, 160

J
John W. Henry, 6
Jones, Alfred WInslow, 1
Jones, Meredith, 30
Jones, Paul Tudor, 171

K
Kat, Harry M., 73, 152
Key person risk, 99
Kirschner, Sam, 34, 36
Kurtosis, 76

L
Lakeshore International Fund, 141
Lancelot, 6
LDI. *See* Liability Driven Investing
Lehman Aggregate index, 76
Leverage, 17–19, 169–170
  extreme, 158
  fixed income returns, 19
  risk, 91–92
Liability Driven Investing (LDI), 15–16
Lipper, 45
Liquidation, forced, 170
Liquidity mismatch risk, 90
Liquidity risk, 85–87
Long-short strategies, 6

Long-Term Capital Management (LTCM), 18,
  81, 98, 156–158, 164
LTCM. *See* Long-Term Capital Management

M
Macro strategies, 6
Malkiel, Burton G., 73, 74
Managers. *See also* Investment Policy Statement
  (IPS)
  articulation of the investment process, 121–122
  bottom-up hedge fund analysis, 141
  database for, 53
  due diligence, 42
    ranking model, 135–136
    summary, 131, 132–134
  generation of ideas for the portfolio, 123
  investor valuation, 128
  monitoring and risk management, 222
  performance and fees, 222–223
  personnel reviews, 185–186
  a prime brokers, 43–45
  recruiting
    at conferences and industry events, 45–46
    with industry publications, 46–47
    through incubators and platforms, 47–48
    through professional networks, 54–56
    with unconventional sources, 53–54
    with web sites and databases, 48–53
  report of due diligence findings, 131
  responsibilities, 200–202
  risk, 85
  search, 41–60, 57
  selection, 199–200, 222
Maounis, Nicholas, 165
MAR. *See* Minimum Acceptable Returns
MarHedge, 45
Marin Capital Partners, 141
Marino, Daniel, 159, 160
Marino, Matthew, 160
Market risk, 85, 94–95
Master feeder structure, 117–118
Maximum drawdown, 52
Mayercap LLC, 34
Meriwether, John, 156
Merton, Robert C., 156
Mindich, Eric, 3
Minimum Acceptable Returns (MAR), 15–16,
  20, 75, 191
Model risk, 96, 98
Modern Portfolio Theory (MPT), 16, 74–76,
  82, 147–148

Moody's, 22–23
Moore Capital, 28
Morningstar, 22–23
Morningstar Risk-Adjusted Return (MRAR), 23–24
MotherRock, 3, 81, 162–165
MPT. *See* Modern Portfolio Theory
MRAR. *See* Morningstar Risk-Adjusted Return
MSCI EAFE Index, 142
Multi-strategies, 6

N
NASDAQ, 68, 106, 145, 147, 149, 160
NAV. *See* Net Asset Value
NDA. *See* Nondisclosure agreement
Net Asset Value (NAV), 62, 88
    risk, 99–100
New York Mercantile Exchange (Nymex), 162
New York Times, 4
Nondisclosure agreement (NDA), 108
NS Utility, 6
Nymex. *See* New York Mercantile Exchange

O
Oak Street Capital, 6
Omega Advisors, 159
1.618 Group LLC, 171
On-site visit, 111–112, 120–126
Opal, 45
Operational risk, 84, 89–90
Ospraie Management, 168–169
Outperformance, 37

P
Paloma Partners LLC, 165
Peak Ridge Capital Group, 172
Peak Ridge Commodity Volatility fund, 172
Peer analysis, 71–72, 91, 181–182
Pension funds, 4–5
Pension Protection Act of 2006 (PPA), 20–22
Performance analysis, 61–79, 174–175, 233–247
    benchmarking, 68–71
    drawdown analysis, 77
    frequency distribution of monthly returns, 65
    good performance, 78–79
    hedge fund indexes, 73–74
    historical performance, 176
    improbable performance, 79
    long and short, 64, 65–66
    measurements, 63–65
    modern portfolio theory, 74–76

number verification, 67
peer analysis, 71–72, 91, 181–182
performance standards, 66–67
standards, 196–19
trends, 179–181
PerTrac Financial Solutions, 30
Pioneering Portfolio Management (Swensen), 13
Portfolios
    alternate investments, 13–16
    construction, 139–153
    determinants of performance, 12–13
    diversification, 19–20
    domestic equity, 192
    exposures, 175, 178–179
    fixed-income, 194
    international equity, 193
    manager's generation of ideas for, 123
    optimization, 147–153
    position summary, 177–178
    real asset, 194
    test versus model of, 142–147
PPA. *See* Pension Protection Act of 2006
PPM. *See* Private Placement Memorandum
Private Placement Memorandum (PPM), 18–19, 117
Prudent Man Rule, 21
Putnam, Judge Samuel, 21

Q
Quantum, 6
Questionnaires. *See* Due Diligence Questionnaire; U.S. Equity long/short managers proposal questionnaire

R
Renaissance Asset Management, 6, 98
Reputation risk, 93–94
Reuters, 93
Review of Financial Studies (DeMiguel, Garlappi, and Uppal), 150
Risks. *See also* Hedge funds, risk management
    business continuity risk, 188–189
    categories, 84–85
    complexity risk, 98–99
    concentration risk, 89
    counterparty risk, 94
    credit risk, 95–96, 97
    derivatives risk, 100–101
    hedge fund risk matrix, 84
    high watermark risk, 87–89
    key person risk, 99

Risks (*Continued*)
  leverage risk, 91–92
  liquidity mismatch risk, 90
  liquidity risk, 85–87
  manager/investment risk, 85
  market risk, 85, 94–95
  model risk, 96, 98
  net asset value instability risk, 99–100
  operational risk, 84, 89–90
  process, 91
  regulatory and legal risk, 188
  reputation risk, 93–94
  risk/return comparison, 82
  sensitivity to assumptions risk, 99
  short selling risk, 92
  submerged, 94
  transparency risk, 90–91
Ritchie, A.R. Thane, 93
Ritchie Capital, 93
Robertson, Julian, 1
Russell indexes, 74, 78, 179
Russia, 157

S
SAC Capital Advisors LLC, 28, 111, 165
Saha, Atanu, 73, 74
Sail Pacific Explorer, 6
Salomon Brothers, 156
SAM. *See* Separate Account Management
Scholes, Myron, 156
SEC. *See* Securities and Exchange Commission
Sector strategies, 6
Securities, fixed income, 195–196
Securities and Exchange Commission (SEC), 4,
  22, 41, 66, 106, 188
  sample ADV form, 203–217
Sensitivity to assumptions risk, 99
Separate Account Management (SAM), 13–14,
  136
1794 Commodore, 6
Sharpe ratio, 50, 76
Short selling risk, 92k
Skewness, 51
Socially Responsible Investing (SRI), 20
Soros, George, 1, 171
Sortino ratio, 50–51, 76
S&P 500, 71, 73, 74, 76, 142
SRI. *See* Socially Responsible Investing

Standard deviation, 50
Statistical measures, 49–53
Steinhardt, Michael, 1
Sterling ratio, 51–52
Submerged risk, 94
Swensen, David F., 13

T
Taxes, 224
Technology, 108–109
Terrapin, 45
Third party vendors, 105–106, 127, 129–130,
  186–187, 189
Time Weighted Return (TWR), 62–63
Trading, 130, 198–199
  leverage, 2
  process and systems, 232–233
  strategies, 6
TransCanada Corp., 165
Transparency risk, 90–91
Tremont Capital Managaement, 73
Trends, 179–181
Tudor, 28
TWR. *See* Time Weighted Return

U
UHNW. *See* Ultra-high net worth
Ultra-high net worth (UHNW), 13
U.S. Bankruptcy Court, 170
U.S. Congress, 4
U.S. Department of Labor, 22
U.S. Equity long/short managers proposal
  questionnaire, 229–248. *See also*
  Investments
U.S. Tax Code, 117, 118

V
Value at Risk (VaR), 107

W
Wall Street Journal, 54, 93
Washington Post, 4
Whittier, John, 160
Wolverine Asset Management, 6, 109
Wood River Capital Management, 7, 106,
  160–162
WorldCom, 81

Printed in the United States
By Bookmasters